BOUNDARIES  ON

RELIGION, CULTURE, AND PUBLIC LIFE

Religion, Culture, and Public Life

SERIES EDITORS

Alfred Stepan and Mark C. Taylor

THE RESURGENCE OF RELIGION calls for careful analysis and constructive criticism of new forms of intolerance, as well as new approaches to tolerance, respect, mutual understanding, and accommodation. In order to promote serious scholarship and informed debate, the Institute for Religion, Culture, and Public Life and Columbia University Press are sponsoring a book series devoted to the investigation of the role of religion in society and culture today. This series includes works by scholars in religious studies, political science, history, cultural anthropology, economics, social psychology, and other allied fields whose work sustains multidisciplinary and comparative as well as transnational analyses of historical and contemporary issues. The series focuses on issues related to questions of difference, identity, and practice within local, national, and international contexts. Special attention is paid to the ways in which religious traditions encourage conflict, violence, and intolerance and also support human rights, ecumenical values, and mutual understanding. By mediating alternative methodologies and different religious, social, and cultural traditions, books published in this series will open channels of communication that facilitate critical analysis.

After Pluralism: Reimagining Religious Engagement, edited by Courtney Bender and Pamela E. Klassen

Religion and International Relations Theory, edited by Jack Snyder

Religion in America: A Political History, Denis Lacorne

Democracy, Islam, and Secularism in Turkey, edited by Ahmet T. Kuru and Alfred Stepan

Refiguring the Spiritual: Beuys, Barney, Turrell, Goldsworthy, Mark C. Taylor

Tolerance, Democracy, and Sufis in Senegal, edited by Mamadou Diouf

Rewiring the Real: In Conversation with William Gaddis, Richard Powers, Mark Danielewski, and Don DeLillo, Mark C. Taylor

Democracy and Islam in Indonesia, edited by Mirjam Künkler and Alfred Stepan

Religion, the Secular, and the Politics of Sexual Difference, edited by Linell E. Cady and Tracy Fessenden

Recovering Place: Reflections on Stone Hill, Mark C. Taylor

BOUNDARIES OF TOLERATION

Edited by
ALFRED STEPAN
and
CHARLES TAYLOR

Columbia University Press
New York

Columbia University Press
Publishers Since 1893
New York Chichester, West Sussex
cup.columbia.edu

Library of Congress Cataloging-in-Publication Data
Boundaries of toleration / edited by Alfred Stepan and Charles Taylor.
pages cm. — (Religion, culture, and public life)
Includes bibliographical references and index.
ISBN 978-0-231-16566-2 (cloth : alk. paper) — ISBN 978-0-231-16567-9 (pbk. : alk. paper) —
ISBN 978-0-231-53633-2
1. Toleration—Philosophy. 2. Group identity 3. Social values I. Stepan, Alfred C.

HM1271.B68 2014
179' 9—dc23 2013025560

Columbia University Press books are printed on permanent and durable acid-free paper.
This book is printed on paper with recycled content.
Printed in the United States of America

c 10 9 8 7 6 5 4 3 2 1
p 10 9 8 7 6 5 4 3 2 1

JACKET DESIGN: Archie Ferguson

To Mark Kingdon,
who made these conversations possible.

CONTENTS

BOUNDARIES OF TOLERATION

INTRODUCTION

ALFRED STEPAN AND CHARLES TAYLOR

HOW CAN PEOPLE of diverse religious, historical, ethnic, and linguistic allegiances and identities live together? And that means: without violence and without the domination of some by others, without inflicting suffering on each other? This is certainly one of our major preoccupations today. But it has recurrently preoccupied people and societies throughout history. Even when domination of some by others was considered normal and inevitable, rulers often tried to avoid its more brutal forms.

To help us begin our reconsideration of toleration in the widest possible way, we invited Salman Rushdie, the Booker Prize–winning novelist of *Midnight's Children*, to inaugurate our deliberations. Rushdie has lived with, and thought profoundly about, religion and the boundaries that demarcate intolerance from tolerance, and even those that cross over beyond tolerance, to mutual respect. Though condemned to death for apostasy by Ayatollah Khomeini's fatwa for his novel *Satanic Verses,* Rushdie reflects broadly and beautifully over his childhood visits to the mutually tolerant Sufi-Hindu culture of Kashmir and the fact that his father chose the surname Rushdie after Ibn Rush'd, the brilliant twelfth-century scholar known in the West as Averroës, who pioneered nonliteralist interpretations of the Qur'an. Rushdie analyzes why this tradition is now under great attack and suggests how it might be recovered. He uses poetic reflections to illuminate how the great Mughal leader Akbar created a culture of tolerance, and finally mutual respect, that transcended much of his despotic origins. This and much more. Read, enjoy, and reflect.

In the rest of this volume a series of distinguished philosophers, historians, sociologists, and political scientists take up Rushdie's suggestive challenges. The question they all address is how can people of diverse allegiances and identities live together.

The language in which these questions were thought out in the classical literature of Western civilization was that of toleration. The milestones in what we in the West understand as our progress toward a better form of society, our liberal democracy, were marked by edicts of toleration, by Locke's *Letter on Toleration*, by appeals to toleration. This was part of the natural language of human discourse in the West from the sixteenth century onward.

But, recently, the term *toleration* has come under attack. Many people want to argue, in our multicultural societies today, that we have gone beyond toleration, and that there is something demeaning to the beneficiaries in talk of tolerating this or that group.

In this volume a number of us recognize that the classical argument for toleration implies that the very act of proposing to tolerate a group, or a practice, or a way of life was already to presuppose that there was some problem with this group: they were dangerous or disturbing to social peace or unpleasant or distasteful. Normally, states would take measures to counteract these negative features, perhaps expelling the group or isolating it or forbidding or limiting some of their group practices. However, the state may have decided to forbear from applying these measures, at least to the full extent. Such forbearance is a key part of this literature on toleration.

The possible motives for states and individuals of such toleration are many and multilayered. We may think that forbearance leads to greater social harmony, that it will arouse less conflict, less mutual hostility than taking the road to repression. Or some may argue that a given group is not as dangerous as had been assumed—see Locke's argument for tolerating dissenters (although not atheists and Catholics). Alternatively, we may tolerate out of compassion or humanitarian feeling.

But in all these cases we are still admitting that there is something wrong with the target group or practice, something which would normally call down on them some negative measures, even though we find reasons to suspend or mitigate these. We can see why the word *toleration* can offend today, since many of us would like to see ourselves as part of a multicultural, liberal society, where (a) differences—of culture, of religion, of sexual orientation, etc.—are not seen as threats to good order or good taste, but on the contrary as potential enrichment; and thus (b) where immunity to special negative treatment is secured not by arguments mitigating deserved discrimination, but by rights. Measures securing individual rights and forbidding discrimination are inscribed in all the charters that are a fundamental component of contemporary democratic constitution building.

It is clear that the logic of toleration, and that of multicultural rights entrenchment, are quite different from each other. How can anyone say that I am receiving as a fruit of toleration something that I have a right to? We would probably also agree that a politics of rights is a more satisfactory arrangement than a politics of tolerance. It is more in keeping with human dignity when we are insured against special negative treatment by right, rather than by the wisdom of governments or majorities who may see good reasons to mitigate this treatment in our case. In that sense, rights take us "beyond toleration." However, even though we are happy to analyze politics beyond toleration, we believe that the concept and practice of toleration are both still essential.

Essential, because we can raise the serious question whether we have really succeeded in transcending altogether the logic of toleration, and whether banning the word may not blind us to the case for forbearance in certain situations that still recur. There is a liberal zealotry which can be as short-sighted and inhumane as the other modes—religious, national, ethnic—that we see in history; and many of these older modes can hide themselves in liberal garb. The present wave of Islamophobia spreading in the Western world is a good case in point: xenophobic and exclusionary sentiments that give themselves what seem impeccable liberal and feminist credentials can be unleashed without restraint.

These are among the questions that will be discussed in this book. We want both to explore the issues and forms of toleration in different contexts and the real possibilities of going beyond toleration in certain circumstances. Part 1, "Classical Western Approaches to Toleration," examines conceptual debates about toleration mainly in the classical Western context. Part 2, "Before and Beyond Classical Approaches to Toleration," documents some largely unexplored variants of toleration in non-Western cultures, some of which predate classical Western arguments about toleration and some of which go beyond toleration to mutual respect practiced well before the creation of modern multiculturalism in the West.

Part 1 opens with a penetrating study by Ira Katznelson, called "A Form of Liberty and Indulgence: Toleration as a Layered Institution," of the logic of toleration and of the different sites and configurations that it has assumed in Western history. It also contains a warning against too quickly assuming that we have transcended the need for such tolerance. The next two chapters are a debate about secularism and its relationship to toleration between Charles Taylor and Akeel Bilgrami. Charles Taylor, in his chapter "How to Define Secularism," offers a reconceptualization of secularism for the new era of multiculturalism, that is, for societies which contain major religious and cultural differences, but which claim to go beyond toleration in their management of these differences. Akeel Bilgrami follows with "Secularism: Its Content and Context," which argues that Taylor's new definition accommodates multiculturalism so much that it might make it difficult to utilize secularism to condemn, and, indeed, make illegal, some dangerous forms of intolerance. In the final essay in part 1, "Half-Toleration: Concordia and the Limits of Dialogue," Nadia Urbinati presents a fascinating historical study of a road not taken. She describes the early post-Reformation notion of "Concordia Christiana," which offered a formula for the harmonious coexistence of Christian confessions that did not appeal to toleration, but rather to a humanist ideal of concord drawn from Cicero. Her chapter explains how Concordia did not succeed and why the route out of discord and conflict in the modern European tradition turned out to be that of developing toleration.

Our choice in this volume to look at the world history of toleration in part 2 helps make it absolutely clear that arguments for the use of toleration and its analogues were not, as is often argued, developed first in Western Europe and only then diffused to non-Western cultures. Rajeev Bhargava in his "Beyond Toleration: Civility and Principled Coexistence in Asokan Edicts" argues that Emperor Asoka, who ruled much of India from 269–232 B.C.E., during a period of internecine religious conflict, helped reduce such sectarian slaughter by installing, in thirty different locations throughout the Indian subcontinent, stone pillars to advance arguments against intolerance and for civility and principled coexistence. For example, Asoka's Rock Edict VII argues that he "wishes members of all faiths to live everywhere in his kingdom. For they all seek mastery of the senses and purity of mind." Rock Edict XII goes beyond the boundaries of seventeenth-century Western ideas of toleration, which imply that a group should be tolerated despite being disliked, by asserting that King Asoka "honours men of all faiths." He argues that all faiths deserve respect and that everyone should guard "one's speech to avoid extolling one's own faith and disparaging the faith of others. . . . . The faiths of others all deserve to be honoured. . . . Concord alone is commendable, for through concord men may learn and respect the conception of Dharma [faith] accepted by others."

A major task that must be done before toleration can become a powerful conceptual variable in the social sciences is the creation of better analytic categories concerning the boundaries of toleration. The chapter by Karen Barkey, "Empire and Toleration: A Comparative Sociology of Toleration Within Empire," pays particular attention to the boundaries between intolerance and tolerance and develops analytic categories of what factors contribute to boundary changes. Barkey poses, and convincingly answers, a fascinating comparative question. Why and how did the Ottoman Empire, which started with greater ideological arguments and governmental mechanisms for toleration of diversity than the Habsburg Empire, with its confessional absolutism, cross paths with the Habsburgs in the eighteenth century, when the Ottomans embarked on a route of intolerance and persecution of the very groups they had gladly tolerated while the Habsburgs declared an Edict of Tolerance?

Sudipta Kaviraj's chapter, "Modernity, State, and Toleration: Exploring Accommodations and Partitions," strongly contests what he considers modern social science's tendency to view the question of toleration through a simple linear narrative. He also contests the dominant views of many modernist

Indian nationalist historians who see Indian history as a chronicle of unceasing religious tension. Kaviraj offers a fundamentally new, nonlinear, history of religious conflict, accommodation, and intermittent periods of tolerance and intolerance over twenty-five hundred years.

In the concluding chapter of the volume, "Muslims and Toleration: Unexamined Contributions to the Multiple Secularisms of Modern Democracies," Alfred Stepan subjects the widespread assumption of a democratic deficit in the Muslim world to close empirical examination. He documents that over 400 million Muslims outside of the West actually live in countries normally classified as democracies by both of the two most authoritative annual surveys of democracies in the world. He examines how and why Muslims in Indonesia, Senegal, as well as the 180 million Muslims in democratic India, rejected any early Rawlsian idea of keeping religion out of the political arena. Rather, in a form of cocelebration of all religions, and policy cooperation with secular authorities, Muslims helped craft new forms of democracy and toleration, adding to the repertoire of the modern world's multiple democratic secularisms. In Indonesia these practices have led to 97 percent of boys between the ages of thirteen and eighteen being literate and 96 percent of the girls. In India, in a survey of 27,000 respondents, 71 percent of Hindus and 71 percent of Muslims affirmed that "democracy is always preferable." The same survey documented the counterintuitive finding that, for Hindus, Muslims, Christians and Sikhs, "the greater the intensity of religious practice, the greater the intensity of support for democracy." Fortunately, there are more routes out of intolerance and toward toleration and democracy than standard accounts of secularism normally recognize.

RELIGION AND THE IMAGINATION

SALMAN RUSHDIE
WITH GAURI VISWANATHAN

Below is an edited transcript from the public discussion Rushdie had with Gauri Viswanathan, Class of 1933 Professor in the Humanities at Columbia University, on the occasion of the launch of the Institute for Religion, Culture, and Public Life, November 6, 2008, at Columbia University.

GAURI VISWANTHAN: It's a real pleasure to be here with you, Salman. Thank you for joining us in the launch of the institute and I want very much to thank Nick Dirks and Mark Taylor for inviting me to be a part of this conversation. Salman, your novels team with stories within stories that get at different levels of religious experience, and you often turn to myth, miracles, and magic to reflect on that experience. Let me begin by asking a simple question, not about religion and the imagination, the title of this session, but about religion as imagination. If, as could be argued, conceptualizing an unseen power inherently involves human imaginings of the divine, what does the literary imagination add? Or what work does it do that is different from the religious imagination? Do you see yourself trying to recover, through literature, the impulses of a religious imagination before it freezes into theology, before experience turns into a theological, ethical construct?

SALMAN RUSHDIE: Well, the first thing to say is that all literature began as sacred literature. That is to say, the beginnings of writings are religious, that the oldest written material that we have is all the product of one or another religious experience. It's a long time, if you look at the history of literature, before literature separates itself from that articulation of religion. So there is something profound in the origins that link them.

The other thing is that religious language has had such a powerful effect, I think, on all of us, whether we are religious or not, that there aren't words to express some things except religious words. For instance, if you think about a word like the *soul,* what does that mean if you are not a religious person? I don't believe in an afterlife or a heaven or a hell and so on, and yet I feel that when I use that word it has some meaning. What could that meaning possibly be? There isn't a secular word for that feeling that we are not only flesh and blood, that there is, as Arthur Koestler, said "a ghost in the machine." Whether you are religious or not, you feel obliged to use language that has been shaped by religion in order to express things that may not have a religious purpose. So that's a constant battle. But I think you are right to say that I'm not interested in devotion, and in that sense I'm not interested in writing books that express anything other than interhuman devotion, which is temporary.

VISWANATHAN: At the same time, I've read several writings of yours where you talk about both the beauty and the terror of religion, the ability of religion to inspire profound feelings of great beauty and majesty as well as to incite great bloodshed.

RUSHDIE: Yes, I was being polite.

VISWANATHAN: But I remember that you wrote this very evocative passage—I think this was when you were in King's College. You had gone to give a talk and you spoke about the architecture . . .

RUSHDIE: Yes, that's true. You know, I grew up as a student looking out of my window at King's College chapel, and it's hard not to believe in the capacity of religion to create beauty when King's College chapel is outside your window, this exquisite thing. Then I was asked to speak there, and one of the things that I thought would never happen to me in my life is that I would deliver the sermon in King's College chapel. There are moments when your life surprises you.

And I have to tell you, apropos of nothing, I learned from doing that why priests speak the way they do. It's because of the echo. They said to me, "You know, it's ninety-two feet high, it's stone, there is no carpet, and if you speak in an ordinary speaking voice then your echo comes back at you and no one can hear a word you are saying." And—so you have to—speak—like this. You have to say—what you have to say—in this way. And suddenly you understand how preachers do it, and it's because of the echo. There is a metaphor lurking in there somewhere.

VISWANATHAN: So do you see something about aesthetics that does have that religious sensibility?

RUSHDIE: Yes, what I'm saying is, I think there are different ways of getting there. It's quite clear that religion has inspired people to create things of incredible beauty and also that people of no religion have created things of incredible beauty. So there is nothing intrinsic about religion that makes it the way of getting there, but it is *a* way of getting there. I think it's true that you can listen to great religious music, for example, you can look at icon painting, you can read Milton or Blake, and you can easily see the power of religious belief to create or to help to create beauty. And for me the great, the most useful thing has been the power of religion to create very strong metaphors. I've gone back often to what I call dead religions, what's more commonly called mythology. But remember that the great Greek myths were once the religion of Greece, and Roman mythology was once the religion of Rome. It had all the apparatus of priests and anathemas and so on to defend it. Now that it doesn't have that, we can simply look at it as text and, of course, you find in these stories astonishing amounts of meaning compressed into very, very small amounts of words.

When I was writing *The Ground Beneath Her Feet*, for example, I was studying the Orpheus myth. Now, you can express the whole story of Orpheus and Eurydice in less then one hundred words. It doesn't really require more than five or six, what, ten sentences maybe, and yet the amount of complexity pushed into that very small story is almost inexhaustible. You have this very complex examination of the relationship between love, art, and death, and you can turn it this way and that way. You can say that this story tells us—shows us—the power of art inspired by love to overcome death. Or, if you are feeling more pessimistic, it can show us the power of death to destroy love, even when love is guided by art.

There isn't a single reading; there are many readings. That's something that living religions also have in common. There is not a single way of reading the text; there are very rich and complex ways of reading these texts. If you're in the text business, you're very interested to see how much power can be concentrated in how little in these ancient works. So it's been very important for me to examine that.

VISWANATHAN: In fact, *The Ground Beneath Her Feet* is the novel I wanted to talk about a little bit. You have pairs of contrasting characters in this novel such as the ultrarationalist Sir Darius and the miracle-chasing wife, Lady Spenta. For Sir Darius, every intellectual effort begins with the death of the gods, and he seeks out a secular origin prior to all religion, whereas his wife searches for enchantment. And in *The Enchantress of Florence*, your most recent novel, you have Akbar as a modern man who questions the existence of God and presides over spirited debates in the tent of the new worship between competing philosophical schools. Yet the same rationalist skeptic has created his imaginary Queen Jodha, and he lives in a world steeped in magic and miracles. So I wanted to ask you how you reconcile these two images cohabiting the same world, these super-rationalist figures who are highly skeptical and who privilege human effort over religion and yet, at the same time, are encompassed by this world of miracles and magic.

RUSHDIE: Yes, I don't reconcile them. That's the thing: I just allow them go on arguing inside me as well as outside. It's true that if you are involved in the making of imaginative writing there is a powerful argument implicit in what you are doing against pure rationalism, because what you are doing often is not reasonable. The way in which a story is created or an imaginative piece comes to life, there is a mystery in it, and you can't deny that is so. There is a bit of me—I guess the bit of me that is sitting here—that is quite rationalistic. I would argue, not unconventionally, that religion comes after reason and that, actually, religious texts were invented by people and that gods, indeed, were invented by human beings in order to answer the two great questions of life, "Where do we come from?" and "How should we live?" It seems as if every religion is based on an attempt to answer those questions, the question of origin and the question of ethics.

I would say, and I have often said, that I don't need religion to answer either of those questions. Because, on the question of origins, the one thing you can say about every religion ever invented is that they are wrong. The world was not created in six days by a sky god who rested on the seventh; the world was not created by the churning of primal material in a giant pot; the world was not created by the sparks unleashed by the friction of the udders of a gigantic cow against the boulders of a bottomless chasm. All these things might be pretty, but they are not true. And so it seems to me that religion just has nothing to say on the question of origins. And on the question on ethics, it seems to me that whenever religion has got into the driving seat on that question, what happens is inquisition and oppression.

So it seems to me not just uninteresting, but not valuable to turn to religion. I don't want the answers to come from some priest. I would prefer them to come from this, from the process of debate and argument and the kind of thing for which this institute has been set up. Actually, the first thing you accept in that situation is that there are no answers. There isn't an answer; there is only the debate. The debate itself is the thing from which flows the ethical life. So that is what I would say, and that is what I think. But when I'm writing, something weird happens, and the result is these books, which clearly do contain a large amount of what you would call supernaturalism. I find that as a writer I need that in order to explain the world I am writing about. As a person I don't need it, but as a writer I do. So that tension is just there. I can't reconcile it, it is just so.

VISWANATHAN: I'm very interested in what you just said now about debate and argument as being part of the formation of religion. I remember in an earlier conversation we had, when we talked about *The Satanic Verses*, you said that you were attempting to depict the convulsions that take place at the birth of any new religion, which you described as a history often marked by discord and disagreement. You had said, and I quote, "There are scenes in *The Satanic Verses* in which the early religion is persecuted and early members of the religion are verbally and physically abused by the mob in the city now called Mecca, and some of that abuse is there in the novel and some of these sentences were taken out as my abusive view of Islam." Then you ask, "If you're going to make a portrayal of the attacks on a newborn faith, how can you do it without showing the attackers doing the attacking? If then those attacks are made into your view, it is a distortion."

So I think your observation about religious debates of the past being turned into contemporary heresies goes right to the heart of the problem that those writing religious histories have, of always having to contend with mainstream accounts. Your effort, as far as I can tell, has been to depict alternative histories, with stories and traditions not represented in mainstream history. So it raises a very important point about the difficulties of representing religious debates when those arguments might have been effaced from the historical record or exist only as fragments, leaving traces on various textual traditions, which are then reconstituted as sacred traditions. In bringing that suppressed religious history of dissent, disagreement, and disputation back to the forefront of our consciousness, do you think that writers almost inevitably end up participating in those debates? Or do you think a reasonable distance can be maintained? What you said in that earlier conversation was that what you were trying to do in depicting the early history of Islam was turned into your heretical pronouncement, and you were trying to emphasize that distinction.

RUSHDIE: Yes, I think that it ought to be possible simply to say, "This is something like what might have happened at the beginning, at the birth of this religion." It ought to be possible to say that, neutrally, without seeming to be on one side or another. Clearly, what happened in the case of *The Satanic Verses* was that there was an assumption that I was on one side rather than the other and that, therefore, my meaning should be found in the hostility rather than in the defense. It's a shame that's what happened, but it is what happened. I think, on the whole, it must be possible in any open society to discuss openly how things happen. I think it's a great shame in the world of Islam that so much interesting contemporary scholarship about the origins of Islam is not acceptable. And the reason it's not acceptable is because of the insistence on the divine origin of the text.

Now, if you insist that the text is the uncreated word of God, then presumably the social and economic conditions of the Arabian Peninsula in the seventh century after Christ are not important, because God operates on a larger canvas than that. If, however, you are willing to historicize the text and to look at its creation as an event inside history rather than above history, then immediately what we know about the history of the period opens up and illuminates the text. I think one of the scholarly tragedies, right now, is that it's not really acceptable to do this inside much of the Muslim world.

To give just one example, in the Qur'an, the Bible stories are strangely varied from the versions that exist in the Old and New Testaments so that in the chapter of the Qur'an called Miriam, which is about the birth of Christ, Christ is born in an oasis in a desert under a palm tree. Now, the reason for this is clear. Allow me to historicize for a moment: The prophet did not begin to prophesy until he was over forty years old, and before that he had a long period as a traveling merchant, a very successful one. On those journeys, at oases and at way stations he would have met the only Christians who were present in the Arabian Peninsula at the time, who were Nestorian Christians. And Nestorian Christianity made local variations, local adaptations of Bible stories, so, in fact, the story about Christ being born under a palm tree in an oasis is a Nestorian story. It existed in the Nestorian tradition before the Qur'an, and the version in the Qur'an is more or less identical to that. So immediately you can see that this version arrives the way it does in this text because of the life experience of this man. But this is something you can't say because it negates the divine origin of the text.

So this is the problem that is faced. I'll answer your question about whether one can approach this neutrally, whether one can simply say, "This is probably what happened." Even that statement now becomes embattled, because there is already an explanation of how these things happened, and if you try to diverge from that explanation you are seen as the bad guy. I have often spoken about Ibn Rush'd; maybe I should slightly rehearse that again, because I am not really called Rushdie. My father made up the name. My grandfather was called Muhammadin Halifid Elvi because he came from Delhi, but my father decided that was too much of a mouthful and so he invented Rushdie. The reason he invented it was because he was an admirer of the philosopher Ibn Rush'd, known to the West as Averroës. And I grew up with this accidental message, or this message in a bottle, from my father, which was contained in my surname. So, at a certain point, I had to find out about Ibn Rush'd, and it's very interesting that he was one of the people who, in the twelfth century, tried to fight the literalist interpretation of the Qur'an and did so with great brilliance and scholarship and, as we can now see from the history of the world, lost that battle. But one of the arguments he made I have always found to be very beautiful, and so I offer it.

He said that if you look at the Judeo-Christian definition of God it differs from the Muslim definition in one important particular, which is that the Jews and Christians say that man was created by God in his own image. What that sentence clearly suggests is that there is some relationship between the nature of man and the nature of God, created in his own image. Islam says the opposite, that God has no human qualities. In fact, it suggests that it would demean God to suggest that He had anything as minor as a human quality. He has divine qualities. And so Ibn Rush'd argued that language, also, is a human quality, and, therefore, it was unreasonable to expect or suggest that God spoke Arabic, because God presumably spoke "God." As a result, even if you believe the story literally, when the archangel appears on the mountain and delivers the message to the prophet, he, understanding it in Arabic, is already making an active interpretation. He is already taking something which arrives in nonlinguistic form and isunderstanding it linguistically—something which arrives as a divine message which he is transforming into human comprehension.

So it was argued that if the original act of receiving the text is already an act of interpretation, then further interpretation is clearly legitimate. That was his attempt, I think probably the most brilliant attempt, to destroy the power of literalism from inside the text, and from inside what is already said and accepted. Well, that didn't work, unfortunately, though I wouldn't mind having another go. Because it is true, and it is very sad, that of all the great world religions this is the one which is born entirely inside recorded history. We really know what was happening at the time, and so it's the one that can be studied as an event inside history, as an economic, social, cultural, political, world historic event. It's actually not difficult to see the ways the conditions of the time impinge upon the Qur'an as a text and help to shape it, and it's a tragedy that you're not allowed to do that. I guess I tried to do that and there were people who disapproved.

VISWANATHAN: Then, would you say, that literature is probably one of the most effective mediums for historicizing religion, especially for its early formations, one which can, as you say, put the spotlight on religion as recorded history?

RUSHDIE: Well, it's a way of getting people to read it. More people read novels than scholarly texts. I'm sorry to say that in this room, but it's true. Of course, a lot of this would not have been possible had it not been for very, very detailed scholarship of a sort that is never going to be a mass-market event, but we can steal it, use it, profit by it.

VISWANATHAN: Let's look at Akbar, one of the major figures in your last novel, *The Enchantress of Florence.* Would you see the historical presence of competing beliefs as a model for experiments with intellectual and religious pluralism, such as the one Akbar created with this tent of new worship?

RUSHDIE: Well, he's attractive, isn't he? Because he had this open-mindedness on the subject of religion. I don't know that it was complete openness; it was more pantheism than open-mindedness, more of a belief that all religions were ways of worshiping the same god, described and named differently, but essentially the same. And, as you know, he tried to invent a religion which expressed that idea, the so-called Din-i-Ilahi, and it didn't catch on. People in the end preferred their differences to the idea of unity, and I think that's one of the poignancies about the project of Akbar. The so-called Ibadat Khana, the house of worship, the place of debate . . .

VISWANATHAN: But it's not even a house, it's a tent.

RUSHDIE: Well, I made that up.

VISWANATHAN: But that's what's so interesting in this little conceit that you have.

RUSHDIE: Well, what interests me is that. If you read the story, the history of Akbar and this place, the Ibadat Khana, the chamber where all these philosophies met every day in debate, it's clear that it was a very important place in the court. And yet in what remains of Fatehpur Sikri, the capital city, nobody knows where it was. The building is lost, and nobody has any idea of where in the site it might have been. It's very strange that a building which was clearly so important in the life of the court should have vanished without leaving a trace. So from that I just decided, well, maybe it was never a permanent building in the first place. The Mughals were incredible tentmakers. They made very elaborate multistory tents, and, in fact, you can say that the architecture of the Mughal period is a rendering in stone of some of the principles of the tentmakers and that the architecture in some ways derives from the tentmaking. So, I thought, maybe it's a tent, and then I thought, maybe that's kind of appropriate because ideas are not permanent. Ideas are things in flux, and they move and shift, and you can pick them up here and put them down over there, so maybe a tent is the right place to discuss ideas.

VISWANATHAN: Is Akbar an ideal for you in any ways?

RUSHDIE: No. I worry about the idealization of Akbar because I think that a lot of that is backwards projection. We want to have a liberal, tolerant, almost kind of democratic man in the sixteenth century, but he was a despot, Akbar, and he was not interested in not being a despot. He was a man jealous of his power and he exercised it. I think the thing I was interested to write about was that conflict in him, between the self that was disputatious and open-minded and the other self that didn't want anybody to argue with him. You can't understand him simply as one or the other. The thing that is colossally important about him is that he tried so hard to break down the barriers between the peoples of India, the barriers created by their different belief systems. I think that it is a heroic action, and it was followed by his son and his grandson. Jahangir, Shah Jahan, the next two emperors, essentially followed that project. Then after that came Aurangzeb, who did a great deal to unmake the project. But, yes, I think it's admirable.

But there are limits to it. There is a story that preexists, which I didn't make up. It's a legend, but it's a legend that I thought was interesting because it shows the possible limits of such a project. The story is that the court musician, Dansen, created this raga, which was the raga of fire, and sang it so beautifully that his skin began to burn and at the end of the music there were actually burns on his body. So Akbar said to him, "Go home and rest and get well." He came from the city of Gwalior, so he went back to Gwalior to rest and recover. In Gwalior he met these two girls called Tana and Riri who were famous for the beauty of their singing. They sang to him the Megh Malhar, the song of the rain, and the rain fell, and it was magic rain and it washed away his burns. The emperors, hearing this story, astonished, invited these girls to the court so that he could celebrate them. And in the girls' family there was a conversation, and the problem was that these were Hindu girls from a Hindu family, and they did not wish to go to the court of a Muslim king. Yet they felt that, if they were to refuse to go, then the king would be angry and there would be reprisals against their family and so on. They didn't know how to say yes, and they didn't know how to say no, and so they committed suicide.

And it just struck me, if you were that kind of king, if you were the kind of king who believed that the borders between religions could be broken down and that people could all live together in mutual understanding, what a shock it must be to discover that there are people who would sooner die, sooner die than buy into that project. And it seemed to me that that was the limit of it. That's why I'm saying it's not idealistic. Here's a project, but there are limitations to the project. There are people who will not do that, and we have to recognize that and see why that is and what comes out of that.

VISWANATHAN: Well, I think it's very interesting, the position that you are taking about the idealization of Akbar, because there is certainly one strand of thought, especially in India, that holds Akbar as this proto-secular, syncretic figure.

RUSHDIE: Yes, and some of that is true.

VISWANATHAN: Yes, in fact, I was thinking of Armartya Sen's book *The Argumentative Indian*, where he makes the strong claim that the diffusion of argumentative traditions in Indian life, cutting across social classes and shaping the Indian social world and culture, has helped to make heterodoxy the natural state of affairs in India and even goes so far as to link it to the development of democracy. Would you go in that direction?

RUSHDIE: Far be it for me to argue with Armartya Sen, but why not? Look, Amartya uses Ashoka and Akbar as early examples of the development of a kind of Indian intellectual tradition which he espouses and values, which he offers as intrinsically Indian tradition—not something imported from outside. The idea that this kind of open, disputatious, secularist principle can be discovered from inside the Indian tradition rather than from outside, it is, of course, important, and I would not disagree with him about that. But the problem with selecting a couple of exemplars and saying this is what the Indian tradition comes from immediately makes one want to say that there are opposite exemplars. Why is it Akbar who is the model and not Aurangzeb? Why is it that the fifty years of tolerance of the reign of Akbar should be the model rather than the fifty years of oppression and violence of the reign of Aurangzeb only three kings down the line?

Ashoka and Akbar were both enormously impressive figures, and it's perfectly right to try to derive from them, if you like, an Indian tradition that one would want to have. The reason why I resist doing only that is that there is also a countertradition, a tradition of Muslim oppression of Hindus and Hindu oppression of Muslims, and the unwillingness of those two sides to compromise or get along. That's part, unfortunately, of the tradition too. And that's not just about India; that's true anywhere you look. You can find models as shining examples in the past to say that these are the people to look to see where the present comes from and where the future should come from, but you always have to recognize that there is a counterexample. Certainly, if you are writing novels, it's very difficult to be only on one side of the fence. You have to be on both sides of the fence. You have to give the devil the best tunes.

VISWANATHAN: Well, with this vision, Akbar's vision of new intellectual and religious pluralism that you depict, it's very dispiriting to reach the end of the novel and see that vision disintegrate. There are these very powerful lines. In fact, I'm going to just quote . . .

RUSHDIE: You are going to give away the end of the novel?

VISWANATHAN: No, I'm not giving it away. I think history has already given away the end of the novel, but "Once he has gone, all he thought, all he had worked to make his philosophy and way of being, all that would evaporate like water. The future would not be what he hoped for but a dry, hostile, antagonistic place, where people would survive as best as they could and hate their neighbors and smash their places of worship and kill one another once again in the renewed heat of the great quarrel he had sought to end forever, the quarrel over God. In the future, it was harshness not civilization that would rule."

It's an extremely bleak sense of the very possibility that Akbar had worked so hard to achieve in his life.

RUSHDIE: Yes, sorry about that. It is bleak. It *is* bleak, but, you know, look at the world we live in. Look at it! I don't want to be singing some happy song while people are slitting each other's throats and throwing bombs at each other all over the place. Just look at it. I mean, what is this? We live in a harsh world. We don't live in this world of tolerance and happiness and music and dance. We live in a world of death and bombs and destruction and hatred and distrust, etc., etc. As President Bollinger was saying, I hope that something on Tuesday can change that—and I believe that maybe something happened that will change that—but it's difficult to live at this moment in the history of the world and be an optimist. It's difficult.

VISWANATHAN: Do you think there is some kind of perfect order? Some perfect world which resists even being represented through your imagination?

RUSHDIE: No, I have no utopian tendencies.

VISWANATHAN: But you do have a sense of alternative political futures.

RUSHDIE: That's what I'm saying. I believe in the argument, and if you are by nature satirical in your imagination it's always easy to see what you don't like. I am good at seeing what I don't like. Much, much harder to work out what you do like, and often you can be wrong about the things you think you do like. I mean let's hope we are not, this week, because this week I do feel optimistic. It's an odd feeling, one that I am not familiar with. Actually, the worst thing I can say is that the last time I felt a little bit like this was after the election of Tony Blair, and look what happened. So I am just hoping this isn't a rerun of that story. I don't think it is.

VISWANATHAN: Well, maybe I can take you back to your more bleak outlook on life.

RUSHDIE: Yes, let's be bleak! I like that.

VISWANATHAN: *Shalimar the Clown* . . .

RUSHDIE: *Bleak House* . . .

VISWANATHAN: *Shalimar the Clown* offers a terrifying glimpse into a world of religious extremism that preys on minds and hearts tortured by longing and betrayal in order to serve its own violent purposes. Yet, in your hauntingly lyrical evocation of Kashmir, the counterpoint to religious extremism is not necessarily secularism—at least that's what I think—but religion restored to a more expansive and more inclusive practice.

RUSHDIE: Exactly. I remember, and I think many people my age who have any knowledge not just of India but of other parts of the Muslim world can remember, another idea of Islam, one that had more or less nothing to do with what walks around the world calling itself Islam nowadays, one in which it was OK to argue about things and to talk freely and to live at peace with other people and so on. It wasn't perfect, because none of us are perfect, but it was possible.

I remember my parents' generation. I remember growing up in that world of people who were in many cases devout Muslims. My grandfather went on the hajj to Mecca. He said his prayers five times a day every day of his life, and his children and his grandchildren, being grandchildren, would make horrible fun of him and ask him why he spent so much time with his bottom higher than his head. And, instead of getting cross with us, he would laugh at us and encourage us to come and have a talk about it. I remember the Sufi Islam of Kashmir, the way in which that Islam was affected by its contiguity with Hinduism and the way in which the Hinduism of Kashmir was affected by its proximity to that Islam, so that, for instance, as I said somewhere in the novel, in Kashmir you have these little shrines of Sufi saints all over the place and people would stop and make offerings. Well, as a Muslim you're not supposed to worship anyone but the one God; you're not supposed to go and do puja at the shrine of Sufi saints. Yet that's what everybody would do, and, interestingly, even the Hindus would do it. Hindu truck drivers would stop by the road and put a flower or offering at the shrine of a Muslim Sufi saint.

That's something interesting and rich, I think, that developed in Kashmir; this composite culture that was neither completely Hindu nor completely Muslim, and for a while it worked, and now it has been destroyed. I think the loss of it is a thing to grieve over, not only in Kashmir, but in many places of the Muslim world. I'm old enough to remember what places like Beirut were like in the 1950s and '60s. They were great cosmopolitan cities, great seats of culture. And to see the way that has been destroyed leads one to say there may be many things for which one can blame the United States, but the self-destruction of Muslim culture by other Muslims is a self-inflicted wound, and it is a grievous wound. In that novel I tried to write about that other, to my mind, more beautiful approach to the world. You're right that the answer to religion is not no religion, but another way of thinking about religion, another way of being in the religion.

VISWANATHAN: Engaging with the richer currents of religion?

RUSHDIE: One of the characters in *The Enchantress of Florence* is asked by Akbar, just before he has his head chopped off, what his idea of paradise is, since he is on his way there. He says that in paradise the words *religion* and *argument* mean the same thing and that there is no suppression in religion. This reminds me of the very great line in the first paragraph of Saul Bellow's novel, *The Adventures of Augie March*. He says, "there is no fineness or accuracy in suppression; if you hold down one thing, you hold down the adjoining." That openness to ideas is something which I don't think should be seen as being antithetical to religion. You only have to look at Jesuit argument. I went to speak at Yeshiva College last year, and I had a very hard time because they're all trained in disputation. So there I was with a thousand students, sort of embryonic rabbis whose entire discipline was to tear apart the argument of the person next door. God, it was difficult. I'm not going there again.

VISWANATHAN: Well then maybe you can confirm or deny something I had read somewhere, that you actually enjoy speaking to religious audiences?

RUSHDIE: Did I say that? I wasn't telling the truth.

VISWANATHAN: But if I can just stay on *Shalimar* a little bit longer. The social ostracism and violent death of Boonyi, your central female character in that book, I think are among the most memorable parts of the novel. In fact, I think they are among the most memorable passages I have read anywhere among your work. You wrote in a *New York Times* op-ed piece in December 2005, and I quote, "Multiculturalism has all too often become mere cultural relativism under cover of which much that is reactionary and oppressive, of women, for example, can be justified." You referred to a couple of notorious recent cases of women, Imrana in India and Mukhtar Mai in Pakistan, women who were very brutally victimized, but the object of your critique in this article is not just the religious authorities and judicial systems that defer to them in India and Pakistan but also the international community that refuses to get involved, saying, "Oh, that's their culture, and that has to be respected even if it offends us."

So, this question of relativism is a very interesting one in your work. It seems to work for you when it comes to resisting the notion of a single origin from which all things and beings derive, but you draw the line on relativism when it becomes a way of saying that cultural difference cancels out a single standard of justice. I think the question of these women becomes an extremely important one in this discussion. Obviously, this is a very difficult question, not difficult in answering but maybe more difficult in framing the argument against relativism without appearing to reinstate a single standard of values that represents some kind of universal, which, too, at another level, you might want to resist.

RUSHDIE: Well, OK, I don't know how unfashionable this is, but I think there are universals. I think there are things that are universally true, and I think there are such things as universal rights. The reason I think it is not culturally specific. The argument made by relativists is that it is culturally specific to argue that there are universals. I think there are other ways of approaching it. One way of approaching it is to say that there are things which are essential to our nature as human beings wherever in the world we come from, and—to go back to what I was saying about Ibn Rush'd—one of those essential characteristics that we all share is the characteristic of language, of speech, what Steven Pinker calls the language instinct. We learn English, we learn language, because we are hardwired to learn language. Our DNA is such that it enables us to learn this very complicated thing without any clues. So we are a language animal, we are an animal that has always from the beginning used language in order to understand itself and in order to define and shape the kind of creature that it is. If you begin to restrict, limit, forbid, circumscribe the ways language can be used, you are committing an offense which is not culturally specific. You are committing an existential offense. It is an offense against the nature of the animal that we are.

We are the language animal, and we have to be allowed to use language to understand ourselves. Therefore, to defend the freedom of language as a universal human right seems to me justifiable not by appeal to this or that cultural tradition, but simply to the biology of the beast. This is the thing that we are. You take language away from the human beings, you take humanity away from them. So it seems to me that it is possible, in this way, to argue for the universality of certain rights. We are a dreaming animal. We live very richly through the things that we imagine. Were it not for the capacity of imagination, there would be very little progress in human existence. You have to imagine a wheel before you can make a wheel; you have to imagine the hyperlink before you can construct the hyperlink. First you dream it, and then you make it so. All through human history imagination precedes reality, and things move constantly through the border between imagination and reality. What starts as a dream becomes reality. So, again, to start restricting our ability to dream and envision, and to tell us that there are things we can dream about and other things that are bad dreams that we must not have, is a crime against humanity.

It's not about whether you are Muslim or Christian or Chinese or American. It's about the kind of creature that we all are and have always been. That's why I think that there are such things as universals, because we are remarkably alike. I forget, because I'm not a scientist, what the figure is, but there is some ridiculously high quantity of our genetic code that is common to all human beings. There is 2 or 3 percent variation that accounts for all this diversity. We are much more the same than we are not. If that is true, then there must be things which apply to all of us.

I think relativism is the dangerous death of liberalism. If you will justify anything that anybody does because it comes from their tradition, it means you abdicate your moral sense; you cease to be a moral being. "Oh yes, let them kill novelists because it is what they do. We personally don't kill novelists, but if it's their way then they must kill novelists." For some reason I feel an objection to that position.

In the article you mention, which talks about the oppression of women, if you were to take religion away as the justification, nobody would tolerate that for a minute. The kind of limitations that women have been placed under, the crimes committed against women in the name of religion, are so profound, and yet somehow people don't get as agitated about them as if the same thing had been committed by someone who wasn't using God as the reason. Well, that seems like nonsense to me.

That's why I'm saying that to be tolerant and open and argumentative doesn't mean that you don't have a moral sense. You still have moral responsibility. You still have to make choices. You still have to say, "This is right; that is wrong." Female circumcision, wrong! I don't care what mullah says so. Death of a novelist is usually wrong, although in some cases one could make exceptions. I promised not to talk about Dan Brown . . .

VISWANATHAN: Well, I think that's an excellent place to end. Salman has very graciously agreed to accept questions from the audience.

AUDIENCE MEMBER 1: Yes, thank you. I really enjoyed your remarks, but I just felt like I needed to challenge you on that last part. Are you in fact saying that men oppress women because of religion? Because of God?

RUSHDIE: No, I'm saying that often they use it to justify their oppression.

AUDIENCE MEMBER 1: Yes, because my impression was that every religion justifies it, in which case it can hardly be the religion.

RUSHDIE: The example I was giving in that article was of a case in North India a couple of years ago, when a woman was raped by her father-in-law. This was a Muslim woman, all parties, wife, husband, father-in-law, all Muslim, and the local Islamic seminary decreed that because this had happened she was now to be considered unclean to her husband and he should therefore divorce her. The husband and wife appeared to genuinely love each other and not wish to be divorced, and yet enormous social pressure was put on them to divorce, for this religious reason. In that case the secular system did rather well; it arrested the father-in-law, tried him, found him guilty, and sent him to jail. But, in spite of that, and in spite of it being quite clear that she had in no way consented to this act, the religious authorities maintained that she was now somehow dirty, soiled goods. It struck me that it was a kind of obscenity to use ideology to justify such a thing.

AUDIENCE MEMBER 1: But is it, perhaps, also an example of a male-dominated religion using religion to rationalize what are actually more biological masculine behaviors?

RUSHDIE: Yes.

AUDIENCE MEMBER 1: I don't want to blame the religion necessarily.

RUSHDIE: I look forward to the creation of the female-dominated religion.

AUDIENCE MEMBER 2: I'm just wondering about your comment that relativism is the death of liberalism, because I'm surprised that you think liberalism itself is a coherent entity, a coherent idea. You say that we have to draw the line at things like female circumcision, that that's clearly wrong. But you have to invoke some sort of timeless, incontrovertible standard that no one could question in order for liberalism to gain the kind of coherence it wants to have. It seems to me that there is no argument you can make against the person who disagrees with you that female circumcision is wrong. If they ask why it is wrong, then you're eventually going to end up in a kind of regress circularity. It seems to me that liberalism just pretends to be tolerant when actually it is intolerant. I'm not saying there is any alternative, but you're actually invoking intolerance. We should be intolerant towards female circumcision or whatever else. We should be intolerant towards the murder of authors.

RUSHDIE: Well, this is the question that Columbia University's President Bollinger asked at the very beginning: Where are the limits of tolerance? Maybe violence and its justification by an appeal to a religious authority is a point at which you could place a limit on tolerance. You know, this is a question-and-answer session, and it would take a longer conversation to thrash this out, but I hear what you're saying. It's not a coherent philosophy, liberalism. But in its essence it believes itself to be an approach of openness and tolerance towards the world, and yet that can lead it to accept actions which are oppressive. The longer conversation, we can have another time.

AUDIENCE MEMBER 3: Thank you, Mr. Rushdie, for being here. Do you think your wide readership and status as a writer is due in part to your oppression, and therefore your writing has had greater power because of what you have faced? How do you reconcile that? Would you have preferred to be in a place where you may not have been oppressed but perhaps lose power as a writer?

RUSHDIE: Yes.

AUDIENCE MEMBER 3: So there's no doubt? Is there a balance? Obviously, you had to go through some pretty terrible events.

RUSHDIE: Lots of writers are oppressed. Whether their work continues to be interesting or not, in the end, has to do with the work and not the oppression. Oppression can bring you some short-term attention, but it does not bring you long-term attention. There are a lot of people now who don't remember the attack on *The Satanic Verses* or who can't, if they were too young. It happened twenty years ago, and to anybody under thirty it must feel like ancient history. I don't think they were drawn towards my books because I was famously oppressed. Actually, I was doing just fine before then and would have been quite happy, thank you very much, to chug along at that level, having my books translated into forty languages and selling millions of copies. You know, that was fine.

But then, you're right there was a kind of spike of attention that happened around 1989, but it's long gone. I think that if any of this stuff that I've done continues to be of interest—including *The Satanic Verses,* by the way—in the end it will have to be in terms of the text itself. The rest of it is just a passing thing. But if you're asking me whether I'd rather it hadn't happened, then yes, I'd rather it hadn't happened. On the whole, if you could in your life possibly avoid being sentenced to death by the tyrannical leader of a foreign power, who then sends international mercenaries after you to carry out the sentence, I would on the whole recommend it.

AUDIENCE MEMBER 4: I wanted to pursue the issue of tolerance a little bit more. I wonder if tolerance, being the European concept that it is, with roots in the war between religions in the 1500s, is tolerant enough as a concept? Related to that, whether, when we discuss religion versus secularism, *religion* is another term, another concept, that is fundamentally a Latin one, and whether we are exporting, just by talking about religion universally, a criterion of unification of languages and traditions that is violent in and of itself?

RUSHDIE: No. You see, I'm sorry to appear to criticize the terms of your question, but I think that those of us who come from the country of Mahatma Gandhi would question whether the idea of tolerance was a Western idea. In fact, as you know, one of his wittier remarks was when he was asked what he thought of Western civilization, he replied, he thought it would be a good idea.

AUDIENCE MEMBER 4: Well, one could speak of hospitality instead of tolerance.

RUSHDIE: Well, to put it in nontheoretical terms, the desire of human beings to get along with each other is not culturally specific. The desire of human beings to be able to put up with their neighbors, even if they play the radio too loud or pick their noses, is something which, in the end, we all kind of feel. I think we try to get along with each other, and I feel that's a thing that does not have to do with culture. It's a thing that we have to do every day; we try to get along with people next-door even if they're not like us. All this is sort of elevating that to a much grander scale. I do think there is a perfectly nonculturally specific idea of tolerance which can be used in this context. I'm not a theoretical person; if you want philosophy, apply elsewhere. I make things up. So I can tell you what I believe, but why would you trust me? I'm a novelist. So I think I'll just leave it there.

AUDIENCE MEMBER 5: I think this question may be a little on the philosophical side, but I'll ask it anyway. You stated that, in religion, there's nothing inherent that inspires beauty, because there are people that are nonreligious who can create beauty. Likewise, I was wondering if you would apply this to the case of evil, so that you have obviously people inspired by religion who do evil things, but there are also people who are not inspired by religion and they do evil things. In that case there is nothing specific to religion that would inspire humans to evil. So I just wanted to see if your statement on beauty could also be applied to evil.

RUSHDIE: Yes, of course, certainly. Absolutely, yes.

AUDIENCE MEMBER 6: I have a very basic question related to *Satanic Verses*. Gibreel Farishta is a character who lives in delusions and, in the end, he turns very self-destructive. He commits suicide, but in the real world, including the world of Prophet Mohammed, prophets or any self-proclaimed prophets don't commit suicide. They are not self-destructive; they actually benefit from their delusions. How do you explain that?

RUSHDIE: I can think of at least one suicidal prophet, Jim Jones, but I agree it's a minority. One of the reasons I wrote that book was that I did not find it very easy to understand the messianic cast of mind. The way I try to understand things is to find a way of telling a story about them and get inside the people and try and see how I can make them behave in a way that's credible to me. That's why I tried to do it in that book. Well, a lot of prophets, of course, don't have time to commit suicide because other people kill them. They crucify them upside down or the right way up and so on, so there is that. It's a short career, usually. Very few prophets need old age pensions. I mean Moses, Abraham, these are exceptions. On the whole, they just get killed, because, in the end, no one can stand them. So, does that answer your question?

AUDIENCE MEMBER 6: Well, not really, because self-proclaimed prophets like Osho and others, they own a lot of wealth, they become celebrities . . .

RUSHDIE: That's true. I'm sorry, I wasn't thinking at the exalted level of Radjneesh; I was thinking more of Jesus Christ, the slightly less significant prophet. No, I don't have a theoretical answer, but I think it is true that there is something that is genuine which is the mystical experience. When I say genuine, I mean, subjectively genuine.

If you look at accounts given by mystics of the nature of their experience, they're very, very similar. If you look at what the prophet Mohammed is reported as having said about the nature of receiving the prophecy in the Hadith of the Prophet, it's remarkably similar to what you would find in the accounts of Saint John the Divine or Joan of Arc. There clearly is a phenomenon, which we call revelation, which happens to certain numbers of people and clearly is a very powerful thing for those people to experience. And it fuels, in some of them, a desire to promulgate that, to send that outwards. Other mystics remain inturned; there isn't a kind of proselytization desire, but sometimes there is a desire to go out and preach. I guess the profundity of the experience is such that it fuels that drive for a lifetime. I mean, the character in my novel is insane, and far be it for me to suggest that that was true of other prophets (or, if I did, I would suggest it at another time). What I mean is, it's not relevant to this conversation. I think it's just that whatever that thing is that happens in the human mind, that creates the experience of enlightenment, or revelation, whatever you want to call it. It's clearly a very profound experience, and it gives people the fuel which often carries them through a lifetime. Maybe that's why they don't kill themselves, but, speaking as someone to whom this has not happened, I am unable to authoritatively answer your question.

AUDIENCE MEMBER 7: You mentioned that at the time of your grandfather there was more Sufistic kind of practicing going on in Kashmir and probably all of South Asia, India, and Pakistan. So I wanted to tell you the good news that it still happens, and the number of people going to shrines is increasing rapidly. There is no decrease in that. Secondly, when you speak of the open-mindedness of Akbar, don't you think that Akbar was a great politician who knew that without the support of the Hindus, especially the Rajputs, he could not establish his kingdom in India, and so he kept marrying girls from Rajput families because he wanted to do that? Would you call that open-mindedness or more the shrewdness of a politician?

RUSHDIE: I don't deny that he was a very shrewd ruler who knew how to, as you say, make alliances and so on. But, remember, this is not by any means the first Muslim kingdom in Indian. There were Muslim kingdoms in India for a couple of centuries before the Mughals. None of the others had ever tried to rule in this way. To give just the most obvious example, this thing called the Jizya tax was a tax imposed on non-Muslims, and so there was a communally unfair taxation system where a non-Muslim paid more taxes then a Muslim did. One of the first things that Akbar did was to abolish the Jizya tax and make people equal under the law.

Of course, there is an element of politics in it, as there would be for any ruler, anytime, anywhere. You have to make the calculation about whether it would play, whether it would work, whether in the end it would benefit you or not benefit you to act in a certain way. But it was a very original idea of Akbar's to try to rule by consensus rather than by oppression. It's an unusual thing given the family he comes from. This is the direct bloodline of Genghis Khan and of Temür, who came to Delhi and killed fifty thousand people. These are his direct ancestors. He himself was illiterate with a childhood of enormous brutality all around him and great personal risk in much of his childhood. He comes to the throne at the age of only fourteen and decides he doesn't want to rule like that. It's an extraordinary thing that a man of that background would become a ruler of that kind. It would have been much more likely that he be another kind of ruler; that's the tradition he came from. So that's why he is an interesting figure: because there was a transformation there, and, in a way, you couldn't believe that man would be that kind of king. So I don't think there is a contradiction. I think you can be the politician and, if you like, the philosopher. He was a kind of philosopher king, which is in itself a deep contradiction in terms. He was that oxymoron.

AUDIENCE MEMBER 8: You speak of the "AND" as though it's a memory and something of the past, celebrating Islam "AND" Hinduism, celebrating secularism "AND" religion. I am wondering if you have any recommendations for the ways educators and writers can move beyond "tolerance" and return to the honoring and celebration of diversity of thought and truths?

RUSHDIE: Well, the bee in my bonnet is the one that I talked about earlier, which is historical context. I am a historian insofar as I have any academic discipline at all. Actually, what I have is academic indiscipline, but that was my degree subject. I think that unless you put things in a historical context you can't understand what they are. To me, it's a great loss to Muslims in the Muslim world that they cannot historicize the birth of the philosophy or the religion by which they live. So I think that would be what I would recommend: Teach the context, not just the text. It is very important to teach the context and then you begin to see why the world is what it is, why ideas are what they are, why they took the path they took rather than another path.

AUDIENCE MEMBER 9: Thank you so much for coming. If you don't mind: What do you live for?

RUSHDIE: What do I live for? Dinner.

1

CLASSICAL WESTERN APPROACHES TO TOLERATION

A FORM OF LIBERTY AND INDULGENCE

Toleration as a Layered Institution

IRA KATZNELSON

The Duke of Buckingham thus expressed himself in favour of a Toleration: My Lords; There is a thing called liberty, which . . . is, that the people of England are fondest of; it is that they will never part with. . . . This, my Lords, in my opinion can never be done without giving an Indulgence to all Protestant Dissenters. It is certainly a very uneasy kind of life to any man, that has either Christian charity, humanity, or good-nature, to see his fellow-subjects daily abused, divested of their liberties and birth-rights, and miserably thrown out of their possessions and freeholds, only because they cannot agree with others in some opinions and niceties of religion, which their consciences will not give them leave to consent to. . . . Methinks, in this notion of persecution a very gross mistake, both as to the point of Government, and the point of Religion. . . . It makes every man's safety depend on the wrong place; not upon governors, or a man's living well toward the civil government established by law, but upon his being transported with zeal for every opinion, that is held by those that have power in the Church that is in fashion. . . . My humble motion to your lordships is, that you would give leave to bring in a Bill of Indulgence to all Protestant Dissenters.

—HOUSE OF LORDS, OCTOBER 1675, *COBBETT'S PARLIAMENTARY HISTORY OF ENGLAND*, VOL. 4: *COMPRISING THE PERIOD FROM THE RESTORATION OF CHARLES THE SECOND, IN 1660, TO THE REVOLUTION, IN 1688*

Toleration is profoundly important. It addresses some of the most difficult and persistent features of human social relations. Combinations of hierarchy and loathing across group lines recur frequently in recorded history, notably, but not exclusively, when cultural pluralism takes religious form. The pervasive, protean, and passionate qualities of religious imaginations and identities combine belief with practical social organization. Hand in hand, religious and political contention can create markers of solidarity, incommensurability, and enmity that expose different faiths, especially minority faiths and their adherents, to zealotry and danger. Often led by specialists in violence, such processes under conditions of diversity that designate people and practices as unacceptable have been persistent in human history.

As Bernard Williams observed, toleration "is necessary when different groups—moral, political, or religious—realize that there is no alternative to living together, that is to say, no alternative except armed conflict, which will not resolve their disagreements and will impose continuous suffering."[1] An alternative to oppression, suffering, and violence, toleration is most needed in circumstances that make respect, cooperation, and social peace difficult to obtain. "We need to tolerate other people and their ways of life," Williams ruefully noted, "only in situations that make it very difficult to do so."[2] Toleration thus is motivated and should be judged by its capacity to manage deeply felt commitments in inconvenient conditions.

Toleration is a virtue.[3] It is not, however, a simple good. In the recent past, a significant number of philosophers and political theorists have probed and debated toleration's meaning, complexity, and ambiguity. They have understood it to be a concept that is "grim and limited," even if immensely valuable.[4] Grim because it is premised on dislike and disapproval. Limited because its rules, combining law, intellectual justification, and social practices, are contingent on self-discipline by the powerful, and offer a form of liberty more qualified than a right.

Toleration is what George Fletcher calls an unstable virtue. Hovering between "an impulse to intervene and regulate the lives of others, and . . . an imperative—either logical or moral—to restrain that impulse,"[5] it never is simply fixed or secure, for it is inherently controversial. Its very existence, its conditions for the accommodation of disliked beliefs and social practices, and its substantive range cannot but be deeply contested and often fiercely resisted, not always unreasonably. Toleration implies circumstances that make it possible and reasons that make it desirable.[6] Both are uncertain.

Curiously, discussions and considerations of such matters have played little if any role in scholarly literatures in history and the social sciences that detail and seek to understand contentious and often violent engagements across the lines of religion and ethnicity, nation, and race. Toleration has yet to function analytically as a theoretically inscribed variable, in part because the philosophical literature designates toleration as self-abnegation by powerful actors but stops short of fashioning the concept in sufficiently differentiated fashion to make it a tool for systematic historical and empirical research. As a result, the separation between philosophical inquiry and such investigations has remained quite stark. My goal, by contrast, is to encourage the integration of toleration "into the current primary social science concerns and analytical methods," which is how J. P. Nettl identified his objective in considering the modern state as a multilayered conceptual variable.[7]

What Sudipta Kaviraj has written about religion as "many different things," and thus with "an indeterminacy of reference," holds for toleration as well. Like religion, toleration refers to a range of institutional fields, spanning "an ethical order, a social order, philosophical systems, political institutions."[8] The sources, qualities, and strategies of human diversity and prospects for toleration all vary. How, I ask, might we specify toleration's various dimensions and identify elements of its formation and topology in both settled and unsettled times? Without such analytical instruments it is not possible to advance a program of inquiry and research that can construct both richer descriptions and better causal explanations about particular historical situations and thus help identify forms of toleration we might wish to have.

I

It is easy to confuse toleration with what it is not. Toleration does not connote being unconcerned. Toleration exists despite caring. That is, toleration designates a willful decision to permit disliked groups, beliefs, or practices to persist despite the ability to do otherwise. Toleration is least required when different groups who dislike each other's values and ways of life are nonetheless indifferent. Toleration is least secure when it is based not on principles but on "a Hobbesian equilibrium, under which the acceptance of one group by the other is the best that either of them can get" given the temporary balance of forces.[9] Toleration is most likely to succeed when it is underpinned by persuasive argument and sustained by values both internal and external to it, when it is supported by practical arrangements that make its performance more likely, and when public authorities are willing to act when fanaticism threatens to override group inhibitions and self-policing.

As a site of applied ethics combining normative and practical elements, toleration hovers in an uncertain zone between, though often overlapping with, respect and recognition, on the one side, and persecution and oppression, on the other. A condition of toleration is the existence of persons and ways of thinking and behaving that elicit more than mild dislike or discomfort, but antipathy often closer to outrage and revulsion.[10] Without such aversion, toleration so overlaps respect and recognition that it loses its distinctiveness. Dislike is often an antecedent to action. To be tolerant is to accept and refrain from action despite the absence of indifference. "Intermediate between wholehearted acceptance and unrestrained opposition,"[11] the concept designates a family of conceptions that support such self-discipline. Unlike cultural and moral relativism characterized by the absence of judgment, and unlike multicultural respect based on a normative approval of human diversity, toleration "*presupposes* . . . negative judgment or condemnation. To tolerate something or someone," as Steven Lukes rightly notes, "is to abstain from acting against what one finds unacceptable."[12] Toleration is not passive endurance, for it entails more than just not doing, but a reflective not doing, a self-conscious acceptance despite dislike and disapproval. Other considerations intervene to motivate either a temporary or permanent suspension of action, notwithstanding an often potent disposition to act.

As a willful act of omission, a deliberate silence or restraint, a suspension of commitment, and a willingness to share geographic and political space with others who deviate from true belief, correct values, and proper behavior, toleration is less a matter of social justice than of forbearance in the face of diversity.[13] Toleration implies targets of disapproval, asymmetric relationships, and the absence of self-regulating regard. That is, it presumes circumstances in which members of at least one group view negatively the ideas and deeds of at least one other. Notwithstanding, those who could act to restrict others do not. They might condemn, but do not intervene despite their ability to do so; "we do not speak of the weak tolerating the strong."[14] Toleration thus restrains action consistent with disapproval. Such self-control requires either cost-benefit calculations that toleration is a necessary means to some more valued end or more principled justifications, based on religious convictions, secular skepticism, or other values that can trump the desire to impose religious and ethical uniformity on persons one wishes were not present or who one hopes would lead their lives differently.[15] Not requiring respect or appreciation of difference, the central "problem of toleration," as Susan Mendus identifies it, is "explaining how it can be right to permit what is wrong."[16]

Toleration implies the capacity to not tolerate.[17] It is a rejection of available intolerance. Toleration curbs behavior by those capable of repression, but does not insist that the beliefs motivating the restrained wish to act against others be given up. Toleration, in short, is based on an insistence that those who have the ability to curb others should voluntarily refrain, even when they are convinced that such actions would be just and means of repression are at hand. This is more than sufferance, for toleration compels decisions not to deploy such available instruments.

Toleration has thus been defined by Andrew Cohen as "an agent's intentional and principled refraining from interfering with an opposed other (or their behavior, etc.) in situations of diversity, where the agent believes she has the power to interfere."[18] Actors with power, Preston King elaborates, decide "to endure, suffer, or put up with a person, activity, idea, or organization" despite their moral or practical aversion. Given the intensity of dislike, toleration is "an act of extraordinary self-restraint,"[19] especially by public authorities who command sovereign powers and law. Understood this way, toleration is not a matter of private judgment but a contested feature of public policy whose indulgences extend liberty.

It hardly needs saying that, in the West, it was the Reformation that projected toleration beyond considerations of heresy and the status of non-Christians, the two sets of questions that had concerned the Church and some rulers in medieval Europe. Toleration, to be sure, possesses an etiology older than ideas and developments in the early modern period. But it was Christian civil war that transformed toleration from a concern with peripheral people by religious authorities and political rulers to a set of questions located at the very center of European public and private life. When John Rawls explained why he had turned from the mode and content of reasoning, above and outside human particularity, that had characterized *A Theory of Justice*'s search for a comprehensive liberalism to focus, by contrast, in *Political Liberalism* on potentially irreconcilable human differences among persons who do not all share a single comprehensive doctrine, he highlighted the Reformation's radically unresolved moment when "rival authoritative and salvationist" forms of Christianity, each "dogmatic and intolerant," faced off while seeking to control and secure protection from secular authorities.[20]

Almost no one in the sixteenth century considered toleration to be a good thing. At a moment when the political was so deeply embedded in the language of God and his creation, and the human condition was understood as an aspect of a larger cosmic structure, conflict tended to be total. Unlike various syncretic and open religious faiths, like Islam in India, the forms of western Christianity were unitary and closed. In France, *tolerer* was used by partisans of a tough line against heresy to denote subjection to an evil, a course of action they despised. During the broadside wars of the Reformation, polemicists often treated toleration as an unwelcome sanction for licentiousness and iniquity, an endorsement of great mistakes, a threat to the seriousness of theology and the depth of doctrine, and thus a recipe for disorder. As a negative slur, the term was "mainly used pejoratively," Alexandra Walsham writes, "denounced . . . [as] a diabolical device, the hallmark of the Beast, 'the last and most desperate design of Antichrist,' 'the whore of Babylon's backdoor.'"[21] Only a minority expressed a contrary conviction to the effect that "we should refrain from mutual slaughter in the name of our differences of opinion on the matter of the Holy Trinity, the sacrament of the Eucharist or predestination, since God, in the Last Judgement, will not ask us about our theological opinions, whether right or wrong, but about whether we tried to live by the commandments of the Gospels."[22]

Today, the location of key arguments has shifted, but aspects of the underlying structure remain present, especially in articulated doubts that toleration is too generous because it goes hand in hand with an abandonment of judgment and thus relinquishes the quest for truth. Stipulating that "I refrain from reacting aggressively to things I strongly dislike or disapprove," Leszek Kolakowski advised that toleration risks insisting that "I refrain from expressing—or indeed holding—any opinion, and sometimes even to condone every conceivable type of behaviour or opinion in others," for its teaches "that when we persist in our beliefs, even if we do so without aggression, we are *ipso facto* sinning against tolerance." Toleration thus can produce a neglect for fundamental values. It can become not just a means to tolerate those held by others but can induce people to become indifferent to their own. Toleration, Kolakowski further cautioned, can turn "against itself" and thus can produce a circumstance that "destroys the conditions of its own existence."[23] Taken too far, toleration may exact too high a price if its suspension of judgment and action comes at the expense of egalitarian values or human rights. This, famously, was the view of Brian Barry.[24] A century and a quarter earlier, Walter Bagehot similarly worried that when toleration becomes too democratic it risks negating liberal values. Further, there is a republican line of criticism that worries lest toleration "weaken the civic and moral virtues that are necessary for self-government."[25] For those who hold this constellation of views, toleration threatens to become a dangerous snare that leads to the suspension of necessary disagreement, even to the absurdity of sanctioning the bad and the ugly.[26] If, as John Gray, notes, "the objects of toleration are what we judge to be evils," or at least are "undesirable, false, or at least inferior,"[27] why should such objects not be reined in?

Today, such views vie with a strong countercurrent that also is sharply critical of toleration, but for rather different reasons. Much contemporary criticism has followed a line of argument pioneered in Thomas Paine's denunciation of toleration in *Rights of Man* as condescending, filled with cultural contempt. Serving to reinforce the laddering of power, he wrote, toleration "is not the *opposite* of intolerance, but is the counterfeit of it. Both are despotisms.

The one assumes to itself the right of withholding Liberty of Conscience and the other of granting it. The one is pope armed with fire and faggot, and the other is the pope selling or granting indulgences."[28] Premised on judgments that denigrate the cultural other, toleration thus advances, rather than curtails, human domination by proceeding without appreciating competing values or regarding minority practices as legitimate. Subjecting such beliefs and behavior to undue scrutiny, toleration demands the provision of reasons that the dominant group does not stipulate for itself.

On this understanding, toleration's combination of disdain and the power to control with merely provisional decisions to self-restrict is sinister, a soft glove covering a hard fist of power. Toleration is too limited in its reach, too cold in its treatment of the weaker other, and misleading in its putative broadmindedness. It stops short of recognizing diverse communities of fate and affect, and it underestimates the legitimate depth of ethical conflict, whether religious or secular. Lacking appreciation or ample respect for the full range of human ways of living, toleration fails to take deep diversity properly into account in collective life and decision making, and thus neglects the imperatives of multicultural citizenship.[29] Worse, as Wendy Brown put the point, toleration as a helpmeet to unequal cultural and political authority is "depoliticizing, regulatory, and imperial,"[30] and, as Herbert Marcuse notably insisted, it can operate not to advance but repress diversity.[31]

It is impossible to simply reject or set aside these distinct lines of objection, which, simultaneously, are quite accurate yet not quite convincing. They pivot on toleration's conditional approval of difference, an inherent feature. And they are right, of course, to observe that toleration requires suspending critical judgment and that it always risks self-important arrogance, for, as Lukes has noted, "the tolerator is not merely exercising power; he is also claiming authority," the authority of treating disapproval as legitimate.[32]

As an ethical and political site, toleration is not a clear-cut or uncomplicated virtue. By insisting on the necessity to suspend some, though not all, judgment, and by often lacking a sense of cultural equality, it inhabits a location charged with tension. Measured against truth, it necessarily shrinks in scale; measured against equal regard, it contracts in appeal. But measured against the long history of human depredation, it nonetheless remains an essential asset. A world without toleration is fraught with danger. Absent toleration, unbridled conflict and coercion produce stark worlds of winners, who defeat pluralism, and losers, for whom the costs of engagement can be very high, even ultimate.[33]

Hardly a single or fixed position, toleration should not be measured against idealized worlds. Rather, it has to be considered as a complex set of views and means embedded in actual, and often threatening, historical arrangements and circumstances. Toleration, moreover, never can be absolute, as it inherently competes with other values that actors also hold. Despite his deep commitment to toleration, Bernard Crick cautions that it "can never always be right to be tolerant; there are occasions on which we should be intolerant."[34] Toleration must not simply mean that anything goes. But reciprocally, toleration does impel real latitude for demographic, cultural, social, and political heterogeneity and thus in fact can open up possibilities for wider and warmer forms of respect and recognition. Like purgatory, toleration is a site with paths that run in more than one direction.

II

It makes little sense to set toleration aside. Decent human life cannot do without it. Rather, we might ask whether, when, and how it can help organize and manage human diversity in ways that are less dreadful and less unjust than all-too-common alternatives. However penetrating, sharp critiques of toleration, Brown rightly concedes, should not move us to a position "rejecting tolerance outright, declaring it a necessarily insidious value, or replacing tolerance with some other term or practice."[35] Without toleration, members of disliked groups often are compelled to live on a plateau of anxiety, subject to hierarchies of humiliation. By offering the prospect of social peace, moreover, toleration is instrumentally valuable and not just for the vulnerable.

Toleration's achievements and significance grow the more we recognize its jagged genealogy and uneven legacies, the more we acknowledge its uncertain, precarious, and porous crosscurrents, the more we understand that human differences always can be exploited to advance "the evil of cruelty and fear."[36] By reducing fear and insecurity, toleration, can serve as a condition for, not an enemy of, a commitment to diversity and cultural respect. Whether this extension actually happens, of course, poses a contingent and important historical challenge.

After all, toleration has not been the norm in human history. Most of the time, situations marked by deep cultural and religious pluralism have produced persecution. "Correct" ideas and behavior are imposed through coercion to correct beliefs and acts that the dominant party believes to be primitive, or repulsive, malicious, or barbaric. Grounded in deeply felt world views, moreover, such profound disapproval cannot be dismissed as simply unreasonable. It thus is a matter of great and compelling importance to understand why, when, and how stronger parties abstain from restrictive deeds and permit liberty for ideas and practices that range from the unloved to the robustly reviled. Unfortunately, such questions demand a concept that moves beyond definition to become a tool for rigorous and systematic empirical inquiry.

That, we currently lack, in part because the main literatures that have documented the history of toleration have tended to divide rather too crisply into opposing evolutionary and realist camps. Focusing on the history of ideas, the first offers a chronicle of ethical achievement. It records how ever broader and appealing ideas advanced to transcend civil disabilities for religious minorities. This record demonstrates toleration's dramatic evolution from early modern Europe, when it mostly was thought to be undesirable, to the nineteenth century, when toleration achieved a positive valence, as one "sketch of the struggle for religious liberty of the last four hundred years" put things, that brought about a "complete emancipation" by the mid-nineteenth century.[37]

Appreciative narratives portraying the history of toleration as a stirring line of progress long have dominated English historiography. This is the story of a lineage that takes us from Sebastian Castellio to Roger Williams and, decisively, to John Locke and on to John Stuart Mill. Now classic texts written in the first half of the twentieth century by H. F. Russell Smith, A. A. Seaton, T. Lyon, and especially W. K. Jordan,[38] as well as an assertive revival of such work,[39] appreciatively detail transformations to theories of religious toleration after the break with Rome in 1534 and the Act of Supremacy making the Queen the head of the Church. Jordan's still unsurpassed four-volume survey chronicles these years as an era of "one of the most momentous changes in the history of English thought," a shift from medieval conceptions of toleration inside "an organic conception of Christian life" to "the legal guarantee of free belief and the free exercise of that belief." After a period of religious extremism, Anglican thought grew more moderate, the dissenting sects started to embrace religious liberty, and "the secular forces" of political necessity, rationalism, and skepticism became more prominent. On this influential view, early modern toleration in England thus was "one of the most significant advances the human race has ever achieved," the opening of a process that produced a sequence of ever more generous and inclusive ideas that bonded with the body of thought we have come to call liberal.[40]

During the past quarter-century, a growing number of historians have called this history of unfolding ideas into question. They stress the expedience and expose the limits of toleration in a world marked by might and command in numerous case studies that reveal the persistence of bias and bullying even in such relatively tolerant locations as early modern Basle, Strasbourg, or the Dutch Republic. In Basle, nonconformists never were safe or free from the dangers of persecution protected by law. Though a relative haven, Strasbourg witnessed the official harassment of nuns, demonstrations against Catholic priests and services, assaults on Anabaptists, and anti-Calvinist displays. The city's laws stifled religious argument, limited which services people could attend, forced religious instruction, and mandated baptism within six weeks of birth. Even in the Netherlands, where the seventeenth-century Dutch Republic was a haven, toleration often was deployed by public authorities and church figures in purely instrumental ways as part of an elaborate system of bargaining for advantages in the context of a shifting balance of power in the various towns. Such realism, stressing how toleration was the cry of the weak and disappointed, underscores how toleration was crafted only when it was advantageous. Toleration, it stresses, was a pragmatic accommodation to the balance of forces, "a function of *raison d'état* rather than a matter of principle."[41]

Each viewpoint sees itself as an antagonist to the other. From the perspective of the first, what is most striking is how the zone of toleration has expanded notwithstanding pressures of bigotry, fanaticism, and persecution.

From the perspective of the second, the history of ideas is thought to have substituted teleology for an awareness of just how unusual, situational, and evanescent toleration has been and how often it has been entwined with intolerant refusals to grant full membership even in liberal polities.

These are fictitious choices. The one does not falsify the other. Toleration never was an uncomplicated extension of freedom. Exclusions and patterns of persecution did not melt away when leading thinkers such as Locke or John Toland shifted toleration from a site for theological debate about heresy and religious difference to become a political and legislative question under conditions of religious pluralism. Still, their texts, and the vast array of reflections and arguments that circulated and were debated in early modern England, did powerfully widen the available intellectual and political space. Precisely because realist histories are convincing when they stress lapses and dangers, the expansion to the scope of toleration's ideas and protections gains in importance.

The hundreds, perhaps thousands, of tracts, essays, and books, ranging from the ephemeral to the enduring, that have sought to advance visions of toleration have possessed two vital features. Written to enlarge the range of possibilities, these texts have offered what Rawls called "realistic utopias," designs close to social reality yet still distant from immediate realization.[42] By insisting on the worth of toleration in difficult historical circumstances, such writings have pushed out the boundaries of what otherwise could not be supposed or conceived, and they have suggested constellations of means with which to confront and contain coercion and bloodshed. The best of these works, like Locke's *Letter on Toleration*, link arguments for why it is desirable or necessary to potentially, if not yet actually, feasible visions and policies on the understanding that toleration designates a distinctive, fragile, and controversial zone of authoritative institutions.

This, certainly, is how Locke saw toleration. As an alternative to Christian civil war, he advanced toleration as a practical and pressing solution, as a set of means to establish secure borders between political authority and civil society and among religious rites and doctrines, each "Orthodox to it self." It was "the refusal of Toleration to those that are of different Opinions," he argued, rather than Europe's diversity of religious doctrines and practices as such, that "has produced all the Bustles and Wars, that have been in the Christian World, upon account of Religion." Toleration, on this account, is not predominantly an idea—though it surely is that, if a complex one—but a set of institutional arrangements that can serve to demarcate official policies and relationships across group lines. Toleration should do so, Locke famously advised, by distinguishing "exactly the Business of Civil Government from that of Religion" and by settling "the just Bounds that lie between the one and the other."[43]

Such proposals have sought to advance the practice of toleration by connecting abstract norms to determinate historical circumstances by way of robust institutional proposals. These writings also have grappled with judgments about how to distinguish two kinds of wrongs: those that can or should be tolerated in order to secure a good or prevent something worse and those that should not because toleration would either protect something too awful or bring about a dangerous or otherwise unbearable outcome. These are amongst the hardest questions to adjudicate in public life, and it is good to possess rich examples of attempts to grapple with them.

III

The challenge that is most urgent is not choosing between an emphasis on ideas or on social reality. Nor does it make sense to pursue the stylized debate political theorists have been conducting about whether or not to appreciate toleration, as if toleration is a singular set of ideas and practices. If we are to assess toleration, we must do so in situational contexts armed with analytical distinctions that can guide scholars to consider toleration as a complex institutional site that can be apprehended with the goal of understanding its range, dimensions, and configurations. By treating toleration as a family of conceptions and practices that has varied and mostly widened over time, though not in simple or linear fashion, it should be possible to probe and compare arrangements across times and places, pose better questions about the character and consequences of such variation, and construct explanations that account for why particular arrangements were selected. How can we unpack the appropriately tight definition of toleration offered by Cohen (which, as you recall, designates toleration as "an agent's intentional and principled refraining from interfering with an opposed other [or their behavior, etc.] in situations of diversity, where the agent believes she has the power to interfere") into dimensions that can be identified and analyzed distinctively and in combination? If toleration comprises an institutional family encompassing acts of intentional self-restraint by capable public authorities regarding disliked persons, beliefs, and actions, how, in short, might we construct the concept as a layered instrument that designates aspects whose variation can be assayed systematically? What might such an agenda for social scientists and historians look like?

Consider how the debate between the historians of ideas and the realists might be transformed into a treatment of the normative status of toleration, ranging from a situational necessity advanced reluctantly, ungenerously, and resentfully to toleration as a cherished value. Justifications for toleration can vary significantly, from the entirely practical to the doctrinal, whether religious or secular in character. Given situations, moreover, can shape relations among actors who locate toleration quite differently along such a continuum, thus animating disagreement not only about whether toleration should exist, but about its grounding, security, and character.

Toleration is protean. In unsettled early modern Europe, a good many kinds and forms differently combined claims to freedom of conscience, the separation of spiritual and secular authority, and notions of love for neighbors and weaker brethren. Variously motivated, toleration's patterns of abnegation and its combinations of liberty and indulgence took many forms. These included toleration as a private, thus passive and covert, expression of belief; de facto toleration that resulted from a lack of resources to enforce conformity; toleration as an interim strategy because the balance of contending forces permitted no other solution; and toleration in which rulers sanctioned pastoral latitudinarianism, with religious authorities deciding not to peer too closely into men's souls. Not just the content but the geography of toleration differed and fluctuated, sometimes limited to particular localities but other times applicable over wider territories, including nation-states and zones of conquest.

As these possibilities unfolded, and as various thinkers sought to find grounds to justify alternative courses of action, it was already clear that toleration was not a singular or unitary possibility, for it varied too much from place to place to be that. If we understand tolerators as persons with the capacity not to tolerate, there was a multiplicity of such actors within the Church and within various governing authorities in empires, states, and towns who possessed the ability to define and implement an array of different public policies to deal with those they disliked. In turn, there were diverse driving forces that produced dislike and a variety of disliked persons and practices. These, in turn, varied by social distance from those who might choose to tolerate them. The degree of difference might be relatively small, as in distinctions between Lutherans and Calvinists, or very great, as between the highly dissimilar Spanish and Inca, or located in a zone in between, as in relations between Christians and Jews, who clearly were neither Christian nor quite full outsiders, for they were inscribed within Christianity's grand narrative.

Just as tolerators and tolerated are not of one piece, neither is the relationship between dislike and disapproval. Not just the content but the degree, intensity, and scope of dislike can vary and thus the degree of self-restraint or modification of dislike required by toleration. The sources and character of diversity are not fixed or homogeneous. As an empirical matter, moreover, there is no precise mapping that connects the qualities of dislike to the taking of decisions to tolerate. Less dislike does not necessarily produce more toleration. And toleration can be shaped over time either by a reduction to the intensity of dislike or by decisions to permit belief and action despite dislike.

Such decisions take in different sites and possibilities. Most important is toleration's substantive content and extensiveness as an authoritative institution. Central to debates and decisions about toleration in early modern Europe was a lack of agreement about how many aspects, zones, or spheres of life were to be covered. These questions became especially pressing and vexing with the development of modern states claiming unique sovereignty over people and territory. As their authoritative institutions crafted ties with diverse civil societies, often marked by religious heterogeneity, they had to define the content of their people and the meaning of their territory. For toleration, these matters raised questions and offered choices that have persisted ever since as matters for official and public adjudication about the conditions of safety for the physical, mental, and spiritual lives of disliked persons and for the terms of their incorporation into the polity and society.

These options cluster into five distinctive, if overlapping, categories, each of which is a site for the expression, adjudication, and management of inter-group dislike. In each, toleration—understood not as a fixed noun but as a cluster of practices and norms—can be characterized as a three-actor game in which public authorities manage relations, fashion institutions, and adjudicate conflicts between majorities and disliked minorities in the civil societies they seek to govern. In each, authorities have to assess the degree of danger and the degree of opportunity offered by human heterogeneity. Each thus has profound implications for the degree of danger and opportunity experienced by the vulnerable. For both the dominant and the vulnerable, moreover, the capacity to impose and the capacity to shape and resist themselves are variables, at each of these levels.

First is the question of toleration in the sense of sheer physical presence. Will those with the capacity to exclude people from places abide their company and agree to share geography with persons they find objectionable? On a continuum from extrusion to full spatial integration, many options appear, including various forms of residential segregation.

Second is the issue of physical security. Will public authorities supply policing to provide members of disliked minorities with protection from violence? Ranging from none to absolute guarantees, the mechanisms of policing can vary. These include providing authorization for groups to self-police to the provision of public forceful protection backed and enforced by law.

Third is the acquisition of means to livelihood. Will disliked minorities be granted access to a limited or wide array of economic opportunities and occupational roles? Tolerated groups must have some means of material sustenance, but the extensiveness of these possibilities can vary considerably.

Fourth is the scope of autonomous cultural expression. How different and how visible are disliked groups permitted to appear and behave within the public sphere? Here the continuum spans the range from a hidden presence to open, even welcome, diversity, both religious and secular. Here too lie questions about the range of cultural matters toleration will cover. At the low end, just one, perhaps a different language or the right to build a church; at the high end, ideas and practices limited only by some universal moral and political values.

Fifth is the character and degree of civic membership. How, if at all, are they included in both military and civil institutions? Do persons who belong to disliked groups gain access to the rights, rituals, and symbols that characterize collective political life? In the wide space between none to all, there is an abundance of options, perhaps especially under democratic conditions. Further, answers to these questions are not fixed. While overall there has been a trend toward civic inclusion, there remain examples of segmented extrusion, even mass killing, of minority-group persons who had become full citizens.

The abnegation of action that is the central hallmark of toleration always proceeds along with affirmative decisions about toleration's character, content, and scope. Decisions about toleration at each of these levels are loosely coupled. That is, there is a degree of independence, which varies in different historical situations, with regard to whether and how toleration is practiced at each level. These need not vary together or in the same direction in particular times and locations. As Preston King has underscored, "it makes no sense to speak of being 'tolerant' of an item in every degree and on every level. One may be completely tolerant of an item in full degree on every level save at least one; one may be tolerant of an item in some degree on one level and no others."[44] Toleration rarely is complete or inclusive.

From this perspective, toleration is best understood not as possessing a bimodal character with peaks of yes or no, but as configurations composed of conditions within and across these five dimensions, each of which is arrayed on a continuum from less to more. Toleration thus can be more or less comprehensive, more or less active.[45] Proper-name history concerning a specific place thus consists of situations that combine circumstances at each level at a particular moment. By attending to these aspects and their arrangements, it becomes possible to assemble cases comparably while protecting their singularity. The goal of such scholarship on toleration, in the language of the philosopher Hugh Stretton, would be to offer "an organization of possibilities . . . being the sort of theory which leaves open the question whether people are doing what people would invariably do in these uniquely complicated circumstances, or are doing one of those comparatively few things which people . . . choose to do in such circumstances."[46] Such interrogative theory constructs what toleration actually has meant in given settings. But it also invites a wide array of causal questions that can help craft accounts that explain why these details were chosen by toleration's authorities.

The study of toleration requires the further development of the concept as a layered variable. As historians, we mainly study variation and particularity, but we want to do so in a manner that allows us to compose cases and instances for meaningful comparisons within and across time. So we need these kinds of tools. As historians of ideas, we aim to do better than consider one thinker at a time or compose lineages that risk becoming teleological, and this kind of approach can help. As social scientists, we require good objects of explanation—that is, systematically composed variations about subjects that matter—about which we try to identify mechanisms and provide causal accounts.

Treating toleration's complex arrangements of liberty and indulgence in a manner comparable to how Nettl considered the state as a conceptual variable thus is a first step toward good and useful work. It begins with the understanding that, like all institutions, toleration's combinations of principles and prudence makes peaceful human life possible by predictably regulating the character and terms of political, economic, and social transactions. As distinctively configured in particular times and places, and patterned by contexts, situations, human preferences and decisions, toleration, like other institutions, in turn conduces thought, sentiments, and behavior.

With toleration as a conceptual variable, it becomes possible to probe distinctive historical cases more methodically and revealingly by offering theoretically grounded tools with which to ask similar questions across a wide array of cases, across time and space, without reducing the particularity of any. To the contrary, this kind of interrogative theory deepens an appreciation of how specific instances are configured distinctively, all the while constructing them in a manner that can facilitate meaningful comparison. With historical information organized this way, it should also become more likely that we can come to better understand the conditions for moving toward and beyond toleration as well as fateful conditions when the vectors are reversed. With the range of potential options having widened under modern conditions to encompass both warm multiculturalism and the radical evil of genocide, fewer subjects are more pressing.

NOTES

1. Bernard Williams, "Toleration: An Impossible Virtue?" in David Heyd, ed., *Toleration: An Elusive Virtue* (Princeton: Princeton University Press, 1996), p. 18. Also see Thomas Scanlon, *The Difficulty of Toleration* (Cambridge: Cambridge University Press, 2003), and an earlier version, "The Difficulty of Tolerance," in Heyd, *Toleration*, pp. 226–39. Scanlon stresses how tolerating difference leaves persons open to the disturbing possibility that the character and terms of their society might then move in directions they deeply oppose when the value of toleration is granted priority over special claims to promote particular values and ways of life. Similarly, Jeremy Waldron has argued that toleration never is cost free. Its accommodations are also impositions. Jeremy Waldron, "Toleration and Reasonableness," in Catriona McKinnon and Dario Castiglione, eds., *The Culture of Toleration in Diverse Societies* (Manchester: Manchester University Press, 2003).
2. Bernard Williams, "Tolerating the Intolerable," in Susan Mendus, *The Politics of Toleration in Modern Life* (Durham, NC: Duke University Press, 2000), especially pp. 65–67.
3. Peter Laslett distinguishes toleration as a virtue, a political virtue, from an ideal in "Political Theory and Political Scientific Research," *Government and Opposition* 6 (April 1971): 219.
4. Bernard Crick, "Toleration and Tolerance in Theory and Practice," *Government and Opposition* 6 (April 1971): 160.
5. George Fletcher, "The Instability of Tolerance," in Heyd, *Toleration,* p. 158.
6. For a discussion of the possibility conditions and basic structure of toleration, see Glen Newey, *Virtue, Reason, and Toleration: The Place of Toleration in Ethical and Political Philosophy* (Edinburgh: Edinburgh University Press, 1999), especially pp. 1–52.
7. J. P. Nettl, "The State as a Conceptual Variable," *World Politics* 20 (July 1968): 559.
8. Sudipta Kaviraj, "On Thick and Thin Religion: Some Critical Reflections on Seculrisation Theory," in Ira Katznelson and Gareth Stedman Jones, eds., *Religion and the Political Imgaination* (Cambridge: Cambridge University Press, 2010), p. 339.
9. Williams, "Toleration," p. 21.
10. The inclusion of persons is rejected by some recent theorists of toleration, who insist that toleration focuses only on behavior, not individuals or groups; others wish to restrict objects of toleration exclusively to persons. I see no persuasive reason to make this choice a priori. For an example of the former, see Robert Paul Churchill, "On the Difference Between Non-Moral and Moral Conceptions of Toleration: The Case for Toleration as an Individual Virtue," in Mehdi Amin Razavi and David Ambuel, eds., *Philosophy, Religion, and Questions of Intolerance* (Albany: State University of New York Press, 1997), especially pp. 193–98; for the latter, see Heyd, "Introduction," in *Toleration,* p. 14.

11. Scanlon, *The Difficulty of Toleration*, p. 226.
12. Steven Lukes, *Moral Relativism* (New York: Picador, 2008), p. 40. Similarly, Walsham notes how "to tolerate is to permit or endure, to abstain from taking steps to restrain something and to refuse to make a fuss; it is a conscious act of omission. . . . It can all too easily be mistaken for mere indifference or apathy, and vice versa." Alexandra Walsham, *Charitable Hatred: Tolerance and Intolerance in England, 1500–1700* (Manchester: Manchester University Press, 2006), p. 269.
13. "A dark side of tolerating diversity is that—as the Latin root tolerare connotes—it involves the enduring of something disagreeable, perhaps even abhorrent." Edward Langerak, "Pluralism, Tolerance, and Disagreement," *Rhetoric Society Quarterly* 24 (Winter-Spring 1994): 95.
14. Lukes, *Moral Relativism*, p. 40.
15. These values are necessary, but not sufficient conditions. Richard Tuck, in this vein, has usefully shown how skepticism, often seen as an important new underpinning for toleration in early modern Europe, often gave rise to just the opposite, as individuals sought to tame the great variety of incommensurable religious and secular moralities. Richard Tuck, "Skepticism and Toleration in the Seventeenth Century," in Susan Mendus, ed., *Justifying Toleration: Conceptual and Historical Perspectives* (Cambridge: Cambridge University Press, 1988), pp. 21–35. Mendus distinguishes "three kinds of justification of toleration . . . (i) that toleration is a requirement of prudence; (ii) that toleration is a requirement of rationality; and (iii) that toleration is a requirement of morality." Susan Mendus, "Introduction," in Susan Mendus and David Edwards, eds., *On Toleration* (New York: Oxford University Press, 1987), p. 3.
16. Susan Mendus, "Review of John Christian Laursen, Religious Toleration: *'The Variety of Rites' from Cyrus to Defoe* (New York: St. Martin's, 1999)," *American Political Science Review* 54 (March 2000): 176.
17. "A person will be said to be tolerant only where he has the power not to be tolerant." Preston King, "The Problem of Tolerance," *Government and Opposition* 6 (April 1971): 197.
18. Andrew Jason Cohen, "What Toleration Is," *Ethics* 115 (October 2004): 69. A similar definition can be found in Preston King, *Toleration* (London: Allen and Unwin, 1976), p. 22. There are many such definitions in the literature by philosophers and political theorists. In a more elliptical instance, Raz defines toleration as "the curbing of an activity likely to be unwelcome to its recipient or of an inclination so to act which is itself morally valuable and which is based on a dislike or an antagonism toward that person or a feature of his life, reflecting a judgment that these represent limitations or deficiencies for him, in order to let that person have his way or in order for him to gain or keep some advantage." Joseph Raz, *The Morality of Freedom* (Oxford: Oxford University Press, 1986), p. 254.
19. King, "The Problem of Tolerance," pp. 172, 175; also see Preston King, *Toleration* (London: Allen and Unwin, 1976), p. 22.
20. Writing a text that "applies the principle of toleration to philosophy itself," Rawls sought to understand how "a just and free society" can be possible "under conditions of deep doctrinal conflict with no prospect of resolution." The stakes, he rightly insisted, are high. "The wars of this century," the introduction to the paperback edition's concluding paragraph

observes, "with their extreme violence and increasing destructiveness, culminating in the manic evil of the Holocaust, raise in an acute way the question whether political relations must be governed by power and coercion alone," a circumstance made ever more likely should reasonable conceptions and practices of toleration be absent. John Rawls, *Political Liberalism,* exp. ed. (New York: Columbia University Press, 2005), pp. xxiii, 10, xxviii, lx.

21. Walsham, *Charitable Hatred,* pp. 4–5. Later, during the nineteenth century, there was significant public debate about whether toleration, thought by some to be an attack on religion by rationalists and agnostics, might bring the continuance of social morality into question. For a discussion, see John P. Halsted, "Walter Bagehot on Toleration," *Journal of the History of Ideas* 19 (January 1958): 119–28, especially p. 119.
22. Leszek Kolakowski, "On Toleration," in *Freedom, Fame, Lying, and Betrayal* (London: Penguin, 1999), pp. 34–35, 39.
23. Ibid., pp. 36–37.
24. Brian Barry, *Culture and Equality: An Egalitarian Critique of Multiculturalism* (Cambridge: Harvard University Press, 2001).
25. Steven Kautz, "Liberalism and the Idea of Toleration," *American Journal of Political Science* 17 (May 1993): 610.
26. Edward Langerak, "Pluralism, Tolerance, and Disagreement," *Rhetoric Society Quarterly* 24 (Winter-Spring 1994): 95.
27. John Gray, "Toleration: A Post-Liberal Perspective," in *Enlightenment's Wake: Politics and Culture at the Close of the Modern Age* (London: Routledge, 1995), pp. 18–19. Gray primarily questions toleration on other grounds, those of its insufficient regard for human difference.
28. Thomas Paine, *Rights of Man* (London: Penguin, 1984), p. 107. Rejecting condescension, T. S. Eliot famously announced, "The Christian does not want to be tolerated." Cited in Maurice Cranston, "John Locke and the Case for Toleration," in John Horton and Susan Mendus, eds, *John Locke: A Letter Concerning Toleration in Focus* (London: Routledge, 1991), p. 78.
29. Will Kymlicka in *Liberalism Community and Culture* (Oxford: Clarendon, 1991), and *Multicultural Citizenship: A Liberal Theory of Minority Rights* (Oxford: Clarendon, 1995); and Bhikhu Parekh, "Minority Practices and Principles of Toleration," *International Migration Review* 30 (Spring 1996): 251–84. For discussions and evaluations, see Christian Joppke and Steven Lukes, eds., *Multicultural Citizenship* (Oxford: Oxford University Press, 1999); and Rajeev Bhargava, Amiya Kumar Bagchi, and R. Sudarshan, eds., *Multiculturalism, Liberalism, and Democracy* (New Delhi: Oxford University Press, 1999).
30. Wendy Brown, *Regulating Aversion: Tolerance in an Age of Identity and Empire* (Princeton: Princeton University Press, 2006), p. 205.
31. Herbert Marcuse, "Repressive Tolerance," in Robert Paul Wolff, Barrington Moore Jr., and Herbert Marcuse, *A Critique of Pure Tolerance* (Boston: Beacon, 1965).
32. Steven Lukes, "Social and Moral Tolerance," *Government and Opposition* 6 (April 1971): 224.
33. A thoughtful reflection about toleration as of "pivotal importance" in confronting the evils of slavery and of racialized anti-Semitism is David A. J. Richards, "Toleration and the Struggle Against Prejudice," in Heyd, *Toleration,* pp. 127–46.

34. Crick, "Toleration and Tolerance in Theory and Practice," p. 144.
35. Brown, *Regulating Aversion,* p. 205.
36. Judith Shklar, "The Liberalism of Fear," in Nancy Rosenblum, ed., *Liberalism and the Moral Life* (Cambridge: Harvard University Press, 1989), p. 29.
37. Roland H. Bainton, "The Struggle for Religious Liberty," *Church History* 10 (January 1941): 95, 119.
38. H. F. Russell Smith, *The Theory of Religious Liberty in the Reigns of Charles II and James II* (Cambridge: Cambridge University Press, 1911); A. A. Seaton, *The Theory of Toleration Under the Later Stuarts* (Cambridge: Cambridge University Press, 1911); T. Lyon, *The Theory of Religious Liberty in England, 1603–39* (Cambridge: Cambridge University Press, 1937); W. K. Jordan, *The Development of Religious Toleration in England,* 4 vols. (London: George Allen and Unwin, 1932–1940).
39. Jonathan Israel, "Toleration in Seventeenth-Century Dutch and English Thought," in Simon Groenveld and Michael J. Wintle, eds., *The Exchange of Ideas: Religion, Scholarship, and Art in Anglo-Dutch Relations in the Seventeenth Century* (Zutphen: Walburg Pers, 1994); Perez Zagorin, *How the Idea of Religious Toleration Came to the West* (Princeton: Princeton University Press, 2003); and John Coffey, *Persecution and Toleration in Protestant England, 1558–1689* (Harlow: Pearson Education, 2000).
40. Jordan, *The Development of Religious Toleration in England,* 1:17.
41. Ole Peter Grell, Jonathan I. Israel, and Nicholas Tyacke, "Introduction," in Ole Peter Grell, Jonathan I. Israel, and Nicholas Tyacke, eds., *From Persecution to Toleration: The Glorious Revolution and Religion in England* (Oxford: Oxford University Press, 1991), p. 1.
42. John Rawls, *Law of Peoples* (Cambridge: Harvard University Press, 1999), pp. 11–23.
43. John Locke, *A Letter Concerning Toleration,* ed. James H. Tully (Indianapolis: Hackett, 1983 [1689]), pp. 32, 55, 26.
44. King, "The Problem of Tolerance," p. 186.
45. For advocacy of a more active and comprehensive version of toleration, see Jack Knight, "Institutionalizing Toleration," in Ingrid Creppell, Russell Hardin, and Stephen Macedo, eds., *Toleration on Trial* (Lanham, MD: Lexington, 2008), pp. 31–47.
46. Hugh Stretton, *The Political Sciences: General Principles of Selection in Social Science and History* (London: Routledge and Kegan Paul, 1969), p. 327.

HOW TO DEFINE SECULARISM

CHARLES TAYLOR

EVERYONE AGREES TODAY that modern, diverse democracies have to be "secular" in some sense of this term. But what sense? The term (along with the corresponding French term *laïcité,* and its derivatives) has more than one sense. There are in fact many different meanings, but I believe that we can get to a crucial issue if we single out two key conceptions.

On one view (A), secularism is mainly concerned with controlling religion. Its task is to define the place of religion in public life and to keep it firmly in this location. This doesn't need to involve strife or repression, provided various religious actors understand and respect these limits. But the various rules and measures that make up the secularist (or *laïque*) regime all have this basic purpose.

On the other view (B), the main point of a secularist regime is to manage the religious and metaphysical-philosophical diversity of views (including non- and antireligious views) fairly and democratically.[1] Of course, this task will include setting certain limits to religiously motivated action in the public sphere, but it will also involve similar limits on those espousing non- or antireligious philosophies. (For instance, the degree to which either can discriminate in certain relations like hiring). For B, religion is not the prime focus of secularism.

The case I would like to make here is that B is much superior to A, at least for our time. The popularity of A is to be explained by certain Western histories of struggle in which secularist regimes came to be. But our present predicament is for the most part rather different than the one which generated these conflicts. It is above all one of growing diversity in all Western democracies. For these reasons, B is more appropriate.

Let's look at what B involves a little more closely. In fact managing diversity involves a complex requirement. There is more than one good sought here. We can single out three, which we can class in the three categories of the French Revolutionary trinity: liberty, equality, fraternity. (1) No one must be forced in the domain of religion or basic belief. This is what is often defined as religious liberty, including, of course, the freedom not to believe. This is what is also described as the "free exercise" of religion, in the terms of the U.S. First Amendment. (2) There must be equality between people of different faiths or basic belief; no religious outlook or (religious or areligious) Weltanschauung can enjoy a privileged status, let alone be adopted as the official view of the state. Then, thirdly, (3) all spiritual families must be heard, included in the ongoing process of determining what the society is about (its political identity), and how it is going to realize these goals (the exact regime of rights and privileges). This (stretching the point a little) is what corresponds to "fraternity."

These goals can, of course, conflict; sometimes we have to balance the goods involved here. Moreover, I believe that we might add a fourth goal: that we try as much as possible to maintain relations of harmony and comity between the supporters of different religions and *Weltanschaungen* (maybe this is what really deserves to be called fraternity, but I am still attached to the neatness of the above schema, with only the three traditional goods).

Why do I think that this diversity model (B) is superior to the religion-focused model (A)? One reason is that it is more evenhanded. If we look at the three goals, they are concerned respectively, with (1) protecting people in their belonging and/or practice of whatever outlook they choose or find themselves in; with (2) treating people equally whatever their option; and (3) giving them all a hearing. There is no reason to single out religion as against nonreligious, "secular" (in another widely used sense), or atheist viewpoints.

Indeed, the point of state neutrality is precisely to avoid favoring or disfavoring not just religion positions but any basic position, religious or nonreligious. We can't favor Christianity over Islam, but also religion over against nonbelief in religion or vice versa.

One of the ways of demonstrating the superiority of the three-principle model of secularism over that which is fixated on religion is that it would never allow one to misrecognize the regime founded by Atatürk as genuinely secular, making light as it does of the fundamental principles and even of the separation of state and religious institutions.

This also shows the value of the late-Rawlsian formulation for a secular state, which cleaves strongly to certain political principles: human rights, equality, the rule of law, democracy. These are the very basis of the state that must support them. But this political ethic can be and is shared by people of very different basic outlooks (what Rawls calls "comprehensive views of the good"). A Kantian will justify the rights to life and freedom by pointing to the dignity of rational agency; a utilitarian will speak of the necessity to treat beings who can experience joy and suffering in such a way as to maximize the first and minimize the second; a Christian will speak of humans as made in the image of God. They concur on the principles, but differ on the deeper reasons for holding to this ethic. The state must uphold the ethic, but must refrain from favoring any of the deeper reasons.

The idea that secularism makes a special case of religion arises from the history of its coming to be in the West (as does, indeed, the name). To put it briefly, there are two important founding contexts for this kind of regime, the U.S. and France. In the U.S. case the whole range of comprehensive views, or deeper reasons, were in the original case variants of (Protestant) Christianity, stretching to a smattering of Deists. Subsequent history has widened the palette of views beyond Christianity and then beyond religion. But in the original case the positions between which the state must be neutral were all religious. Hence the First Amendment: Congress shall pass no law establishing religion or impeding the free exercise thereof (or something like this).

The word *secularism* didn't appear in the early decades of American public life. But this was the sign that a basic problem had not yet been faced. Because the First Amendment concerned the separation of church and state, it opened the possibility of giving a place to *religion,* which no one would accept today. Thus, in the 1830s, a judge of the Supreme Court could argue that while the

First Amendment forbade the identification of the federal government with any church, since all the churches were Christian (and in effect Protestant), one could invoke the principles of Christianity in interpreting the law.

For judge Joseph Story, the goal of the First Amendment was "to exclude all rivalry among Christian sects," but nevertheless "Christianity ought to receive encouragement from the state." Christianity was essential to the state because the belief in "a future state of rewards and punishments" is "indispensable to the administration of justice." What is more, "it is impossible for those who believe in the truth of Christianity, as a divine revelation, to doubt, that it is a special duty of government to foster, and encourage it among the citizens."

This primacy of Christianity was upheld even later in the nineteenth century. As late as 1890, thirty-seven of the forty-two existing states recognized the authority of God in the preambles or in the text of their constitutions. A unanimous judgment of the Supreme Court of 1892 declared that if one wanted to describe "American life as expressed by its laws, its business, its customs and its society, we find everywhere a clear recognition of the same truth . . . that this is a Christian nation" (*Church of the Holy Trinity v. United States*, 143 U.S. 457 at 471).

In the latter part of the century, resistance began to build to this conception, but a National Reform Association was founded in 1863 with the following goal: "The object of this Society shall be to maintain existing Christian features in the American government . . . to secure such an amendment to the Constitution of the United States as will declare the nation's allegiance to Jesus Christ and its acceptance of the moral laws of the Christian religion, and so as to indicate that this is a Christian nation, and place all the Christian laws, institutions, and usages of our government on an undeniable legal basis in the fundamental law of the land." After 1870 the battle was joined between the supporters of this narrow view, on one hand, and those who wanted a real opening to all other religions and also to nonreligion. These included not only Jews but also Catholics who (rightly) saw the "Christianity" of the NRA as excluding them. It was in this battle that the word *secular* first appears on the American scene as a key term, and very often in its polemical sense of non- or antireligious.[2]

In the French case, laïcité came about in a struggle *against* a powerful church. The strong temptation was for the state itself to stand on a moral basis independent from religion. Marcel Gauchet shows how Charles Renouvier laid the grounds for the outlook of the Third Republic radicals in their battle against the church. The state has to be "moral et enseignant." It has "charge d'âmes aussi bien que toute Église ou communauté, mais à titre plus universel." Morality is the key criterion. In order not to be under the church, the state must have "une morale indépendante de toute religion," and enjoy a "suprématie morale" in relation to all religions. The basis of this morality is liberty. In order to hold its own before religion the morality underlying the state has to be based on more than just utility or feeling; it needs a real "théologie rationnelle," like that of Kant.[3] The wisdom of Jules Ferry, and later of Aristide Briand and Jean Jaurez, saved France at the time of the Separation (1905) from such a lopsided regime, but the notion stuck that laïcité was all about controlling and managing religion.

If we move, however, beyond such originating contexts, and look at the kinds of societies in which we are now living in the West, the first feature that strikes us is the wide diversity not only of religious views but also of those that involve no religion, not to speak of those that are unclassifiable in this dichotomy. Reasons (1), (2), and (3) require that we treat evenhandedly all of these.

This fixation on religion is complex, and it is bound up with two other features we often find in the debates on secularism: the first is the tendency to define secularism or laïcité in terms of some institutional arrangement, rather than starting from the goals as I proposed earlier. And so you hear mantra-type formulae, like "the separation of church and state" or the necessity of removing religion from public space ("les espaces de la République," as in the recent French debate). The second follows from the first or may easily seem to. If the whole matter is defined by one institutional formula, then one must just determine which arrangement of things best meets this formula, and there is no need to think further. One cannot find oneself in a dilemma, as will easily happen if one is pursuing more than one goal, because here there is just one master formula.

Hence one often hears these mantras employed as argument stoppers, the ultimate decisive response that annuls all objections. In the U.S., people invoke the "Wall of Separation" as the ultimate criterion, and hyper-republicans in France cite laïcité as the final word. (Of course, if one consulted the First Amendment of the U.S. Constitution one would find two goals mentioned, the rejection of establishment and the assurance of "free exercise." It is not inconceivable that these could conflict.)

This kind of move amounts, from the standpoint I'm adopting here, to a fetishization of the favored institutional arrangements, whereas one should start from the goals and derive the concrete arrangements from these. It is not that some separation of church and state, some mutual autonomy of governing and religious institutions will not be an inescapable feature of any secularist regime. And the same goes for the neutrality of the public institutions. These are both indispensable. But what these requirements mean in practice ought to be determined by how we can maximize our three (or four) basic goals.

Take for example the wearing of the hijab by Muslim women in public schools, which has been a hot issue in a number of Western democracies. In France, pupils in public schools were famously forbidden the headscarf, seen as a "signe religieux ostantatoire," according to the notorious Loi Stasi of 2004. In certain German Laender, pupils can wear it, but not teachers. In the UK and other countries there is no general interdict, but the individual schools can decide.

What are the reasons for this variation? Plainly, in all these cases, legislators and administrators were trying to balance two goals. One was the maintenance of neutrality in public institutions seen (rightly) as an essential entailment of goal (2): equality between all basic beliefs. The other was goal (1), ensuring the maximum possible religious liberty or, in its most general form, liberty of conscience. Goal (1) seems to push us toward permitting the hijab anywhere. But various arguments were made to override this in the French and German cases. For the Germans what was disturbing was that someone in authority in a public institution should be religiously marked, as it were. In the French case an attempt was made to cast doubt on the proposition that wearing the hijab was a free act. There were dark suggestions that the girls were being forced by their families or by their male peers to adopt this dress code. That was one argument that was frequently used, however dubious it might appear in the light of the sociological research carried out among the pupils themselves, which the Stasi Commission largely ignored.

The other main argument was that the wearing of the headscarf in school was less an act of piety than a statement of hostility against the republic and its essential institution of laïcité. This was the meaning behind the introduction of the concept of "signe ostantatoire." A smaller discrete sign would be no problem argued the Stasi Commission, but these attention-grabbing features of dress were meant to make a highly controversial statement. It was in vain that Muslim women protested that "le foulard n'est pas un signe."

So on one level we can see that these different national answers to the same question reflect different takes on how to balance the two main goals of a secular regime. But on another level the dilemma and its resolution remain hidden under the illusion that there is only one principle here, say, laïcité and its corollary of the neutrality of public institutions or spaces ("les espaces de la République"). It's just a matter of applying an essential feature of our republican regime; there is no need or place for choice or the weighing of different aims.

Perhaps the most pernicious feature of this fetishization is that it tends to hide from view the real dilemmas that we encounter in this realm, and which leap into view once we recognize the plurality of principles at stake.

We should be aware that this fetishization reflects a deep feature of life in modern democracies. We can see why as soon as we ponder what is involved in self-government, what is implied in the basic mode of legitimation of states that they are founded on popular sovereignty. For the people to be sovereign, it needs to form an entity and have a personality.

The revolutions, which ushered in regimes of popular sovereignty, transferred the ruling power from a king onto a "nation" or a "people." In the process, they invent a new kind of collective agency. These terms existed before, but the thing they now indicate, this new kind of agency, was something unprecedented, at least in the immediate context of early modern Europe. Thus the notion "people" could certainly be applied to the ensemble of subjects of the kingdom or to the nonelite strata of society, but prior to the turnover it hadn't indicated an entity that could decide and act together, to whom one could attribute a *will.*

But for people to act together, in other words, to deliberate in order to form a common will on which they will act, requires a high degree of common commitment, a sense of common identification. A society of this kind presupposes trust, the basic trust that members and constituent groups have to have, the confidence that they are really part of the process, that they will be listened to and their views taken account of by the others. Without this mutual commitment, this trust will be fatally eroded.

And so we have in the modern age a new kind of collective agency. It is one with which its members identify, typically as the realization/bulwark of their freedom and/or the locus of their national/cultural expression (or most often, some combination of the two). Of course, in premodern societies, too, people often "identified" with the regime, with sacred kings or hierarchical orders. They were often willing subjects. But in the democratic age we identify as free agents. That is why the notion of popular will plays a crucial role in the legitimating idea.[4]

This means that the modern democratic state has generally accepted common purposes or reference points, the features whereby it can lay claim to being the bulwark of freedom and locus of expression of its citizens. Whether or not these claims are actually founded, the state must be so imagined by its citizens if it is to be legitimate.

So a question can arise for the modern state for which there is no analogue in most premodern forms: what/whom is this state for? whose freedom? whose expression? The question seems to make no sense applied to, say, the Austrian or Turkish Empires—unless one answered the "whom for?" question by referring to the Habsburg or Ottoman dynasties, and this would hardly give you their legitimating ideas.

This is the sense in which a modern state has what I want to call a political identity, defined as the generally accepted answer to the "what/whom for?" question. This is distinct from the identities of its members, that is, the reference points, many and varied, which for each of these defines what is important in their lives. There better be some overlap, of course, if these members are to feel strongly identified with the state; but the identities of individuals and constituent groups will generally be richer and more complex, as well as being often quite different from each other.[5]

In other words, a modern democratic state demands a "people" with a strong collective identity. Democracy obliges us to show much more solidarity and much more commitment to one another in our joint political project than was demanded by the hierarchical and authoritarian societies of yesteryear. In the good old days of the Austro-Hungarian Empire, the Polish peasant in Galicia could be altogether oblivious of the Hungarian country squire, the bourgeois of Prague, or the Viennese worker, without this in the slightest threatening the stability of the state. On the contrary, this condition of things only becomes untenable when ideas about popular government start to circulate. This is the moment when subgroups that will not, or cannot, be bound together start to demand their own states. This is the era of nationalism, of the breakup of empires.

I have been discussing the political necessity of a strong common identity for modern democratic states in terms of the requirement of forming a people, a deliberative unit. But this is also evident in a number of other ways. Thinkers in the civic humanist tradition, from Aristotle through to Arendt, have noted that free societies require a higher level of commitment and participation than despotic or authoritarian ones. Citizens have to do for themselves, as it were, what otherwise the rulers do for them. But this will only happen if these citizens feel a strong bond of identification with their political community and hence with those who share with them in this.

From another angle again, because these societies require strong commitment to do the common work, and because a situation in which some carried the burdens of participation and others just enjoyed the benefits would be intolerable, free societies require a high level of mutual trust. In other words, they are extremely vulnerable to mistrust on the part of some citizens in relation to others, that the latter are not really assuming their commitments—e.g., that others are not paying their taxes or are cheating on welfare or as employers are benefitting from a good labor market without assuming any of the social costs. This kind of mistrust creates extreme tension and threatens to unravel the whole skein of the mores of commitment that democratic societies need to operate. A continuing and constantly renewed mutual commitment is an essential basis for taking the measures needed to renew this trust.

The relation between nation and state is often considered from a unilateral point of view, as if it were always the nation that sought to provide itself with a state. But there is also the opposite process. In order to remain viable, states sometimes seek to create a feeling of common belonging. This is an important theme in the history of Canada, for example. To form a state, in the democratic era, a society is forced to undertake the difficult and never-to-be-completed task of defining its collective identity.

Thus what I have been calling political identity is extremely important in modern democratic states. And this identity is usually defined partly in terms of certain basic principles (democracy, human rights, equality) and partly in terms of their historical, or linguistic, or religious traditions. It is understandable that features of this identity can take on a quasi-sacred status, for to alter or undermine them can seem to threaten the very basis of unity without which a democratic state cannot function.

It is in this context that certain historical institutional arrangements can seem to be untouchable. They may appear as an essential part of the basic principles of the regime, but they will also come to be seen as a key component of its historic identity. This is what one sees with laïcité as invoked by many French republicans. The irony is that in the face of a modern politics of (multicultural) identity they invoke this principle as a crucial feature of (French) identity. This is unfortunate, but very understandable. It is one illustration of a general truth: that contemporary democracies, as they progressively diversify, will have to undergo redefinitions of their historical identities, which may be far-reaching and painful.

At this point, I would like to discuss an interesting point that Habermas reminds us of in his paper "Das Politische": originally political authority was defined and justified in cosmic-religious terms. It was defined within the terms of a "political theology." But Habermas seems to think that modern secular states might do altogether without some analogous concept, and this seems to me not quite right.

The crucial move that we see in the modern West from the seventeenth century, the move that takes us out of the cosmic religious conceptions of order, establishes a new "bottom-up" view of society, as existing for the protection and mutual benefit of its (equal) members. There is a strong normative view attached to this new conception, which I've called the "modern moral order."[6] It enshrines basically three principles (on one possible enumeration): (1) the rights and liberties of the members, (2) the equality among them (which has of course been variously interpreted and has mutated toward more radical conceptions over time), and (3) the principle that rule is based on consent (which has also been defended in more and less radical forms).

These basic norms have been worked out in a host of different philosophical anthropologies and according to very different concepts of human sociability. It very soon transcended the atomism that narrowed the vision of its early formulators, like Locke and Hobbes. But the basic norms remain and are more or less inseparable from modern liberal democracies.

The rejection of cosmic-religious embedding thus was accomplished by a new conception of "the political," a new basic norm, which, as Lefort suggests, involved its own representation of political authority, but one in which the central spot remains paradoxically empty. If the notion of sovereignty is retained, no one person or group can be identified with it.

Democratic societies are organized not necessarily around a "civil religion," as Rousseau claimed, but certainly around a strong "philosophy of civility," enshrining the three norms, which in contemporary societies are often expressed as (1) human rights, (2) equality and nondiscrimination, and (3) democracy.

But, in certain cases, there can be a civil religion: a religious view incorporating and justifying the philosophy of civility. This was arguably so for the young American republic. It was adopting a form which was clearly part of God's providential plan for mankind ("We hold these truths to be self-evident, that men were *created* equal . . ."). Or it can alternatively be part of a non- or even antireligious ideology, as with the First French Republic. One can even argue that all-englobing views of this kind seem more "natural" to many of our contemporaries. After all, the principles of our civil philosophy seem to call for deeper grounding. If it's important that we agree on the principles, then surely things are much more stable if we also accept a common grounding. Or so it may appear, and the centuries-long tradition of political life seems to testify to this idea.

For indeed the overlapping consensus between different founding views on a common philosophy of civility is something quite new in history and relatively untried. It is consequently hazardous. And, besides, we often suspect that those with different basic views can't really subscribe to these principles, not the way we do! (Because, as "we" know, "atheists can't have principles or, as [another] "we" knows, "religions are all against liberty and /or equality.")

The problem is that a really diverse democracy can't revert to a civil religion or antireligion, however comforting this might be, without betraying its own principles. We are condemned to live an overlapping consensus.

We have seen how this strongly motivated move to fetishize our historical arrangements can prevent seeing our secular regime in a more fruitful light, which foregrounds the basic goals we are seeking and which allows us to recognize and reason about the dilemmas we face. But this connects to the other main cause of confusion I cited previously, our fixation on religion as the problem. In fact, in many Western countries we have moved from an original phase in which secularism was a hard-won achievement warding off some form of religious domination to a phase of such widespread diversity of basic beliefs, religious and areligious, that only clear focus on the need to balance freedom of conscience and equality of respect can allow us to take the measure of the situation. Otherwise we risk needlessly limiting the religious freedom of immigrant minorities, on the strength of our historic institutional arrangements, while sending a message to these same minorities that they by no means enjoy equal status with the long-established mainstream.

Think of the argument of the German Laender that forbade the headscarf for teachers. These are authority figures, surely; but is our idea that only unmarked people can be authority figures? That those whose religious practices make them stand out in this context don't belong in positions of authority in this society? This is maybe the wrong message to inculcate in children in a rapidly diversifying society.

But the fixation on religion as the problem is not just a historical relic. Much of our thought and some of our major thinkers remain stuck in the old rut. They want to make a special thing of religion, but not always for very flattering reasons.

What are we to think of the idea, entertained by Rawls for a time, that one can legitimately ask of a religiously and philosophically diverse democracy that everyone deliberate in a language of reason alone, leaving their religious views in the vestibule of the public sphere? The tyrannical nature of this demand was rapidly appreciated by Rawls, to his credit. But we ought to ask why the proposition arose in the first place. Rawls's point in suggesting this restriction was that everyone should use a language with which they could reasonably expect their fellow citizens to agree. The idea seems to be something like this. Secular reason is a language that everyone speaks and can argue and be convinced in. Religious languages operate outside this discourse, by introducing extraneous premises that only believers can accept. So let's all talk the common language.

What underpins this notion is something like an epistemic distinction. There is secular reason that everyone can use and reach conclusions by, conclusions, that is, with which everyone can agree. Then there are special languages, which introduce extra assumptions, which might even contradict those of ordinary secular reason. These are much more epistemically fragile; in fact you won't be convinced by them unless you already hold them. So religious reason either comes to the same conclusions as secular reason, but then it is superfluous, or it comes to contrary conclusions, and then it is dangerous and disruptive. This is why it needs to be sidelined.

As for Habermas, he has always marked an epistemic break between secular reason and religious thought, with the advantage on the side of the first. Secular reason suffices to arrive at the normative conclusions we need, such as establishing the legitimacy of the democratic state and defining our political ethic. Recently his position on religious discourse has considerably evolved to the point of recognizing that its "Potential macht die religiöse Rede bei entsprechenden politischen Fragen zu einem ernsthaften Kandidaten für mögliche Wahrheitsgehalte." But the basic epistemic distinction still holds for him. Thus when it comes to the official language of the state, religious references have to be expunged. "Im Parlament muss beispielsweise die Geschäftsordnung den Presidenten ermächtigen, religiöse Stellungnahmen und Rechtfertigungen aus dem Protokoll zu streichen."[7]

Do these positions of Rawls and Habermas show that they have not yet understood the normative basis for the contemporary secular state? I believe that they are on to something, in that there are zones of a secular state in which the language used has to be neutral. But these do not include citizen deliberation, as Rawls at first thought, or even deliberation in the legislature, as Habermas seems to think from the lines I have quoted. This zone can be described as the official language of the state: the language in which legislation, administrative decrees, and court judgments must be couched. It is self-evident that a law before Parliament couldn't contain a justifying clause of the type "Whereas the Bible tells us that p." And the same goes, mutatis mutandis, for the justification of a judicial decision in the court's verdict. But this has nothing to do with the specific nature of religious language. It would be equally improper to have a legislative clause: "Whereas Marx has shown that religion is the opium of the people" or "Whereas Kant has shown that the only thing good without qualification is a good will." The grounds for both these kinds of exclusions is the neutrality of the state.

The state can be neither Christian nor Muslim nor Jewish, but by the same token it should also be neither Marxist nor Kantian, nor Utilitarian. Of course, the democratic state will end up voting for laws that (in the best case) reflect the actual convictions of its citizens, which will be either Christian or Muslim, etc., through the whole gamut of views held in a modern society. But the decisions can't be framed in a way that gives special recognition to one of these views. This is not easy to do; the lines are hard to draw, and they must always be drawn anew. But such is the nature of the enterprise that is the modern secular state. And what better alternative is there for diverse democracies?[8]

Now the notion that state neutrality is basically a response to diversity has trouble making headway among "secular" people in the West who remain oddly fixated on religion as something strange and perhaps even threatening. This stance is fed by all the conflicts, past and present, of liberal states with religion, but also by a specifically epistemic distinction: religiously informed thought is somehow less *rational* than purely "secular" reasoning. The attitude has a political ground (religion as threat), but also an epistemological one (religion as a faulty mode of reason).[9]

I believe we can see these two motifs in a popular contemporary book, Mark Lilla's *The Stillborn God*. On one hand, Lilla wants to claim that there is a great gulf between thinking informed by political theology and "thinking and talking about politics exclusively in human terms."[10] Moderns have effected "the liberation, isolation, and clarification of distinctively political questions, apart from speculations about the divine nexus. Politics became, intellectually speaking, its own realm deserving independent investigation and serving the limited aim of providing the peace and plenty necessary for human dignity. That was the Great Separation."[11] Such metaphors of radical separation imply that human-centered political thought is a more reliable guide to answer the questions in its domain than theories informed by political theology.

So much for the epistemological ranking. But then, toward the end of his book, Lilla calls on us not to lose our nerve and allow the Great Separation to be reversed,[12] which seems to imply that there are dangers in doing so. The return of religion in this sense would be full of menace.[13]

This phenomenon deserves fuller examination. Ideally, we should look carefully at the double grounds for this stance of distrust, comment on these, and then say something about the possible negative political consequences of maintaining this stance. But in this chapter I shall only really have space to look at the roots of the epistemological ground.

I think this has its source in what one might call a myth of the Enlightenment. There certainly is a common view that sees the Enlightenment (*Aufklärung, Lumières*) as a passage from darkness to light, that is, as an absolute, unmitigated move from a realm of thought full of error and illusion to one where the truth is at last available. To this one must immediately add that a counterview defines "reactionary" thought: the Enlightenment would be an unqualified move into error, a massive forgetting of salutary and necessary truths about the human condition.

In the polemics around modernity, more nuanced understandings tend to get driven to the wall, and these two slug it out. Arnold's phrase about "ignorant armies clashing by night" comes irresistibly to mind.

But what I want to do here, rather than bemoaning this fact, is to try to explain what underlies the understanding of Enlightenment as an absolute, unmitigated step forward. This is what I see as the "myth" of the Enlightenment. (One can't resist this jab, because "myth" is often cited as what Enlightenment has saved us from.)

This is worthwhile doing, I believe, because the myth is more widespread than one might think. Even sophisticated thinkers, who might repudiate it when it is presented as a general proposition, seem to be leaning on it in other contexts.

Thus there is a version of what Enlightenment represents which sees it as our stepping out of a realm in which revelation, or religion in general, counted as a source of insight about human affairs into a realm in which these are now understood in purely this-worldly or human terms. Of course, that some people have made this passage is not what is in dispute. What is questionable is the idea that this move involves the self-evident epistemic gain of our setting aside consideration of dubious truth and relevance and concentrating on matters that we can settle and that are obviously relevant. This is often represented as a move from revelation to reason alone (Kant's "blosse Vernunft").

Clearer examples are found in contemporary political thinkers, for instance, Rawls and Habermas. For all their differences, they seem to reserve a special status for nonreligiously informed reason (let's call this "reason alone"), as though a) this latter were able to resolve certain moral-political issues in a way that can legitimately satisfy any honest, unconfused thinker and b) where religiously based conclusions will always be dubious and, in the end, only convincing to people who have already accepted the dogmas in question.

This surely is what lies behind the idea I mentioned earlier, entertained for a time in different form by both thinkers, that one can restrict the use of religious language in the sphere of public reason. We must mention again that this proposition has been largely dropped by both, but we can see that the proposition itself makes no sense, unless something like (a) + (b) is true. Rawls's point in suggesting this restriction was that public reason must be couched in terms that could in principle be universally agreed upon. The notion was that the only terms meeting this standard were those of reason alone (a), while religious language by its very nature would fail to do so (b).

Before proceeding farther, I should just say that this distinction in rational credibility between religious and nonreligious discourse, supposed by (a) + (b), seems to me utterly without foundation. It may turn out at the end of the day that religion is founded on an illusion and hence that what is derived from is it less credible. But, until we actually reach that place, there is no a priori reason for greater suspicion being directed at it. The credibility of this distinction depends on the view that some quite "this-worldly" argument *suffices* to establish certain moral-political conclusions. I mean "satisfy" in the sense of (a) it should legitimately be convincing to any honest, unconfused thinker. There are propositions of this kind, ranging from "2+2=4" all the way to some of the better-founded deliverances of modern natural science. But the key beliefs we need, for instance, to establish our basic political morality are not among them. The two most widespread this-worldly philosophies in our contemporary world, utilitarian and Kantianism, in their different versions, all have points at which they fail to convince honest and unconfused people. If we take key statements of our contemporary political morality, such as those attributing rights to human beings as such, say the right to life, I cannot see how the fact that we are desiring/enjoying/suffering beings, or the perception that we are rational agents, should be any surer basis for this right than the fact that we are made in the image of God. Of course, our being capable of suffering is one of those basic unchallengeable propositions in the sense of (a), as our being creatures of God is not, but what is less sure is what follows normatively from the first claim.

Of course, this distinction would be much more credible if one had a "secular" argument for rights that was watertight. And this probably accounts for the difference between me and Habermas on this score. He finds this secure foundation in a "discourse ethic," which I unfortunately find quite unconvincing.

The (a) + (b) distinction, applied to the moral-political domain, is one of the fruits of the Enlightenment myth, or perhaps one should say it is one of the forms that this myth takes. It would be interesting to trace the rise of this illusion through a series of moves that were in part well-founded and in part themselves grounded on illusions. In another essay I identified three, of which the first two are relatively well traced and the third requires more elaborate description.[14] I'll briefly mention the first two here.

First comes (1) foundationalism, which one sees most famously with Descartes. This combines a supposedly indubitable starting point (the particulate ideas in the mind) with an infallible method (that of clear and distinct ideas) and thus should yield conclusions that would live up to claim (a). But this comes unstuck, and in two places. The indubitable starting points can be challenged by a determined scepticism such as we find in Hume, and the method relies much too much on a priori argument and not enough on empirical input.

But even though his foundationalism and his a priori physics were rejected, Descartes left behind (α) a belief in the importance of finding the correct method and (β) the crucial account that underpins the notion of reason alone. He claimed to be prescinding from all external authority, whether emanating from society or tradition, whether inculcated by parents or teachers, and to rely only on what monological reason can verify as certain. The proper use of reason is sharply distinguished from what we receive from authority. In the Western tradition this supposedly external imposition comes to include, indeed to find its paradigm in, religious revelation. As the marquis de Condorcet put it in his account of the progress of the human mind,

> Il fut enfin permis de proclamer hautement ce droit si longtemps méconnu de soumettre toutes les opinions à notre propre raison, c'est-à-dire d'employer, pour saisir la vérité, le seul instrument qui nous ait été donné pour la reconnaître. Chaque homme apprit, avec une sorte d'orgueil, que la nature ne l'avait pas absolument destiné à croire sur la parole d'autrui; et la superstition del'Antiquité, l'abaissement de la raison devant le délire d'une foi surnaturelle disparurent de la société comme de la philosophie.[15]

Our reasoning power is here defined as autonomous and self-sufficient. Proper reason takes nothing on "faith" in any sense of the word. We might call this the principle of "self-sufficient reason." The story of its rise and its self-emancipation comes to be seen as a kind of coming of age of humanity. As Kant put it, not long after Condorcet wrote, Enlightenment is the emergence of human beings from a state of tutelage for which they were themselves responsible, a "selbstbeschuldigte Unmündigkeit" (a self-responsible nonage). The slogan of the age was *sapere aude*! Dare to know.[16]

The first crucial move is that to self-sufficient reason. The second (2) was to point to natural science as a model for the science of society, the move we see in Hobbes, for instance. I shall not pursue this further here because reductive views of social science have less credibility today, although they are, alas, still present on the scene.

This whole matter deserves much further consideration, more than I can give it here. But I am convinced that this further examination would lend even more credibility to the diversity concept I have been proposing, which amounts to this: What deserve to be called "secularist" regimes in contemporary democracy have to be conceived not primarily as bulwarks against religion but as good-faith attempts to secure the three (or four) basic goals I have outlined. And this means that they attempt to shape their institutional arrangements, not to remain true to hallowed tradition, but to maximize the basic goals of liberty and equality between basic beliefs.

NOTES

1. Rawls would talk here of "comprehensive conceptions of the good." See John Rawls, *Political Liberalism,* exp. ed. (New York: Columbia University Press, 2005).
2. Christian Smith, *The Secular Revolution* (Berkeley: University of California Press, 2003).
3. Marcel Gauchet, *La Religion dans la Démocratie* (Paris: Gallimard, 1998), pp. 47–50.
4. Rousseau, who laid bare very early the logic of this idea, saw that a democratic sovereign couldn't just be an "aggregation"; it has to be an "association," that is, a strong collective agency, a "corps moral et collectif" with "son unité, son *moi* commun, sa vie et sa volonté." This last term is the key one, because what gives this body its personality is a "volonté générale." *Contrat Social* (Paris: Garnier Flammarion, 1966), book 1, chapter 6, p. 52.
5. I have discussed this relation in "Les Sources de l'identité moderne," in Mikhaël Elbaz, Andrée Fortin, and Guy Laforest, eds., *Les Frontières de l'Identité: Modernité et postmodernisme au Québec* (Sainte-Foy: Presses de l'Université Laval, 1996), pp. 347–64.
6. See Charles Taylor, *Modern Social Imaginaries* (Durham: Duke University Press, 2004).
7. Jürgen Habermas, *Zwischen Naturalismus une Religion* (Frankfurt: Suhrkamp, 2005), p. 137. Of course, Habermas is right: official language in diverse democracies must avoid certain religious references (although this shouldn't be stretched to include assembly debates), but this is not because they are specifically *religious*, but rather because they are not shared. It would be just as unacceptable for, say, legislation to be justified by a "whereas" clause referring to an atheist philosophy as by such a clause referring to the authority of the Bible.
8. I am not sure whether I am disagreeing with Habermas or whether the difference in formulation really amounts to a difference in practice. We both recognize contexts in which the language of the state has to respect a reserve of neutrality and others in which freedom of speech is unlimited. We differ perhaps more in our rationales than in the the practice we recommend.

9. Sometimes the obligation of citizens to address their compatriots in the language of secular reason is grounded in an obligation to make one's position intelligible to them. "The self-understanding of the constitutional state has developed within the framework of a contractualist tradition that relies on "natural reason", in other words soely on public arguments to which all persons are supposed to have equal access." Jürgen Habermas "Religion in the Public Sphere," p. 5. But what reason is there to think that "natural reason" offered us a kind of ideological Esperanto? Were Martin Luther King's secular compatriots unable to understand what he was arguing for when he put the case for equality in biblical terms? Would more people have got the point had he invoked Kant? And, besides, how does one distinguish religious from secular language? Is the Golden Rule clearly a move in either one or the other?
10. Mark Lilla, *The Stillborn God: Religion, Politics, and the Modern West* (New York: Knopf, 2007), p. 5.
11. Ibid, p. 162.
12. Ibid, pp. 305–6.
13. Habermas is an exceptional figure; in many respects, of course, but here I want to point out that although he is a major thinker in the epistemological distinction religion/reason (for which I criticize him further on), he most emphatically does NOT share the political mistrust of religion which often goes with this.
14. See "Blosse Vernunft," in Charles Taylor, *Dilemmas and Connections* (Cambridge: Harvard University Press, 2011), chapter 11.
15. Nicolas de Condorcet, *Esquisse d'un tableau historique des progrès de l'esprit humain* (Paris: Flammarion, 1988), p. 225. I have learned a gret deal from the interesting discussion in Vincent Descombes, *Le raisonnement de l'ours* (Paris: Seuil, 2007), pp. 163–178.
16. Immanuel Kant, "Was ist Aufklärung?" in *Kants Werke*, Akademie Textausgabe (Berlin: Walter de Gruyter, 1968), 8:33.

SECULARISM

Its Content and Context

AKEEL BILGRAMI

1

I begin with three fundamental features of the idea of secularism. I will want to make something of them at different stages of the passage of my argument in this chapter for the conclusion—among others—that the relevance of secularism is contextual in very specific ways.

If secularism has its relevance only in context, then it is natural and right to think that it will appear in different forms and guises in different contexts. But I write down these opening features of secularism at the outset because they seem to me to be invariant between the different forms that secularism may take in different contexts. It is hard to imagine that one hasn't changed the subject from secularism to something else, something that deserves another name, if one finds oneself denying any of the features that I initially list here.

First, secularism is *a stance to be taken about religion.* At the level of generality with which I have just described this, it does not say anything very specific or precise. The imprecision and generality have two sources. One obvious source is that *religion,* regarding which it is supposed to take a stance, is itself, notoriously, not a very precise or specifically understood term. But to the extent that we have a notion of religion in currency with some meaning—however imprecisely elaborated—secularism will have a parasitic meaning partially elaborated as a stance regarding it. Should we decide that there is no viability in any notion of religion, and should the notion pass out of conceptual currency, secularism too would lapse as a notion with a point and rationale. The other source of imprecision is that I have said nothing specific or precise about *what sort* of stance secularism takes toward religion. One may think that it has to be in some sense an adversarial stance since surely secularism, in some sense, defines itself against religion. This is true enough, but, still, the very fact that I find the need to keep using the qualifier "in some sense" makes clear that nothing much has been said about the kind of opposing stance this amounts to. Part of the point of this essay is to add a little precision to just this question.

Second, for all this generality just noted, *secularism*—unlike *secular* and *secularization*—is quite specific in another regard. It is the name of a *political* doctrine. So to the extent that it takes a stance vis-à-vis religion, it does so only in the realm of the *polity*. It is not meant—as the terms *secular* and *secularization* are—to mark a highly general and dispersed social and intellectual and cultural phenomenon and process. Unlike the term *secularization,* it is not so capacious as to include a stance against religion that requires redirection of either personal belief or, for that matter, any range of personal and cultural habits of dress or diet or . . . Thus it is not a stance against religion of the sort that atheists and agnostics might wish to take or a stance that strikes attitudes (to say nothing of policies) about the hijab. The increase in a society of loss of personal belief in God or the decrease in church- or synagogue- or mosque-going or the surrender of traditional religious habits of dress or prohibitions against pork may all be signs of increasing secular*ization,* but they are irrelevant to the idea of secular*ism.* And unlike the term *secular,* which is often said to refer innocuously and indiscriminately to all things that are "worldly" in the sense of being *outside* the reach of religious institutions and concerns (outside the cloister, in the mundiality of the world at large, as it were), secular*ism* aspires to be more concentrated in its concern—to not merely *refer* to anything that is outside of that reach, but to focus on something specific (the polity) and attempt to *keep* it or *steer* it outside of some specified aspects of that reach.

Third, secularism, as a stance regarding religion that is restricted to the polity, is not a good in itself. It seeks what is conceived, by those who favor it, to promote certain other moral and political goods, and these are goods that are intended to counter what are conceived as harms, either actual or potential. This third feature may be considered too controversial to be regarded as a defining feature, but its point becomes more plausible when we contrast secularism with a more cognitive (rather than political) stance regarding religion, such as atheism. For atheists, the truth of atheism is sufficient to motivate one to adhere to it and the truth of atheism is not grounded in the claim that it promotes a moral or political good or the claim that it is supported by other moral or political values we have. By contrast, secularists, to the extent that they claim "truth" for secularism, claim it on grounds that appeal to other values that support the ideal of secularism or other goods that are promoted by it. Secularism as a political doctrine arose to repair what were perceived as damages that flowed from historical harms that were, in turn, perceived as owing, in some broad sense, to religion. Thus, when it is said that secularism had as its vast cradle the prolonged and internecine religious conflicts in Europe of some centuries ago, for instance, something like this normative force of serving goods and correcting harms is detectably implied. But if all this is right, then it follows that one would have to equally grant that, should there be contexts in which those goods were not seen necessarily to be goods, or to the extent that those goods were being well served by political arrangements that were not secularist, or to the extent that there were no existing harms, actual or potential, that secularism would be correcting, then one could take the opposing normative stance and fail to see the point and rationale for secularism.

2

I want to now turn from features that *define* or characterize secularism to features of its *justification and basis of adoption.*

In an essay written in the days immediately following the fatwa pronounced against Salman Rushdie, called "What Is a Muslim?,"[1] I argued that secularism had no justification that did not appeal to substantive values, that is to say, values some may hold and others may not. It was not justifiable on purely rational grounds that anyone (capable of rationality) would find convincing, no matter what substantive values they held. I had invoked the notion, coined by Bernard Williams as "internal reasons," to describe these kinds of grounds on which its justification is given.[2] Internal reasons are reasons that rely on specific motives, values, and commitments in the moral psychologies of individuals (or groups, if one takes the view that groups have moral-psychological economies). Internal reasons are contrasted with "external reasons," which are reasons that someone is supposed to have quite independent of her substantive values and commitments, that is, independent of elements in the psychologies that motivate people. Bernard Williams, recapitulating Humean arguments against Kantian forms of externalist rationality and the universalism that might be expected to emerge from it, had claimed that there are no such things as "external reasons." Whether that general claim is true or not, my more specific claim had been that there are no external reasons that would establish the truth of secularism. If secularism were to carry conviction, it would have to be on grounds that persuaded people by appealing to the specific and substantive values that figured in their specific moral psychological economies.[3] Such a view might cause alarm in those who would wish for secularism on a more universal basis. Internal reasons, by their nature, do not provide such a basis. As, I said, internal reasons for some conclusion that will persuade some people, may not persuade others of that conclusion, since those others may not hold the particular substantive values to which those reasons appeal and on which those reasons depend. Only external reasons could persuade everyone since all they require is a minimal rationality possessed by all (undamaged, adult) human minds and make no appeal to substantive values that may be variably held by human minds and psychologies. Alarming though it might seem to some, there is no help for this. There are no more secure universal grounds on which one can base one's argument for secularism.

Charles Taylor has convincingly argued that in a religiously plural society secularism should be adopted on the basis of what Rawls called an "overlapping consensus."[4] An overlapping consensus, in Rawls's understanding of that term, is a consensus on some policy that is arrived at by people with very different moral and religious and political commitments who sign on to the policy from within their differing points of view and therefore on possibly very different grounds from each other. It contrasts with the idea that when one converges on a policy one must all do so for the *same* reason.

What is the relation between the idea that secularism should be adopted on the basis of an overlapping consensus and the idea presented in the earlier paragraph about internal reasons being the only reasons available in justifying secularism? A very close one. The latter idea yields (it lies behind) the former. The relation is this: internal reasons, unlike external reasons, may vary from person to person, group to group. This may give the impression that there simply cannot be a consensus if we were restricted to the resources of internal reasons. But that does not follow. Or, at any rate, it only follows if we assume that a consensus requires that all sign onto something (some policy or political position such as secularism) on the same grounds or for the same reason. In other words, on the basis of an external reason or reasons. But such an assumption is a theoretical tyranny. Without that assumption one could say this. *If* there is to be a consensus on some political outcome on the basis, not of external but of internal reasons, it will presumably *only* be because different persons or groups subscribe to the policy on their own, different, grounds. This just is the idea of an *overlapping* consensus. If there were external reasons for a policy, one could get a consensus on it of a stronger kind and would not need to hold out hope for a *merely* "overlapping" consensus.

Perhaps all this is obvious. However, for reasons having to do with Rawls scholarship, I have been a little wary of this use of the notion of overlapping consensus since in Rawls it has always been a notion embedded in the framework of his celebrated idea of the "original position," i.e., the idea that one contract into policies to live by without knowledge of one's substantive position in society. I find myself completely baffled by why the idea of the original position is not made entirely redundant by the notion of an overlapping consensus. If one did not know what one's substantive position in society is, one presumably does not know what one's substantive values are. If so, the very idea of internal reasons can have no play in the original position. It follows that if one were to adopt an overlapping consensus on the basis of divergent internal reasons that contractors may have for signing onto a policy, then the original position becomes altogether irrelevant to the contractual scenario. Of course, if one were to completely divorce the idea of an overlapping consensus from Rawls's conceptual apparatus within which it has always been formulated (even in his last published work, *The Law of Peoples*),[5] then it would be exactly right to say, as Taylor does, that secularism should be adopted in pluralistic society on the basis of an overlapping consensus. But now the only apparatus one has to burden the contractors with is the capacity for internal reasoning, that is, with psychological economies of substantive values that yield internal reasons. Rawls would not be recognizable in this form of contractualist doctrine. Indeed, one would be hard-pressed to say that one was any longer theorizing within the contractualist tradition at all, which is a tradition in which serious constraints of an "original position" or a "state of nature" were always placed as methodological starting points in the making of a contract. Shorn of all this, one is left with something that is the merest common sense, which would be bombastic to call a social contract. We now need only say this: assuming no more than our capacity for internal reasoning, i.e., our capacity to invoke some substantive values we hold (whatever they may differentially be in all the different individuals or groups in society), we can proceed to justify on its basis another substantive value or policy—for example, secularism—and so proceed to adopt it for the polity. If this path of adoption by consensus, invoking this internalist notion of justification, works in a religiously pluralist society, it will be just as Taylor presents it, an overlapping consensus, with none of Rawls's theoretical framework.

3

The last two sections have respectively presented points of definition of secularism and points of its justification and basis of adoption. I think it is important to keep these two things separate on the general ground that one needs to have a more or less clear idea of what we are justifying and adopting before we justify and adopt it.

In a very interesting recent essay, Charles Taylor has argued that we need to *redefine* "secularism."[6] It is a complex essay with highly honorable political and moral motivations underlying it. But, speaking more theoretically, I don't think it is quite as well motivated. It begins by saying that there have been two aspects to secularism—one, the idea of the *separation of church and state* and the other that the *state maintain a neutral equidistance from different religions within a plural society*. The essay wishes to correct an overemphasis on the first by stressing the importance of the second aspect and wishes to modify the second, too, along the following lines.

In modern societies, we seek various goods, and the three in particular (echoing the trio of goods expressed in a familiar slogan) that remain relevant to secular aspirations are the *liberty* of worship, the *equality* of different faiths, and, finally, more than just equality, we need to give each faith a voice in determining the shape of the society, so there must be *fraternal* relations within which negotiations, with each voice being equally heard, are crucial. What is more, because the first aspect's stress on separation of church and state was too focused on religion, the second aspect's stress on religious diversity should be modified and expanded to include the fact that in late modernity the diversity of pluralist societies contains not just a variety of religious people but nonreligious people as well. Their point of view must also be included in the mix. *All* this is now included in the idea and ideal of a redefined secularism.

So, to sum up his explicit motivations for seeking this more capacious definition of secularism: There is the importance of the state maintaining a neutrality and equal distance from each religion. There is the importance of a society allowing the democratic participation of all religious voices in shaping its polity's commitments. And there is the need to turn one's focus away from just religion to acknowledging and respecting wider forms of cultural diversity and a variety of intellectual positions, including nonreligious ones. These are all worthy motivations, and a society that pursues them would be measurably better than one that doesn't. The question is how does thinking so make a difference to the way we theorize about the meaning or definition of secularism? There is no denying that it makes *a* difference to secularism, but it is not obvious to me that it is just as he presents it.

One of the things he finds distorted about secularism while defined along the unrevised lines that he is inveighing against is that, so defined, it has been too focused on "institutional arrangements." Slogans such as "separation of church and state" become mantras, and, as they do, they suggest institutional arrangements that are fixed. Once done, it is hard not only to change the institutions but also to reconceptualize secularism. What is better in order to maintain both theoretical and institutional flexibility is to allow the ideals in questions (the echoes of liberty, equality, and fraternity) to determine what is needed rather than these slogans, which point to institutional arrangements and stop or preempt conversations about how to theorize secularism. In keeping with this point, he applauds Rawls for starting with certain ideals such as "human rights, equality, the rule of law, democracy" rather than anti-religious (or for that matter, religious principles) and then proceeding to consider the question of secularism to be in line with them.[7]

This is just right, I believe, as are the general moral and political instincts that prompt Taylor's appeal for a redefinition of secularism: the desire for greater flexibility, the desire not to tie secularism to the polemical sense of non- or antireligious, the desire to establish secularism on the basis of an overlapping consensus of internal reasons. The question is, is it wise or necessary to redefine secularism to pursue these instincts and motivations?

4

Let me then turn to a way of characterizing (I say characterizing because perhaps *defining* is too constricting a term for what both Taylor and I are interested in, but I will not always avoid talk of *definition* since it is the word Taylor himself uses) secularism that is, or to put it more cautiously, that may be, at odds with Taylor's. (I add this caution because, despite what it seems to me at present, it may turn out that we are not much at odds and it is really a matter of emphasizing different things.)

I have said that it is a good idea, as Taylor suggests, to *start* with certain ideals that do not mention religion or opposition to religion and *then* move on to talk of political and institutional arrangements involving the role of the state and its stances toward religion. So, just because it is what is most familiar to us in our tradition of political theory and philosophy, let us start within a liberal framework, let us start with some basic ideals and the fundamental rights and constitutional commitments that enshrine them, just as Rawls and Taylor propose. Starting with them as the basic, though tentative, givens, I suggest we embrace Taylor's account only up to a point and then add something that does not seem to be emphasized by him, indeed something that he may even wish to be deemphasizing in his redefinition.

I propose, then, something like the following nonarbitrary stipulation as a characterization of secularism that contains all of the three features I had mentioned at the outset.

(S): Should we be living in a religiously plural society, secularism requires that all religions should have the privilege of free exercise and be evenhandedly treated *except when a religion's practices are inconsistent with the ideals that a polity seeks to achieve* (ideals, often, though not always, enshrined in stated fundamental rights and other constitutional commitments) *in which case there is a lexical ordering in which the political ideals are placed first.*

Much commentary is needed on this minimal and basic characterization.

Here are some miscellaneous points of commentary, in no particular order, that help to situate and motivate (S), thereby showing why, as a stipulation, it is nonarbitrary and where it may seem to depart in emphasis and implication and significance from Taylor's redefinition.

To begin with, (S) makes explicit mention of the sort of thing that Taylor thinks it is important to stress, the evenhanded, neutral distance between different religions in a religiously plural society. However, the "qualifier" that (S) opens with, "Should we be living in a religiously plural society . . . ," is there to point out that secularism is a doctrine that may be relevant even in societies where there is no religiously plurality. If there is a monoreligious society, it is not as if secularism becomes irrelevant. In such a society there may still be point in a lexical ordering of the sort that characterizes secularism in (S). If there are ideals that form the starting point of one's construction of the content of secularism, and one wishes to protect those ideals, then, should the single religion of such a society run afoul of them, the lexical ordering will have a point. Thus secularism has a broader relevance and meaning than one that—as in Taylor's redefinition—only ties it to the idea of being neutral and evenhanded with a plurality of religions as well as various nonreligious points of view. Speaking more generally, though, Taylor applauds Rawls for adopting this starting point where the examples of ideals are basically those of a liberal polity in a society with plural social interests and concerns; there may be other societies in which there is less plurality and so the starting point may formulate other ideals.

The more important point of difference between (S) and the sort of redefinition Taylor is seeking is that, when characterizing secularism, (S) squares with his urge to be nonphobic and accommodating toward religion as well as with his idea to have the state keep a neutral and equal distance between all religions—but then emphasizes something else as well: the lexical ordering. The point of this latter essential element of the characterization is that (S) is a stance that *can* be *adversarial* against religious practices and laws, but *only* when, from the point of view of the ideals one starts with, it needs to be that, i.e., when those practices and laws go against the very thing Taylor himself thinks we should start with—the ideals and goals (formulated without reference to religious or antireligious elements) that a society has adopted.

The fact that one's starting point lies in certain ideals helps (S) to avoid the charge that Taylor makes against some contemporary formulations of secularism, viz., that they start with an assertion of certain institutional arrangements with slogans or mantras such "the separation of church and state." Rather, in the Rawlsian manner of which Taylor approves, (S) starts with certain ideals and goals that the society wishes to adopt, and the lexical ordering suggests that the institutions should be shaped and distributed in such a way that certain priorities articulated in the lexical ordering get implemented. There is certainly more of a stress than in Taylor on the priority over religion of certain goals and ideals formulated in terms independent of religion. Religion and its practices come second to these, if there is ever a clash between them. But, just as Taylor would have it, it is these goals rather than any institutional arrangements that form the starting point.

I had said that the first basic defining feature of secularism is that it is some sort of a stance regarding religion. What sort of stance is (S)? The point in the previous paragraph brings out how, as a stance, it is more adversarial than Taylor wishes secularism to be, but it is by no means obsessively seeking religion out as a target. It is certainly not trying to polemically remove it root and branch from public life, in all its social, cultural and intellectual aspects, in a way often suggested in recent writings by today's doctrinaire atheists. This is because (S) keeps strict faith with the second elementary feature of secularism mentioned at the outset, viz., that it is only and precisely a political stance, a stance regarding religion as it affects the polity. It is not dismayed by or concerned with the presence of religiosity in the society at large or in the personal beliefs of the individual citizens as so much of the ideological urge for secularity in the modern period does. The lexical ordering merely says that if and when there is an inconsistency that arises between certain goals sought to be achieved in a polity that are formulated independently of religion, and the practices of a religion, the former must be placed first and the latter second.

Quite apart from the fact that it is restricted to political matters, the antecedent in the conditional "if and when there is an inconsistency" makes it clear that *even within this restricted domain*, there is no harm to be found in the presence of religion, so long as it does not clash with certain fundamental ideals and commitments of the polity.

What sorts of things are clear examples of the political domain and of the priority being proposed within it, by the lexical ordering? The examples are hardly exotic.

Take a society in which the commitment to free speech is a fundamental ideal of its polity. Assume that it is our starting point, in just the way Taylor urges. Let's, then, also assume that there are religions and religious practices in that society, those of Christianity and Islam, say, but not Buddhism, which have strict commitments to censorship of blasphemy. (S) says that it is important to see secularism as requiring the state to be evenhanded toward religions in general, but not in any case when the lexical ordering comes to have application. And this is such a case. In this case the lexical ordering requires one to spoil the neutrality by favoring Buddhism over Christianity and Islam since the state must place the commitments to blasphemy in these religions second and the commitment to free speech first, in the context, say, of the publication of novels such as *The Last Temptation of Christ* or *The Satanic Verses* in a society such as Britain's with a polity defined upon basic liberal commitments. (It is interesting to note that Britain took a non-neutral stance in a quite different sense than the one I am recommending, weighing down on Islam but, as a result of Mary Whitehouse's campaigns, not on Christianity. It is a question whether this hints at the extent to which established religion is more than merely nominal in Britain.) I will discuss free speech and another example involving gender equality again later, but, for now, I offer this as a rather straightforward example of the occasion on which (S) seems to depart from Taylor's understanding of secularism, by emphasizing the "lexical ordering" ideal over the "neutral and equidistant" ideal of secularism that he favors.

I think in late modern societies committed to liberal ideals of this sort it is a theoretical *loss* rather than gain to allow that a polity has been impeccably secular in *any* case in which it capitulates to the banning of a novel on the grounds that it is blasphemous by the lights of a religion's customs or laws. One may—even in late modern liberal societies—find good moral and political reasons to ban the novel. That is not the theoretical issue I am focusing on. What is theoretically questionable is only that we should describe the ban as falling well within the secular ideal. It may well be that good politics or morals sometimes requires us to put the secularist policy aside. But it is *secularist* policy that we would be putting aside. If a redefinition of secularism were to deny this, that would be a questionable theoretical outcome of the redefinition. The stress on the neutral equidistance ideal over the lexical ordering ideal in a characterization of secularism may well lead to just such a questionable theoretical outcome in cases such as this. A society whose polity banned *both* the Kazantsakis *and* the Rushdie novel, on grounds of their being blasphemous by the lights of two different religions that were being treated neutrally in this twin banning, meets the neutral and equidistant state ideal of secularism but fails to meet (S).

It cannot really be argued on Taylor's behalf that such a twin and symmetrical banning does *not* satisfy the state-neutralist ideal of secularism by pointing out that he has allowed into the groups that the state must be neutral toward, nonreligious people as well. What these religions find blasphemous are not just the expression of a point of view, described innocuously as "nonreligious," it is the expression of views that trash and cartoon and satirize their most cherished and deep commitments with contempt as Rushdie or Kazantzakis (or Buñuel of Arrabal . . .) did. So a state that decided to keep all these things (evenhandedly for both—indeed all—offended religions) out of circulation in bookstores and cinemas would not be failing to be neutral and fair toward a group under the description "nonreligious" people. It would be failing to be fair toward "blasphemers," not exactly a natural or routine category or grouping by any pluralist count of society. So, I assume that the only protection that *blasphemers* can properly expect to get is from secularists who believe in (S), not secularists who wish to be neutral and equidistant between religious and "nonreligious" people. Those last two or three words of the last sentence are too bland a description in the state-neutralist ideal to warrant our saying that such an ideal has the very particular focus needed to count the censorship of something so specific as hurtful and contemptuous writing against a religion as antisecular.[8] What is clearly moving Taylor is that a genuine pluralism in many *contemporary* societies has to acknowledge as a natural grouping in the plural mix not only Hindus, Muslims, Christians but also nonreligious people. Taylor is concerned to respect this development in the pluralism of our time. And what I am saying is that we should certainly grant him that that is a correct way to modify "the neutral and equidistant ideal of secularism" he favors, but then say, even so, that, when we speak of pluralism and its groupings today, *blasphemers* is *not* a natural grouping. As a result, his pluralist motivation here in adding to the mix of things toward which the state must be neutral is not sufficient (not sufficiently particular) to make the case that such censorship would be antisecular by the lights of a state-neutralist ideal of secularism.

If he were to go beyond what are broad and natural groupings to something much more indefinitely detailed in its pluralist count in a society, counting as a group any group (however specifically described, blasphemers being just one example) that could claim that there has been a lapse in neutrality by the state, after the fact of some state action, it is very doubtful that there could be anything at all that a neutralist state secularist ideal would yield by way of policy. That is to say, there would hardly be any policy that would be sanctioned as secular policy when there are an indefinite and limitless number of conflicting groups whose points of view have to be equally respected. Indeed, unless there was some *ex ante* specification of the pluralist elements that a state was to be neutral between, the ideal amounts to nothing that can be interestingly specified at all. What I think we must assume such an ideal envisages, if it is to envisage something plausible, is not that "blasphemers" are *ex ante* counted as a group that must be protected when devising state policies, but rather something like this: Muslims, Christians, Jews, Hindus, etc., as well as "nonreligious" people (*a fragment among whom* will be novelists, filmmakers, etc. that satirize, vilify, one or another religion) must equally have a voice in the policies that a polity will adopt. Whatever policy is adopted once this fraternal deliberation takes place must count as the policies of a secular state according to this ideal. After all, it is the outcome of a state allowing evenhanded voice to all groups. Now *it may turn out* that nonreligious people will want protection for the fragment among them that have offended religions deeply in the novels they write or the films they make. And if they carry the day in the deliberation, then the outcome of this state-neutralist ideal process of decision making will *coincide* with the outcome of a lexical ordering imposed by (S), i.e., they will be co*extensive*, (not cointensive) outcomes. But *it may turn out instead* that the fraternal deliberation with all voices involved yields a policy that evenhandedly bans novels and films considered blasphemous by various religions, and, if it does, the policy will *also* count as secular since the criterion of *fraternal* and *equal* participation of *freely* speaking voices will be satisfied. The point is that (S), however, will *never* count such an outcome as secular, so long as free speech is an ideal one begins with. The adoption of the policy will *always* fall afoul of the lexical ordering that is essential to (S)'s formulation of secularism. And, just for that reason, I am saying, (S) has things more theoretically right about what secularism is.

In a clarifying response in personal correspondence to a draft of this chapter, Charles Taylor makes a point of real importance and relevance for the present in explaining why he thinks a characterization of secularism should not incorporate the first feature of secularism that I had mentioned at the outset, that it is a stance regarding religion. He expresses the anxiety that the sort of lexical ordering I propose, which mentions explicitly the importance of placing one or other ideal or goal of a polity before some *religious* practice or custom or law, might sometimes have the effect of having the secular polity equate some *unrepresentative* element of a religious population with "the religion" in question. The woeful effects of just this sort of thing are familiar from the present cold war being waged against "Islam" on the basis of a few acts of atrocity by a small fraction of Muslims. This is what Taylor says:

> Here's where the hard-line secularist focus on religion alone leads to tragic and destructive moves. They attack "Islam" for instance for female genital mutilation, and for honour killings. And they seem to have a semblance of justification in that the communities who practice these can see them as religiously sanctioned. They tar the whole community with this brush, and drive moderates into the arms of fundamentalists. Whereas, as Anthony Appiah has argued, the most effective way of ending these practices involves making allies with the more orthodox who can effectively convince Islamic societies that they are deviant to the message of the prophet.

As with everything else that prompts him on this matter, this is a humane and politically perceptive concern. But I don't find myself convinced that these considerations, despite their great importance today, are to be diagnosed as flowing from a characterization of secularism that incorporates the lexical ordering in the terms that I have presented it. As I presented it, there is nothing in (S) that constitutes an "attack" on religion as a generality. In particular, when female genital mutilation or honor killings are identified as practices to be placed second in the lexical ordering, Islam, as a generality, is not "under attack." Rather, the claim is entirely conditional: *If* there be a claim by those who practice them that these practices owe to a religion and *if* that claim is correct, then the placing of the practice lower in the lexical ordering than the moral and political ideals they run afoul of would be properly called a "secularist" policy on the part of the state. That is all a characterization of secularism as (S) amounts to. I don't see that, so understood, secularism as a stance regarding religion has the effects Taylor thinks it does. If it should turn out that nothing in the religion in question sanctions these practices, then the ideals and goals of the polity may supersede these practices in a lexical ordering, but that lexical ordering would not be the lexical ordering characterized in (S), which specifically mentions religion. In that case, secularism, being a stance regarding religion, is not a notion that descriptively applies to such a case.

Moreover, though the anxiety that a whole community is being tarred by the brush of practices of a fractional group in the community is a genuine and justified anxiety to have, it is not clear how (S) as a characterization of secularism is responsible for its happening. True, as a formulation of secularism,

(S) mentions religious practices without distinguishing between the numbers that do and do not practice them. But it is not such a general understanding of secularism that gives rise to the public impression that the religion in question is itself to be identified with the practice. What is really responsible for it is an irresponsible media that doesn't care to distinguish finely enough between the practitioners and the rest of the community. And it is not as if states are completely innocent of responsibility, since states, for familiar statist reasons, track whatever the media calls or fails to call attention to. But that a state should be implicated in that sort of thing is independent of whether the state has adopted secular policies as characterized by (S). One of the real sources of difficulty is that states, including liberal states, have no (and, by the nature of the case, cannot have any) political mechanisms by which to introduce *intra*community democratization that would show the practitioners to be an *unrepresentative* minority within the community. Liberal politics has institutions that, via mechanisms like elections, calibrate representation with numbers of people. This happens, as we know, at the federal, state, regional, and even municipal level, but, unlike these levels, religious communities are too dispersed and too imprecisely defined to have such mechanisms. Whether there can be intracommunity democratization of a kind that does not depend on such representative institutions is a subject that needs much more study than it has had in political sociology. Until such democratization, a small fraction within a community, which has the shrillest voice and the most activist presence, may often get to be seen as more representative of the community than it deserves by its numbers to be, since the media will typically pay the most attention to the most audible voices, and the state, for typical reasons of state, will do so as well. This, not secularism as formulated in (S), should at bottom be the diagnosed source of Taylor's quite proper anxiety.

Taylor is rightly anxious too that when there is an equation of a religion with a small fragment of its members and its practices, it can sometimes have the effect of driving ordinary devout people, as he puts it, "into the arms of the fundamentalists." But again it is not clear why secularism as (S) elaborates it has any role to play in this. It is a complex question why nonpractitioners of the practices in question do not always distinguish themselves vocally and explicitly from (the far smaller number of) the practitioners. Speaking more generally, it is a complex question why ordinary devout people remain a large but silent majority and don't speak out against the relatively small numbers of extremists and fundamentalists in their community with whom they share so little by way of ideas and ideology. The answer to such questions would have to invoke a whole range of factors, all of which, I think, are at some distance from (S)—factors that make them feel as if they are letting their side down if they were to be openly critical of anyone in their community, even those whose views and practices they have no sympathy for. In the case of Islam, this defensively uncritical psychology has been bred by years of colonial subjugation, by continuing quasi-colonial economic arrangements with American and European corporate exploitation of energy resources of countries with large Muslim populations, by immoral embargos imposed on these countries that cause untold suffering to ordinary people, by recent invasions of some of these countries by Western powers, and, finally, by the racialist attitudes toward migrants from these countries in European nations. It is these factors that are responsible for ordinary Muslims, who might have otherwise been more willing to criticize fundamentalists in their community, focusing instead primarily on an enemy that is perceived to be external rather than internal.

One might think that the rhetoric of "secularism" (like the rhetoric of "democracy") plays a role in the anti-Islamist drumbeat of propaganda that accompanies these other factors, and therefore it in turn plays a role in making the vast majority of ordinary Muslims unwilling to be critical of the offending practitioners in their midst. That might sometimes be so. But, if and when it is so, the right thing to do is not to ask that secularism be redefined, but to demand that one should *drop* talk of secularism and focus instead on trying to improve matters on what is really at stake: the effects of a colonial past, a commercially exploitative present, unjust wars and embargos, racial discrimination against migrants in Europe, and so on. It is a change in these things, not a redefinition of secularism, that will draw ordinary Muslims out of "the arms of fundamentalists," that will give the vast majority of nonpractitioners the confidence to come out of their silence and their defensive psychologies to distinguish themselves from those whom they find to be a small but extreme and unrepresentative minority in their community's midst.

In the quoted passage, Taylor implies that secularism, as for instance defined by (S), would spoil the chances of making alliances with the orthodox in a community whose voices would have the most chance of bringing about an end of the offending practices. It is perfectly possible for a state to sometimes judge that it would be better for it to forge alliances with the orthodox element in a community to get it to speak up for an end to a certain offending practice rather than adopt a policy like (S) that opposes the practice that the orthodox element gives support to. That would be to surrender secularism for a more effective pragmatic strategy. It would not be to adopt a different ideal of secularism. I myself think that what is needed is for a secular state, as defined by (S), to help provide *internal* reasons to the community, including the orthodoxy that supports the practice, to persuade it to change some of its commitments. Such a strategy is perfectly compatible with a secularism defined in terms of (S) and I discuss how that is so at length in sections 5 and 6 (see particularly note 16 and the text in the main body of this paper to which it attaches.) What is required in order to make this possible is for secularism not to give up on its lexical ordering as formulated in (S) but to seek a *conceptual vernacular* within which it can seek to provide internal reasons that speak to even the orthodox element in a community. Too often secularism adopts the universalist rhetoric of rights in its efforts at persuasion rather than seek *local* concepts and commitments within the community (including even among the orthodox in the community) that might put pressure on the community's own practices and thereby eventually provide the source of internal reasons for change. This is the entire theme of sections 5 and 6.

Though (S) insists sturdily on the invariance of the lexical ordering in all contexts where there is secularism, it allows for much contextual differential in the form secularism may take because it allows for much variation in the ideals that are placed first in the lexical ordering.

Thus, for instance, the values and rights may vary from constitution to constitution, but one can assume that, if it is liberal democracies in late modernity one is concerned with, then there will be substantial overlap of the basic and familiar values—freedom of speech, say, or racial and gender equality, and so on. In other sorts of societies, the ideals may be substantially different and there may be less stress on the basic freedoms and social forms of equality. Thus some socialist societies have stressed economic equality and the right to work more than they have stressed basic freedoms. And there will no doubt be yet other forms of ideals and commitments in yet other societies that the lexical ordering mentioned in the stipulated characterization of secularism will place before the religious practices inconsistent with them. The point is not to lay down very specific ideals that form a definite list. The point, rather, is to stress the role of the priority such ideals (whatever they may be) will have in *the lexical ordering that forms the heart of the characterization of secularism.*

The last point has wider implications that distinguish between (S) and Taylor's redefinition in a rather sharp way. One should be able to characterize secularism independently of whether a polity is authoritarian or liberal in its fundamental orientation. Taylor, as I said, mentions with approval Rawls's starting point in certain rights and other liberal ideals. This is an approval one may share without actually insisting that there cannot be variation in the form that the ideals take or the ideals themselves. The theoretically important requirement is not that there be this or that ideal but that there be ideals that do not get articulated in terms that mention religion or the opposition to religion. All the opposition to religion that the characterization in (S) demands is in the notion of a lexical ordering that follows the initial starting point in these ideals. Thus, by these theoretical lights, so long as there were such ideals motivating a polity, and they played such a role in the minimal demands of a lexical ordering, then (whatever other properties that polity possessed) it meets the necessary and sufficient condition of secularism. So, for instance, on the assumption that there were such ideals that were motivating the political regime that Atatürk imposed on Turkey, and on the assumption that religion and religious practices were always placed second in the lexical ordering as formulated in (S), the authoritarian properties of that regime do nothing to cancel the secularist nature of the regime, whatever else they cancel—for instance, the *liberal* nature of the regime. Not all secularism need be liberal secularism. So also, then, many communist regimes should get counted as secular by this criterion. Someone may find the authoritarian methods by which secularism was imposed in both Atatürk's Turkey and the Soviet Union to be wrong without denying they were committed to secularism. Taylor, who *explicitly* takes it to be an advantage of his redefinition that it rules out Atatürk's Turkey as secular,[9] is on this point at least, quite visibly at odds with (S) as a characterization of secularism. There is a further and symmetrically converse point to be made: just as secularism may bypass liberalism, liberalism may outrun secularism when the liberal goals and ideals one might begin with, such as free speech, say, are concerned to protect those who offend *non*-religious sentiments and concerns, over and above protecting blasphemers. It can't be a reason to redefine secularism that the goals it begins with (when they are liberal goals), which seek to protect one from the illiberality of some religious demands, would also protect one from illiberality coming from *other* sources than religious demands. Liberalism is a wider notion than secular liberalism, which qualifies liberalism to a restricted domain, just as liberal secularism qualifies secularism to a restricted set of cases of secularism.

It is true that that Turkey and some other nations did much else besides meet the minimal requirements of the lexical ordering as articulated in (S). They sought to rule out religion not just in the polity, but in a much more general way, intruding into the cultural life and the intellectual and artistic productions of their citizens. In doing so, they went far beyond the requirements of the lexical ordering. And in doing so they were not merely enforcing secularism in authoritarian fashion, they were enforcing secular*ization* as a broader social process. All this too may be acknowledged without it falsifying the observation of a more minimal property of these polities, which is that they were secular*ist*. As I said in c) earlier, the characterization of secularism on offer in (S) is not by any means committed to rooting out religion in society. The lexical ordering that is the core of the characterization is perfectly compatible with a society that has a great deal of religiosity in its culture and practices. The ideals that are placed first in the lexical ordering could be such as to find acceptable a wide range of religious practices. But, equally, on the other hand, it is not a requirement of secularism, as defined by (S), that secularism should be *in*compatible with determined and authoritarian efforts at imposing secularization in addition to secularism. I had said earlier that because secularism, restricted as it is to the polity, is a narrower notion than secularization, which extends as a process to society at large and its cultural and intellectual life, polities may be secular*ist* with or without the society at large being proportionately secular*ized*. The separateness of these two notions would also have it, of course, that just because there is extreme secularization enforced, as in Atatürk's Turkey, that is not necessarily a sign that secularism must exist. In Turkey, as it happened, secularism did exist, but there can be a society—Tel Aviv society, unlike Jerusalem, I suspect, is one such—that is highly secularized but is embedded in a national polity that is not secularist. Moreover, the separateness of the two notions guarantees that the existence of secularization via authoritarian methods as in Atartürk's Turkey is not a sign that secularism does not exist. Authoritarianism, whether it imposes secularism or secularization, is orthogonal to the criterion by which secularism is defined.

Quite apart from Atatürk, even Richard Dawkins and Christopher Hitchens would not get counted as secularists but *anti*secularists by Taylor's redefinition since they repudiate neutrality between religions and unbelief, the very thing that Taylor demands of secularism, when he says: "Indeed, the point of state neutrality is precisely to avoid favoring or disfavoring not just religious positions but any basic position, religious or nonreligious. We can't favor Christianity over Islam, but also religion over against nonbelief in religion *or vice versa*."[10] But I do think something simple yet deep is under theoretical strain, if these are the implications of a semantic stipulation. I—despite being an atheist—hold no brief for Dawkins and Hitchens, who, in my view, represent one of the least appealing and most irrelevant intellectual stances on religion today. Still, the idea that they as well as the idea that Atatürk should be counted as antisecularists is too counterintuitive, and the redefinition seems to go against our most ordinary understanding and instincts about secularism for reasons that have to do with values that have nothing much to do with secularism at all.

In the last comment, I have urged that we allow that not all secularism is liberal secularism, implying more generally that secularism is only one value among others, and, as a result, it may in some contexts be accompanied by properties that put aside many of the other values that we might cherish. But there is a more radical point to be made: we might, having begun with certain goals and ideals (which make no mention of religion or opposition to religion, just as Rawls, Taylor, and (S) require), find that secularism is a quite unnecessary political doctrine or policy to adopt. We might find that religious practices and customs promote those goals and ideals quite satisfactorily and that it would be a fetish of modernity to think that secularism nevertheless must be adopted by a polity. This is the scenario whose possibility I wanted to leave space for when I was outlining the third defining feature of secularism.

It is how Gandhi thought of the ideal of secularism for India in the early part of the twentieth century, and there was wisdom in that view then. India, because of its distance from Europe, not merely physical but cultural and political, was a good test case for contemplating both secularism's content and its relation to its own history.

If we step back and look at secularism's history from a distance in order to try and view its larger trajectories and patterns, we notice that much of the consolidations of secularism, that is, much of it coming to be viewed as a *necessity* in modern societies, occurred in the context of slow- and long-forming features of European societies. One particular trajectory was central.

In the post-Westphalian European context there emerged a need for states to seek their legitimacy in ways that could no longer appeal to outdated ideas of the divine rights of states as personified in their monarchs. This new form of legitimacy began to be sought by the creation of a new form of political psychology in a new kind of subject, the "citizen," of a new kind of entity that had emerged, the "nation." It was to be done, that is, by creating in citizens a *feeling* for the nation, which generated a legitimacy for the state, because the nation was defined in tandem, in hyphenated conjunction, with a certain kind of increasingly centralized state. This nation-state was to be legitimized by this feeling among its subjects, a political-psychological phenomenon that would somewhat later come to be called national*ism*. In European nations such a feeling was uniformly created in their citizens by a very standard ploy—by finding an *external* enemy *within*, the outsider in one's midst, "the other" (the Irish, the Jews . . . to name just two) to be despised and subjugated. In a later time, with the coming of a more numerical and statistical form of discourse, these would come to be called minorities, and the ploy that I am outlining would be described as majoritarianism. Often *religion* was either central to or was implicated in the way that minorities and majorities were defined, and it was to *repair* the deep and severe damages and scars caused by *this* process that secularism was consolidated as an indispensable necessity in the political life of nations. It came to be seen as a politically constructed guarantee of tolerance in this context, that is to say, in a context of modernity in which a very specific trajectory of nation-state formation was central. It is not that intolerance did not exist in prior times, but the structural necessities set up by new national boundaries and political institutions made the intolerance generated by the self-consciously adopted ploy I have sketched, as something seemingly quite impossible to alleviate in any other way but by the formulation of secularism and the devising of state policies in order to promote it.

Now, it should be possible to say, as Gandhi did, that where such a trajectory had never occurred as it had in Europe, no such repair was needed. It was his view that religions had long pervaded the political life of India, but it was within an ethos of quite unself-conscious pluralism, a syncretic religious culture, within which politics was conducted in *scattered* loci of power, with no highly centralized state seeking to legitimate itself by creating the wrong basis for unity by a self-consciously constructed feeling among its citizens. A unity that was instead an outgrowth of a rooted and syncretic culture within which diverse religions were, without too much strain, in any case relatively tolerant of each other, required no artificial measure and policies, no doctrinal formulations of modernity, under the name of secularism. Whatever the other shortcomings of such a culture, there was nothing measurably damaging of this specific sort to repair, and to impose secularism on one's people under these circumstances would be a mimicry of its colonial masters, a form of cognitive slavery. So it seemed to Gandhi. And, in fact, his greatest anxiety was that the eager modernizers around him in the Indian freedom movement that he led would fall into a form of thinking in which the post-Westphalian European path to modernity, conceived via this new form of state, was seen as compulsory for India as well. When he wrote first about it in the early part of the twentieth century he declared explicitly that it was quite *un*compulsory.

Savarkar, who very deliberately and articulately formulated such a European path of politics for India, with majoritarian methods to achieve feelings of unity in his vision of a modern Indian nation of the future, was Gandhi's chief ideological opponent, and it is not surprising that it was one of his followers who would later assassinate him. Everything Gandhi stood for also stood in the way of such a conception of Indian modernity. As it turned out, Savarkar's thinking had a great deal of influence in India, even within the Congress Party that Gandhi led, and the openly vocal and activist form of majoritarian Hindu nationalism that has emerged in the country since the passing of Gandhi, Nehru, and some of the other leaders of the older generation has made something like secularism seem much more obviously relevant for India than it seemed to Gandhi when he was writing about these matters during the early period of the freedom movement. The point I am laboring in all this is that there may be many ideals—of pluralism, of tolerance—that we start with, just as Taylor asks, but in many societies, there may be no work for the lexical ordering and for secularist doctrine, in general, to do in order to promote those ideals. Secularism is a normative position that is shaped by these ideals in specific contexts where the ideals and goals require it. It is not a goal in itself. Were the ideals present in other political forms and arrangements, the need for secularism would not so much as arise. In my view, it is theoretically sounder to say this than to redefine secularism so that it becomes the appropriate doctrine for all contexts and occasions and always serves the ideals we wish to pursue.

Still, I think one can explore these matters a little more by voicing a protest on behalf of Taylor's redefined ideal of secularism. One might do this by saying that what I am suggesting is the wrong lesson to learn from Gandhi's reaction to the situation in early twentieth-century India. After all, what Gandhi was pointing out was that there was tolerance by each religion of the other and there was equal and free participation of all religions in the syncretic religious culture of the time, and that just *is* secularism in the fraternal as well as the liberty and equality sense that Taylor has outlined. So, if Taylor is right, Gandhi was in favor of, not against, secularism, and his view was that India was always secularist. It may be that, once there is a more centralized state than existed in India in that earlier time, this earlier secularism would have to be recast a bit to be seen as a centralized state being neutral and even-handed among different religions, trying to steer modern society to replicate the syncretism of past times by keeping all religions to be mutually respectful of each others' freely chosen religious practices. But it would essentially be a secularism that was continuous with the past.

A response on behalf of (S) to such a protest will help to bring out in a little more depth the history by which (S) has come to seem necessary.

The view voiced in the protest, I think, would be a quite mistaken reading of Gandhi, who was more clear-eyed about how secularism emerged from a certain history in the West and had certain distinct functions of meeting specific goals that needed to be met as a result of certain developments in Europe in the modern period.

The fact is that the goals and ideals Gandhi articulated were merely those of tolerance and pluralism. But tolerance and pluralism, though they obviously have some relation with secularism (as they do with any number of other political notions and doctrines) are by no means identical with it. And secularism is not a guarantee for those ideals in all contexts. It is neither a necessary nor sufficient condition for tolerance and pluralism. Secularism is a doctrine that is also introduced to further goals of a quite different sort that were not in the forefront of Gandhi's mind, and even when tolerance and pluralism were at the core of what secularism sought to promote it was within a context that I have just sketched, in which this core came to be surrounded by other goals as well. Thus, for instance, it would never occur to Gandhi to be anxious to allow blasphemy to go uncensored. Nor did it particularly worry him that one or other religion, Hinduism or Islam, was running afoul of the ideals of gender equality in its family laws. These were not ideals or goals that were central to what he thought politics should be responding to and pursuing.[11] On the matter of religion, his focus was instead on keeping India removed from a politics in which Hindu majoritarianism entered as a way of creating nationalist feeling in India, thus giving rise to a trajectory in which secularism would be the natural outcome introduced to repair the damage in this.

Now, one might think that a state conceived as neutral among different religions, as Taylor envisages it, *is the best method by which to deal with the damage done by this trajectory*. So why am I resisting calling it secularism?

This is a good question and the answer is that once this trajectory takes its course, the damage is so deep and pervasive and so easily and constantly revived and revisited, that minorities are simply not in a position to ensure that the state, even in a democracy (obviously even less so in more authoritarian regimes), will be able to be evenhanded. Political parties will constantly appeal, for electoral gain to majoritarian tendencies and will not be able to eschew these tendencies after electoral success when they are tenants of the state. This, in turn, gives rise to a *reaction* among minorities to fall into identity politics as a defense, since the state is often unable to withstand majoritarianism and remain neutral. When majorities and minorities are defined in terms of religion in this familiar scenario, there inevitably arises a sense that religion (in the political sphere) *itself* is the problem, even though the historical source of the problem lies in majoritarianism. Recent Indian history has increasingly shown this to be true, a victory, as I said, for the forces of Savarkar over Gandhi, even within the Congress Party, leave alone the Hindu nationalist party. For this general reason (and not merely in India), something more radical was said to be needed, something that—in crucial ways that are necessary to avoid this entire tendency to domination by a majority and religious identitarian reactive responses by minorities—keeps religion out of the polity, so that the temptation of the appeal to religious majoritarianism is preempted at the outset as a legal or constitutional transgression, something the courts of an independently constituted judiciary are there to ensure (though, as it turns out in some recent decisions, it is not obvious that the courts are willing always to do so). Thus this entire trajectory that I've been describing at some length gives rise to an ethos in which something like a lexical ordering of the sort I have mentioned tends to come to the forefront in how a modern polity is conceived. Once conceived this way, the term *secularism* is and has been the natural name for it. And once the conception comes into place, it begins to seem, in this increasingly and *very specifically* modern political ethos that had its origins in post-Westphalian Europe, that it is not sufficient to be neutral and evenhanded among religions.

Moreover, in such an ethos, where religion itself comes to be seen as the source of the problem, whether in its majoritarian exploitation or in its minoritarian reaction to that, new goals (that is, goals beyond merely tolerance and pluralism) emerge, and, though they are defined independently of religion (goals such as free speech, say, and gender equality), one begins to detect that, in light of these new goals, there are shortcomings *in religion*. Thus free speech is now seen as free speech (even) in the face of a religious requirement to suppress deliberate and brazen blasphemy, and gender equality is steered toward gender equality in the face of gender-unjust religious family laws; and so on. Again, as a result, something like (S) alone, therefore, comes to seem like the only policy that could provide the repair and reform of religion, because neutrality and evenhandedness among religions cannot possibly promote these new goals and ideals. It is not enough to neutrally and evenhandedly allow each religion in society its free speech-denying blasphemy laws or its gender-discriminating family laws. These laws are trumped only by the first-placed lexical ordering of free speech and gender equality. Of course, one can still insist that the state neutrally and evenhandedly apply the lexical ordering to each religion, but that still means that the ideal of neutrality and evenhandedness is embedded in (S). It does not constitute a secularism that is independent of (S).

None of this, however, was relevant when Gandhi wrote, as neither issues of blasphemy laws nor of gender inequality were in the forefront of the public agenda surrounding the local, syncretist religious cultures and the politics that surfaced in them. (And this may well be the case in many parts of the world to this day—in many regions of Africa, say, even possibly in parts of the Middle East, though the intense material and therefore cultural gaze on, not to mention interventions in, the latter by Western interests may be comprehensively and decisively changing that.)[12] But they are much more relevant now, and, along with the need for the reversal of social and political damages of religious majoritarian sources for nationalism, they form part of a trajectory that emerged in India *since* the time Gandhi expressed his qualms against a very specific path in European modernity. To describe Gandhi's position of an earlier time in India as secularist, therefore, is to quite fail to see the relevance of a range of developments in India since the time in which he first wrote (the developments of what I had called a specific post-Westphalian trajectory), regarding which he had prescient anxieties about what might be visited upon India if the trajectory was adopted there. If we pay close attention to his anxieties in that period, we can recognize that he was not a proto-secularist but rather that he did not want the conditions in which secularism would seem a necessity at all to occur in India.

To sum up, it has, in general, been the burden of these several comments, a) to f), that I have been making on the nature of (S) to say that its stipulated form of secularism in terms of a certain lexical ordering gives a certain theoretical bite and specificity to secularism, such that it is not all good in all contexts but only a good in some contexts and therefore not always to be embraced even in temporal modernity, if the conditions don't require it for the pursuit of other worthy goals. This specificity also allows one to say that secularism can often be accompanied by bad political and institutional arrangements, such as in Atatürk's Turkey or in Baathist Iraq or in the aggressively authoritarian secularist policies of some communist regimes. It does not see those bad political arrangements and institutions as a reason and occasion to try and redefine secularism so that they don't count as secularist polities at all. Such redefinitions take the bite out of the concept, in much the same way that the redefinition attempted in the idea of "people's democracy" to counter "free democracy" took the bite out of the notion of democracy.[13] The specific formulation of the lexical ordering, moreover, has the strict advantage over the "neutrality and equidistant state" ideal of secularism in disallowing things that would, in our own time if not earlier, intuitively count as antisecular—for example, censorship of works of art and literature on grounds of "blasphemy" against a religion, something that the latter ideal would permit in a given case, on the grounds that it was ready and willing to neutrally permit it in all other cases of blasphemy against all other religions in the society.

I've spent considerable time on these semantic matters with a view to bringing out the content of secularism, using Taylor's interesting and challenging ideas of a redefinition of secularism as a foil. I had said that though I think Taylor's redefinition has worthy moral and political motivations, it is not as well motivated theoretically. (S), by contrast, does not make any attempt at redefinition, it merely tries to elaborate, along modest and minimalist lines, the rationale underlying the instincts behind dogmatic-sounding metaphors such as "the separation of church and state." As such, (S) seems to contain crucial elements that Taylor is trying to redefine secularism *away* from.

I want to turn now from semantic matters, from questions of what is the more plausible and nonarbitrary stipulation by which we define or characterize the content of secularism, to questions of which position is more plausible, no matter how it is defined and what it is called, i.e., whether it is called secularism or not. Thus we might ask: no matter which we think is better described as secularism, is it better to adopt the ideal of a state that is neutral and evenhanded with all religions and nonreligious points of view, and that takes no adversarial stance against religion (thus repudiating the very first feature of secularism that I had presented in section 1), or is to better to adopt (S)?

5

Let me begin by trying to diagnose sympathetically why it might theoretically and philosophically seem to many that Taylor's ideal of a state, neutral and equidistant between religious and nonreligious points of view, is a better position to adopt than (S).

In section 2 I took up the question of what *justified* secularism over and above what defined or characterized it, saying that it was important to distinguish between the two. And, while discussing the justification of secularism, I had invoked Bernard Williams's distinction between two types of justification, one that appealed to internal reasons and the other to external reasons, and had claimed that there are only internal reasons for embracing secularism. I have not argued for nor will I argue for that claim in this chapter, partly for reasons of space, but partly also because I have done so extensively in previous essays.[14] The point of interest in the present essay, as I say in section 2, is that this view is entirely compatible with, and indeed lies behind, the claim that secularism should only be adopted on the basis of an overlapping consensus. On these issues of justification and adoption (rather than those of definition just discussed in section 4) there is complete accord between Taylor's views and the ones expressed in this chapter.

To political philosophers and theorists, it might seem natural to conclude from these commitments on which there is complete accord between us that secularism is fated to be mired in a form of *relativism* regarding moral and political values, and such a relativism may well suggest, in turn, that something like a "neutral state" version of secularism is what we should retreat to, whereas any secularism such as (S) that seeks a somewhat more adversarial stance against religion should be counted not as secularism but as one nonreligious standpoint among other standpoints, including religious standpoints, between which the state is neutral.[15] This approximates Taylor's own favored understanding of secularism.

So, we must ask, whichever we think is best to call secularism, is the neutralist ideal shown to be better than (S) as a consequence of the relativist implications that seem to follow from the stress on internal reasons in the justification of secularism?

The idea is this. If there are no external reasons that support a moral or political standpoint or value (such as secularism, say, or, to keep things even more specific and focused, secular liberalism), if internal reasons are the only reasons one can bring to bear when there is a deep disagreement over values (between, say, such a secular liberalism and one or other religious point of view), then it might seem that something like relativism about these values and points of view is necessarily in the offing. Recall that external reasons are reasons that all will agree on, no matter what their values and substantial commitments may be, and internal reasons appeal only to substantial moral and political commitments of individual citizens. If internal reasons are the only reasons there are for justifications of such values as secularism, the thought that (S) in its secular liberal form will even have the resources to effectively offer such internal reasons to a strongly held religious standpoint (say, for example, a position with strong Muslim identitarian political values) to change its mind might seem too optimistic; and that, in turn, will make it seem as if some antisecular Muslim commitments, such as to the value of censorship of blasphemy, may have their own sort of truth (*relativistically* characterized truth) on their side.[16] And, if that is so, then it would seem only right that a state having to now navigate these different *true* standpoints—(S) in its secular liberal form as well as various religious standpoints such as Islamists and other strongly held religious views—should be neutral and evenhanded with each of them, since each has the prestige of *truth* on its side. This would reduce (S), even in the eyes of those who subscribe to it, to one among other true points of view, including religious ones. Thus the relativism that seems to emerge as a consequence from the points of philosophical *agreement* between Taylor and me, on the primacy of internal reasons and the inefficacy of external reasons, may seem to suggest that the state neutrality ideal is *theoretically* quite well motivated (by this relativism) and (S) less well so, despite all the theoretical points I made in the previous section.

Can this be right? Does this specific argument, via a relativism that flows from the primacy of internal reasons, that I make on sympathetic behalf of Taylor's view, give us a reason to adopt the state-neutralist ideal he favors over (S)? Or, to put it differently, does this specific argument give a state committed to adopting (S) any reason to yield to a more state-neutralist ideal?

I think it is arguable that it does not.

Notice, first, what exactly is meant by relativism, as it seems to follow from the denial of external reasons and the claim that only internal reasons will justify secular liberalism. It means something quite strong. What is meant is that when there are no external reasons, and two parties are in disagreement over some value commitment, *there may in principle be no scope for either party to give even internal reasons to one another.* Internal reasons are dependent on support coming from our substantive values, not something given to us by the very fact of our rationality. Therefore, unlike external reasons, there is no guarantee that internal reasons to subscribe to (S) will be available, since they are dependent on further values that may not be present—in the case under consideration, present in the values held by Islamists. And, in general, it is prima facie possible that in some sorts of value disagreement there will, *in principle*, be no such further values for the parties in the disagreement to appeal to. In that case we will have the kind of impasse mentioned in the formulation, just given, of relativism. The expression *in principle* is doing some serious work in this formulation of relativism. Relativism is a theoretical or philosophical position; it is not just a practical difficulty about how it is sometimes very hard to persuade someone you disagree with on some evaluative matter. The theoretical position is that each party in the dispute may be utterly unreach*able* by the other. This may indeed be cause for alarm to subscribers to (S), and, to the extent that we are alarmed, a concession and retreat to Taylor's redefinition of secularism shows the appropriate respect for each position that has truth on its side because (S) cannot claim greater truth for the ideals it begins with and therefore must drop its claim to a lexical ordering that places those ideals first and religious laws and customs and practices second when they clash. Thus relativism requires that not only are there no external reasons for justifying secular ideals, reasons that all can share and find to be reasons, but there are *no* reasons (not internal ones either) that it can, in principle, find to justify secular ideals to other more religious points of view. Secular liberalism is one truth among many, and not merely one standpoint among many. The latter claim (one standpoint among many) is uncontroversial. But for a secular liberal to allow the former claim (that religious points of view that it often wants to place second in a lexical ordering have the *truth* on their side) would undermine the very priorities asserted in the lexical ordering. A relevantly neutral state of the kind that Taylor recommends is a better form of polity for such a scenario than (S), which has to concede that secular liberalism is just one truth among many. So these considerations of relativism might well motivate the adoption of Taylor's neutralist state rather than a state that adopts the lexical ordering ideal.

But before we concede that this relativism is the fate of (S), given the primacy of internal reasons, some more detailed understanding of what exactly internal reasons are is required.

What is it to find internal reasons to persuade another? Internal reasons are reasons we give to another that appeal to some of *his own values* in order to try and persuade him to change his mind on some given evaluative issue, such as, say, a commitment to censorship of blasphemy. So if a Muslim does have such a commitment, a secular liberal subscribing to (S) can only appeal to some other value of *his* which is *in tension or in conflict* with his commitment to the censorship of blasphemy. To put it very explicitly, one will have to find that such Muslims are committed a) to censorship of blasphemy, and yet that they are also committed b) to various other values that may lend support to the value of free speech. And for (S) to use internal reasons against such Muslims is to stress b) them in an effort to bring them around to discarding a). Of course, if (S) was justifiable on grounds of external reasons, one couldn't appeal to considerations such as b), which is a substantive value. But, in that case, one would not *need* to appeal to such a consideration. It is only because one takes the view that both Taylor and I, following Williams, take, that there are no external reasons, that one is forced to appeal to considerations such as b).

In general, then, the strategy of internal reasons is a strategy that can only work when those against whom it is brought to work are *internally conflicted.*

(It is important to add that conflicts within values need not always take the form of there being blatant inconsistencies among them. In fact it may seldom be that. Much more likely and much more pervasive are conflicts of a more subtle kind, tensions or dissonances between values.)

We can now pull the strands together. Relativism, as I've defined it for the purposes of this chapter's concerns, is a doctrine that holds if there is a certain kind of impasse. It holds if there are, *in principle*, no internal reasons that two parties in a disagreement over values can give to one another. And if the prospect for giving internal reasons turns on the possibility of there being an internal conflict in at least one of the parties involved in a disagreement over values, then that implies that relativism would hold only if both parties in such a disagreement are *completely unconflicted*, that is, if they have perfectly and maximally coherent value economies. In other words, in order for relativism of the sort we are worrying about to be true, it would have to be the case that someone with whom one disagrees over values is not merely never inconsistent (as I admitted, blatant inconsistency might be hard to attribute to political and moral subjects), but they would also have to be *wholly* without any tension or dissonance in their values and desires. That alone makes for a *principled* impasse.

But it is hard to think that ordinary human subjects are so completely without internal conflict in this broad sense. The idea of such a total lack of inner conflict is an extraordinary condition to find in any value economy. Relativism, conceived on this condition, would find instance, it seems, only when two parties in a dispute over a value were *monsters of coherence*. Perhaps some imagined rational automata are maximally coherent in their value commitments, but the idea that ordinary human moral-psychological economies are so is barely conceivable. Thus, so long as Islamists with commitments to blasphemy laws are susceptible to conflicting relations among their commitments, so long as they are not possessed of maximally coherent value economies, the scope of internal reasons to establish secular liberalism even in the face of identity politics is maintained. Maximal coherence being a barely conceivable condition, there is no need to despair about the scope for secular liberal politics to succeed without externalist reasons and arguments.

The point cannot be quite left where it is.

Let it even be conceivable that, at a given time, a particular illiberal moral-psychological economy is highly coherent and unconflicted—at any rate, let it be conceivable, as it surely is, that any conflict or tension that it *does* contain among its value commitments is not as a matter of fact helpful in bringing it around to shedding its antiliberal commitments. It is perfectly possible that, even if Islamists are internally conflicted, these may be on matters that are not relevant to (S)'s efforts to give internal reasons to them to get them to change their mind on censorship of blasphemy. This *still* does not hobble the scope of secular liberalism. Why not? The answer to this question, I think, is central to the epistemology of political and moral values. The answer is *because political philosophy cannot consider moral subjects and political citizens as standing outside of history, in some timeless, unconflicted psychological economy.*

Since citizens are historical subjects, history and the incoming states of information that it provides to those subjects in its course may well *introduce* conflict for them by introducing tensions and dissonance in the relations between their value commitments. Let me give just one example at some distance from the dispute on issues of blasphemy to illustrate what I have in mind. It is now fairly well documented that the large increase in pro-choice attitudes among hitherto even relatively conservative women in America in the third quarter of the last century was a result of their having deliberated their way out of a conflict in their own commitments, a conflict that *emerged* fully only in that period of history, when, as a result of the rise of service industries and the relative decline of heavy manufacturing goods industries, the possibility of a more gender-distributed work force was created. A historical change, which provided greater prospects for employment for women, introduced conflict into the values of even hitherto conservative women, and this in turn gave rise to internal deliberation on their part that resulted in many of them revising their views on the issue of abortion. The point, then, is that even if, at a given time, a value economy seems relatively unreachable by internal reasons because it is relatively coherent and unconflicted, so long as we think of moral-psychological economies as necessarily being *in history*, internal conflicts may be injected by historical developments into moral-psychological economies.

The point is essentially Hegelian, though in Hegel himself it is unfortunately marred because it is nested in terms that were unnecessarily deterministic. But it is a point of the utmost importance for those who think both that (S) can only be justified on the basis of internal reasons and that thinking so entails *no* relativism of the sort we are considering.

This Hegelian idea goes deeper than it might seem. It might seem that all the idea amounts to is that at some later time we might be able to persuade someone with whom we are in disagreement by giving her internal reasons, but, *for now* at least, there is an impasse and so relativism about reasons is true. But this deflationary description misses the real theoretical status of the appeal to the subject-*in*-history. That appeal is precisely intended to repudiate the idea that we should think of subjects as being in slabs of time, with relativism about their values holding in one slab, and possibly passing away in the next. Despite the talk of different times, that would *still* be to conceive the subject essentially synchronically at each slab of time. A genuinely diachronically conceived subject (hardly ever the subject that is considered by analytical philosophers and political theorists writing about morals and politics or anything else), a subject conceived neither synchronically nor in discreetly periodized times, but rather a subject conceived of as essentially historically open-ended, is exactly intended to replace the subject relativized to a time when her values may have a "relative" truth or her reasons a relative closure. Hence the inclination to say, "Relativism *for now*, but not perhaps *later*!" is to not yet quite be on board with the depth of the point that Hegel's stress on the importance of history for our conception of human subjectivity is making. To be fully on board is to see that *no* sort of relativism is sanctioned for subjects conceived essentially diachronically and therefore open to the internal conflicts that history may provide.

I will admit again, however, that my appeal to Hegel here is highly selective, since the fact that history should play this kind of role in our understanding of moral subjectivity (paradoxically) opens things up against the very sort of historical determinism that historicism, in particular Hegel's own historicism, usually suggests. The select element in Hegel that I am applauding is the idea that reason (what I, following Williams, call "internal" reason) does its work in a human subject by bringing about changes of value via deliberation on her part to overcome internal conflicts between values (something that popularizing Hegelians—never Hegel himself—describe overly schematically in dialectical terms of the trio of "thesis, antithesis, and synthesis"), and that one does so very often as a result of conflicts (what in the popular Hegelian representation is called antitheses) that emerge because of incoming states of information provided by specifically historical encounters. Once viewed this way, there is no reason to think that relativism follows upon the loss of external reasons, and so no reason to be pessimistic about the scope of *internal* reasons to be a resource for secular liberal political outcomes. Within this selective Hegelian view of the importance of history and of diachronic subjectivity, the right way to describe what has wrongly been described as this "pessimism" is simply to say that there is no Whiggish *guarantee* of a consummation of the historical process in a secular liberal outcome. That is not pessimism, it is just a recoil from a *deterministic* historicism. One can be as optimistic as one wishes and hold out for history to introduce conflict in the points of view that one wishes to offer internal reasons to in order to change their commitments. Thus secular liberalism can remain committed to its ideals with confidence, and a secular state need not retreat to neutrality between secularism and other religious points of view, even in the face of the most vexed disagreement with these other points of view.

That we should see the significance of history for subjectivity along these lines is, however, not a merely metaphysical position; it is in a rarefied sense itself an *evaluative* position. This point is crucial. After all, someone else may see history as having a rather depressing record in resolving conflict between groups and resist my repudiation of relativism, a repudiation that has *the default* lie in the view that it is always at least possible that new conflicts *internal* to an individual or group will—via internal reasoning—help resolve conflicts *between* individuals or groups. Such a person will simply not find the record in history sanctioning this default position. The default says that when there is an intractable value disagreement between two parties, history may always inject in one of the parties the sort of internal conflict necessary for the other to provide internal reasons to it. The interlocutor here will deny this, saying that the record of history does not justify this to be the default position. I have no purely philosophical or metaphysical argument against such an interlocutor, one that does not agree with me about how to view the significance of history for moral subjects in conflict with one another. To find this interlocutor wrong is, in the end, to assert a value. In fact, we cannot find him wrong without asserting a value, we cannot find him wrong by a nonevaluative argument. And to say that is to assert the priority of the evaluative over the metaphysical.

This needs more patient exposition.

The default position says we must see the significance of history for subjectivity to be as follows: that one always see it as at least *possible* that a dispute in values may be resolved by internal reasoning as a result of the requisite *internal* conflict being introduced into one or other of the disputing parties by the incoming states of information that historical changes provide to their psychological and value economies. It is when the significance of history is viewed along these lines (as allowing such a default position) that we are in turn allowed to turn our backs on the claim of relativism that the deepest disputes in value might constitute an impasse. Such a default allows one to make *no* concession to a possible right or truth or correctness on the side of one's opponent in cases of interesting and deep moral and political dispute. So the hard question remains: *what gives us the right to view the significance of history for moral subjectivity along these line*s? Why may we not see its significance along quite different lines, see history as providing too much evidence for *disallowing* what I claim as at least a necessary and permanent *possibility*? The nested modalities are complicated here, but my interlocutor's idea will be that what I am insisting is a possibility might only be contingently so: there may be no necessity that such a possibility always exists. History is simply not to be viewed in the optimistic way I am viewing it. It is possible that such dispute resolving internal conflicts are introduced into moral subjects by history, but it is possible also that they are not. Why, then, am I insisting that history must be viewed in a way that it *necessarily* leaves it as an open possibility that such a conflict is introduced?

As I admitted, there is no answer to this question (and so there is no justification for taking the default position I do on the significance of history) along lines that are *non*-normative or purely metaphysical. There is nothing in history, nothing in the concept of history and our place in it, when that is conceived in purely descriptive and non-normative terms, that could instruct us to view history as offering us the default position I insist on. To take the default position I do, therefore, is *itself* to take a higher-order *evaluative* stance. And it is only by taking such an evaluative stance that a secular liberal can express the confidence that disputes in identitarian contexts with illiberal tendencies need not ever produce the despondency of saying that perhaps both sets of principles (liberal and illiberal) may have their own sort of right on their side.

What do I mean by saying that it is in the end an *evaluative* stance that gives a secular liberal the confidence to insist on the exclusive rightness of secular liberalism against illiberal opponents, *despite* the loss of externalist reasons and the loss of externalist justifications of liberalism? I mean simply that it reflects a value, a value central to what I think is best conceived as a special and unusual version of *humanism*.

Here is how I have allowed myself to think of it.

When one is in a moral dispute with another, even if it is a bitter and vexed dispute, it is far better to have an attitude of *inclusiveness* toward one's foe that makes one strive to share the truth as one sees it with him, rather than to adopt an *excluding* attitude and say that he may have his own sort of truth or right on his side. The latter is what the relativist pluralist says, and it will be said by anyone who does not see the philosophical and methodological force and insight of the Hegelian notion of a subject and its significance for morals and politics as I am seeing it. For someone who does see that force and that significance, the attitude will be quite the opposite, the value of inclusiveness. This is the value that claims it is far more attractive to say, even to one's bitterest foe in a moral or political conflict, "You must be my brother" than it is to say "You can never be my brother." To insist that he must be your brother, to refuse to allow him his own truth, and to strive to convince him of the truth as you see it and judge it is to show the requisite attitude of inclusiveness toward him. This may seem paradoxical since one is *refusing* him his own sort of truth for his views in the name of seeing him as *one's brother*. But that is just how it is. Perhaps only a subject as perverse and abstract as philosophy can see in this no paradox at all.

I will admit that the rhetoric of "must" versus "never" in my last paragraph to express the contrasting values does not present the best options. I did use the flamboyant rhetoric even so, and presented the options in their most extreme form, in order to bring out the contrast vividly. To care about the truth, as one sees it and judges it, and to care enough for others who do not see it, to strive to share it with them, need not take on the vocabulary which has it that one thinks they "must" be one's brothers and embrace the truth we see. But that vocabulary captures something of the caring that I want to stress here against the relativist form of pluralism that precisely does not care in this way. Opposing such a relativistic form of pluralism, I am saying, involves not merely appealing to the Hegelian notion of subjectivity in the way I do, but also seeing that appeal as an assertion of a value of caring about the truth (as one sees it and judges it), rather than showing an indifference to others who disagree with one, as the relativistic pluralist does when he says that they may have their own sort of moral truth on their side. Such a way of caring for truth therefore itself reflects a caring for *others*, caring enough to want to convince them of the truth. That is the point of the talk of "brotherhood" as a value, a humanist value, that, in this specific sense, is missing in the relativist cast of pluralism.

To many humanists such talk of brotherhood—flowing as it does from an ideal of caring for something so *abstract* as truth and wanting to share that abstract thing with others—will seem too intellectualized a way of talking compared either to the down-to-earth ways in which we talk of the humanist values of brotherhood or to the sentimental, literary cast it has taken on ever since the rhetoric of "sweetness and light." It is brotherhood based on an epistemological value rather than on the usual sort of moral values of solidarity and support that are articulated in standard versions of humanism. To such traditional humanists, the paradox of denying one's moral foe his own sort of rightful moral view in the name of brotherhood will seem to undermine the doctrine from within. But, as I said, there is no paradox here. It is a sign of greatly respecting someone, of including him in humanity, that you deeply want him to believe what you believe to be the truth rather than grant him, as a truth (*his* truth), what you take to be deeply false. I admit that this is an abstract way of configuring the ideal of human inclusiveness. But why should humanism not have highly abstract sources? These sources are precisely what might give the doctrine some further muscle and rigor and therefore make it less dismissible as a musty and pious doctrine.

If I am right, it is, in the end, this abstractly humanistic and evaluative understanding of the role of history in the constitution of human subjectivity in morals and politics that underlies the repudiation of relativism in the realm of moral and political values.[17] (In the more purely cognitive realm of science, the issues are quite different, and responses to relativism need to be constructed along different lines.) What are its implications for our subject of secularism?

6

The goal has been to show that this repudiation of relativism allows a state that has adopted (S) to remain committed to its idea of a lexical ordering. It was intended to preempt the need for a state to abandon (S) and retreat to a neutrality between nonreligious and religious points of view.

If the argument of the last section is convincing, then, though anyone, committed to the idea of an overlapping consensus on some policy such as (S), is committed to a pluralism about *reasons* for subscribing to (S), they are *not* committed to a pluralism about the conclusions and outcomes based on those reasons. This is because the argument allows them to say that they are not committed to merely a relativistic truth for (S), but committed to its truth, *simpliciter*. With right (a right given by the entire Hegelian dialectic I am presenting), (S) takes its own commitments to be true and holds out for them against opponents, given the possibility that history will inject conflicts in their thinking so as to make them come around to its commitments by the internal reasons that those conflicts might introduce into their moral-psychological economies. It holds out for fully secular outcomes and in no way wavers in confidence about the truth of (S), even if it grants that (S) might not be implementable until internal reasons, as a result of historical developments, are available to religious points of view that, in the present, contain illiberal commitments. So, in the examples we considered earlier, it would insist that something like laws requiring censorship of blasphemy or gender-unjust family laws of a religion must be placed lower in the lexical ordering than free speech and gender equality. It would not grant that these laws possess truth, relativistic truth, from within their own larger religious points of view. The whole point of the stress on a Hegelian framework for understanding the role of internal reasons is to ensure that (S) need not make any such concession or compromise on the *exclusive* truth or rightness of its commitments to free speech and gender equality, giving it the right to assert the lexical ordering it favors. Thus (S) will not allow secular liberalism to be demoted to just one truthful standpoint amongst others, as was suggested would happen if relativism were true. This makes all the difference to the question whether we should hold fast to (S) or concede the superiority of a state-neutralist ideal that Taylor has proposed as being better.

The issue can be usefully explored by looking at a very well-known example from India as a test case. In the aftermath of Indian independence, Muslims in India, after much fascinating discussion during the Constituent Assembly debates, were allowed by constitutional provision to live by their own personal and family laws. (I am going to consider this case, ignoring the fact that there *has* been a reform of the Hindu code as it applies to family laws. What this asymmetry between Muslims and Hindus shows is that granting Muslims their own personal laws runs afoul of *both* (S) *and* the state neutrality ideal that Taylor has advocated, but, I am concerned for now only with the fact that Muslims were granted their own personal laws and how that falls short of (S).)

How exactly that awarded outcome of an exception to Muslims in India is to be interpreted is actually a rather delicate matter, and one may see in it two possible ways of conceiving of what the state intended and therefore two possible ways in which the state conceived of itself.

One way to look at this case is to see it as triumph of the kind of pluralism that is suggested by the relativist position. What pluralism, in the relativist form, allows for is the idea that a liberal democratic state will, in the name of minority cultural rights, grant to minorities (in the Indian case, to Muslims) their own special personal laws on divorce, marriage, alimony, etc., even if some of these laws are illiberal in various respects. On this reading, the state may grant to all religions their own *alternative nomic or customary system*, which is a rival system to liberal law, with its own sort of right or truth on its side, and the pluralism that the constitution was committed to must acknowledge that fact.[18] So interpreted, the state can be viewed as approximating a neutralist position, not favoring secular ideals over Muslim personal laws as a lexical ordering would, but instead granting the Muslim demand in the constituent assembly debates that they be allowed to live by their own personal laws.

But the Hegelian considerations I have presented allow another possible reading of the concession to Muslims, which I also think is the more historically accurate one, the one that the framers of the constitution actually had in mind. On this reading, it is not that the Muslim community is being granted its demand for living by its own personal and family laws on the grounds that their standpoint, like the secular standpoint, has truth on its side. Rather the thinking was this: in the aftermath of independence, the Muslims who remained in India and did not migrate to Pakistan lost a great deal—they lost their count in numbers not only due to migration to Pakistan but also due to the killing of Muslims in the pogroms on the Indian side of the newly partitioned borders, they lost jobs, they lost land, in the vital sense of its wide availability in instruction in schools and colleges, they even lost their language, Urdu. In the face of these losses and the demoralization it generated, depriving them of the cultural aspects of their lives that are centered in their family and personal laws would be an inhumane blow for a state to deliver to a minority community. What a secular state, subscribing to something like (S) must, therefore, do is to wait for history to bring into Muslim thinking the sorts of internal conflict that might give them reasons to come around to secular ideals of gender equality and put aside their family and personal laws. But, until then, the lexical ordering that places those laws second to gender equality may be put in *abeyance*—which is not the same as putting the lexical ordering *aside*. One would put it aside only if one thought that the state thinks that there is *truth* on the side of those laws, equal to the truth of ideals of gender equality. But one would put it in abeyance only because it would be *coercive* to implement (S) until the necessary internal reasoning takes place among Muslims.

(I should add as an aside that this issue has been excruciatingly complicated at present by the fact that the demand for reform of Muslim personal law usually comes these days—and for some years now—not from anything recognizable as allowing Muslims to reform them as a result of their own internal reasoning, but rather from a kind of harassment of a minority by the Hindu right wing in the country. That Muslims could be reasonably expected to reform their personal laws by internal reasoning in the face of such harassment would be to utterly fail to understand the psychological preconditions for how internal reasons usually work in a historical context. A group's capacity to change via internal reasoning requires a great deal of psychological security and self-confidence, precisely what is undermined by the demoralization caused by such harassment.)

Returning from the details of this example to the general point: this second reading reveals that a Hegelian framework for thinking of justification by internal reasoning and the adoption of political outcomes by an overlapping consensus preempts any need to think that a state *must* be neutral between secular ideals and religious standpoints. It allows for a full and confident adherence to (S), confident not only about it having the exclusive right on its side on the liberal outcomes at stake, but in the hope that it will provide internal reasons eventually to other opposing illiberal points of view to embrace those outcomes.

How does this square with my project of having secularism applaud Taylor's motives for redefining secularism, while refraining from embracing the position that is articulated in the redefinition?

It does so by distinguishing between what is the *right outcome and the right definition,* on the one hand and, on the other, what are the right ways of *justifying and implementing* the right outcomes, correctly defined. If my argument is effective, the right outcome for a polity, according to a secularist, remains (S), and (S) remains the right stipulation by which secularism should be defined or characterized. It needs no redefinition. But this still leaves open the possibility for us to say that in justifying and implementing (S) we should do exactly as Taylor suggests. We should involve, in the fraternalist manner he rightly proposes, all the voices in the polity, including the antisecularist religious voices, should there be any, just as happened in the Constituent Assembly debates in India where the Muslims were able to make their demands and argue for them. Until those voices find the *internal* reasons to adopt (S), (S) must be held in abeyance. If so, it should be quite possible to allow—without conceding anything theoretically amiss with (S)—that (S) remain temporarily unimplemented, just as happened with Muslim family laws in postindependent India on the *second* reading I gave.[19]

Why exactly should it be possible to allow this? Because the deepest concern behind Taylor's demand of fraternal involvement of all groups, I believe, is that a state must, as far as it is possible, be *noncoercive* in the adoption and implementation of the policies it views as justifiable. (Jeffrey Stout wisely advises me that since states have sanctions backing the laws they make and implement, they are, by their very nature, going to be coercive no matter what, and so a better term to use to describe Taylor's motivation is that he would like the state to be, as far as is possible, *nondominating*. I am happy to follow his advice.) Taylor's concern here is a moral one, and it speaks for a certain conception of politics. What it properly motivates, indeed, what it forces us to do, is to look for the right forms of adoption and implementation of (S). It would be wrong to think that, in doing so, what it motivates and forces are merely things in the practical rather than in the theoretical domain. The entire construction of the role and relevance of the Hegelian notion of subjectivity in the dialectic of this chapter was intended to provide a *theoretical* solution to the problem posed by Taylor's search for a noncoercive and overlapping consensus for the secular outcome or, to put it in my own favored terms, to the problem of implementing a secularism whose justification is based only on internal rather than external reasons. But what this chapter has nevertheless insisted is that this theoretical solution requires neither a redefinition of secularism nor any concession to the superiority of state neutrality ideals over (S). It is an avoidable inference that the nondomination in the adoption of secularism that motivates Taylor's arguments makes a difference to what it is we are adopting or should adopt. It does not lead to another *conception* of secularism.[20] Such secularism as is worth believing in is well characterized by (S).

Yet I have also said that it is not required to believe (S) in all contexts. The relevance of a doctrine of the sort that (S) exemplifies emerged in particular historical contexts when certain political goals could not be pursued without something like the lexical ordering (S) formulates. (S), therefore, is a valuable doctrine to embrace and implement in contexts that approximate those historical conditions and contain those political goals. It is not a doctrine that holds without regard to context, purely on the basis of abstract philosophical arguments or on the basis of glib assertions of the universal reach of a certain familiar form of modernity.

Taylor's own desire to redefine secularism is based—as we saw in section 3—on the argument that a context of modernity has now emerged in which his redefinition is needed. This, as he sometimes puts it, is the context of multiculturalism, in which talk of *toleration* is no longer appropriate. A state neutral between different religious cultures and also nonreligious cultures should constitute the new meaning of secularism in such a multicultural context. I will end with some closing remarks on the relation between (S) and the idiom of "toleration."

What is it about the idiom that seems inappropriate in the present multicultural West? The answer is obvious. It is a familiar and repeatedly made observation that the very idea of toleration presupposes *disapproval* of what is tolerated and a condescending acceptance of what is disapproved of. If, in the context of an aspiring multiculturalism, one wants to improve on or replace the attitude of disapproval with some other moral psychological attitude that cultures (including secular cultures) must exhibit toward one another, it might seem that we have two choices. One is to emphasize a different, less hostile, kind of negative attitude: *indifference* rather than disapproval. And his redefined secular ideal of state neutrality toward different religions might be seen as precisely maintaining such an indifference toward them, neither favoring nor disfavoring any of them, allowing each culture, in turn, to thrive in relative autonomy and with indifference rather than hostility toward one another. The other is to stress a more positive attitude: *respect* rather than disapproval.

Now, it must be admitted that it is exactly indifference that is opposed by the humanism underlying the Hegelian ideal of historical subjectivity in the understanding of secularism as defined by (S). When one finds something appealing in the attitude expressed by "You must be my brother" toward someone with whom one is in moral conflict, it is the appeal of *not* being indifferent to his views. Respect is another matter. As I said earlier, it *is* showing (a rarefied form of) respect of this abstract humanist kind to someone with whom one is in moral disagreement when one seeks to change his mind and make him one's brother. But *for just that reason* one is not showing indifference toward him and his views. So, if indifference is a crucial ingredient in the way in which one must (in multicultural societies) supersede the disapproval implicit in "toleration," does this repudiation of indifference by (S) mean that (S) is retaining the element of disapproval that is presupposed by the idiom of "toleration"? And, if so, should we conclude that the state-neutralist secularist ideal is more apt than (S) for a context in which multiculturalism has taken us beyond the ideal of toleration? I think it would be a mistake to infer that. The moral psychology involved in (S) is more subtle than that conclusion suggests.

First of all, because (S) replaces indifference with a concern to register disagreements and attempt to change the minds of those points of view with which one is in moral and political disagreement, its assumption of disapproval of one point of view for another is never accompanied by any condescension whatever. Even if disapproval of another point of view is present, (S) demands the sort of positive engagement between points of view that leaves no place for condescension. But, for the same reason, it is not at all obvious that there really is even an assumption of disapproval that it really makes, and here is why not. The sorts of efforts that are needed to reach others (with whom one is deeply conflicted) by providing them with *internal* reasons and arguments requires one not merely to get past indifference toward their views but also, in a sense, to get past the disapproval of their views. Now this idea of "getting past" disapproval could, of course, still be interpreted as meaning that the disapproval of others is a necessary condition, even if not a sufficient condition, when one seeks to change their minds in situations of moral and political conflict with them. That is, it could be interpreted as saying that the disapproval must be in place throughout, but it must be *supplemented* by some rational engagement with (rather than merely toleration of) those whom one disapproves of. However, such an interpretation of "getting past" disapproval would not be up for the tasks at hand as I have sketched them in the last many pages. "Getting past" the disapproval would have to really amount to *overcoming* the disapproval and *replacing* it (rather than merely supplementing it) not just with respect but with further more detailed attitudes toward the other, if one is to engage the other with something as *empathy*-demanding as the search for *internal* arguments, arguments in *their conceptual vernacular*, in order to change their minds—since as these last two sections of the chapter make clear, nothing less than that are the tasks at hand.

What these further attitudes that are needed exactly are is a searching question in the moral psychology of politics, and part of the exercise in these last two sections has been to bring us to the point of raising it. There is not enough space to explore this question in any detail in a chapter that is already far too long. But one can convey in a general way the sorts of considerations that will matter in any answer we might give.

Take one sort of example, particularly relevant to a point Taylor raised in his response to me cited earlier. To tap the conceptual vernacular of those one opposes in providing them with internal reasons to change their mind on some particular matter (censorship of blasphemy, say), may often (though not necessarily always) involve tapping elements in their tradition that are themselves religious, even sometimes elements in the orthodox aspects of their religion. There is no reason to think that a secularism such as (S), even though it does in some sense take a stance *against "religion,"* cannot display its own wisdom and appeal by showing how the ideals it seeks have their echoes (or premonitions) in *religious traditions*. As I have said, (S) tends to be most pressingly required when religion emerges in the political arena in a specific way—in the context of majoritarianisms that are peculiarly the product of modern nationalism (to take a contemporary example, Hindu nationalism—and the Muslim identitarian backlash against it—in India of the last twenty years or more). And so, in particular, there is no reason to think that various ideals that (S) seeks to promote in the face of such religious majoritariansim cannot sometimes be argued for by appealing to the commitments of ordinary people that flow from some of the remnants of their *older* religious traditions that are still relatively uncontaminated by the modern contexts that have been marked by majoritarianism. It is not as if these traditions are totally erased in the lives and mentalities of people in modern society. However ruthless modernity's trajectory might be in some parts of the world, so long as it is human mentality and culture that it acts upon, its surface will be more like a palimpsest than some sort of brand new and blank slate. If that were not the case, we would have no use or application for the concept of tradition. And so the thought is that it is quite possible that sometimes religious *tradition* may provide someone the grounds for internal reasons to change his mind away from the *new* majoritarian forms that religion takes in its appearance in political modernity.

I particularly want to stress this for two reasons. First, and less important, because it may seem that just because the entire Hegelian argument of these last two sections is based on a subject's capacity to be redirected in her values by incoming considerations in one's historical future, those considerations can't turn on elements of one's past thinking and traditions. But that would be an elementary fallacy. It is a childish non sequitur to think that considerations that cause one to change one's mind in the *future* cannot contain elements in one's *past* traditions. But the more important reason to stress it is that such a reliance (as I have been stressing in the last page or two) on the conceptual vernacular in the providing of internal reasons necessarily generates elaborately empathetic attitudes of engagement with the traditions and mentalities of those one opposes. If the implementation of a doctrine such as (S) is theoretically elaborated along these lines, it cannot possibly be faulted for failing to have relevance in a context in which we have gone "beyond toleration" to multiculturalism. Being based on a specific form of humanism, (S) admittedly does eschew indifference toward those it opposes, but what it replaces it with—in the sort of detailed engagement that I have been trying to convey—equally takes it decisively beyond the chronic assumption of disapproval that has made the idiom of toleration come to seem so off-beam in the pluralist contexts of multiculturalist modernity.

NOTES

Charles Taylor read a draft of this chapter with much care and acute comprehension and responded with a generous and detailed account of the points on which we are agreed and disagreed. Despite the remaining disagreements, I am grateful to him for the considerable improvements that I was able to make as a result of having to address his response.

1. Akeel Bilgrami, "What Is a Muslim?" *Critical Inquiry* (1992), see also "Rushdie and the Reform of Islam," *Grand Street* 8, no. 4, (Summer 1989), pp. 170–84.
2. Bernard Williams, "Internal and External Reasons" in *Moral Luck* (Cambridge: Cambridge University Press, 1981).
3. I am passing from talk of "truth" of a doctrine to whether there are reasons for believing it that carry conviction. This is not a slip. See note 13, this chapter, for more on this.
4. See Charles Taylor, "Modes of Secularism," in Rajeev Bhargava, ed., *Secularism and Its Critics* (New York: Oxford University Press, 1998). The idea of an overlapping consensus is most fully articulated in John Rawls, *Political Liberalism* (New York: Columbia University Press, 1993).
5. John Rawls, *The Law of Peoples* (Cambridge: Harvard University Press, 1999).

6. Charles Taylor, "Why We Need a Radical Redefinition of Secularism," in Jonathan Van Antwerpen and Eduardo Mendieta, eds., *The Power of Religion in the Public Sphere* (New York: Columbia University Press, 2011).
7. Ibid., see p. 37.
8. India is often described as a secular state that fits the neutral, symmetrically equidistant ideal toward India's different *religions*. (I think this is a mistaken conception of secularism as it has come to be central in the Indian context today. This is not a chapter on Indian secularism, so I can't discuss why that is so here, though some of what I say at the end of this essay on a well-known issue regarding secularism in India has implications for why it is mistaken.) Clearly the point I make about how a state-neutralist ideal of secularism that allows the *symmetrical* banning of books blaspheming against different religions in the society applies to this view of Indian secularism that I find mistaken. But, unlike this idea of Indian secularism, Taylor wishes to add to the mix of standpoints that the secular state must be neutral toward *nonreligion* as well.
9. Taylor, "Modes of Secularism," p. 37.
10. Ibid. (my emphasis).
11. Though not greatly focused on gender inequality, considerations of caste inequality, in particular untouchability, was an issue that was constantly in Gandhi's thoughts.
12. For a fine essay contextualizing issues of blasphemy, which is illuminating on just this sort of point, see Talal Asad, "Reflections on Blasphemy and Secular Criticism," in Hent de Vries, ed., *Religion: Beyond a Concept* (New York: Fordham University Press, 2008).
13. I give this example of the term *democracy* just so as to show that a word can get a "hurrah" status with all sides wanting it for themselves since there will be seeming merit on the side of those who can claim it, thereby taking away from any precise meaning that it might have. I don't mean to suggest that Taylor has the polemical and propaganda motives that surrounded the cold war disputes around "free" versus "people's" democracy debates. In fact, in the case of that term, I think, the way to define or characterize it is to see it as a form of government in which ordinary people have a serious input in the important decisions in their material and other central aspect of their lives. Neither cold war exemplifications of "free" or "people's" democracy met this criterion. On the one hand, elections in "free" democracies were not occasions or sites on which important issues that made a difference to the material lives of people were even so much as raised (all crucial decisions being made by the corporate sectors of society at some distance from the electoral field). And, on the other hand, the very idea of "people's" democracy was not intended (at any rate, not after the soviets and democratic councils in the Soviet Union were dismantled), to give people *input* into decisions on these matters, it was rather a claim to achieve the fulfillment of people's material and other essential needs—thus, even, when this was genuinely achieved, its achievement, however it is described, can't be described as an achievement of *democracy*, by the lights of the criterion, I just mentioned.
14. Apart from the essays mentioned in note 1, see Akeel Bilgrami, "Two Concepts of Secularism," *Economic and Political Weekly* 29, no. 28 (July 1994): 1749–61, reprinted in Bhargava, *Secularism and Its Critics* (New York: Oxford University Press, 2004), and "Secularism and

the Moral Psychology of Identity," *Economic and Political Weekly* 32, no. 40 (October 1997) and reprinted in Amiya Bagchee, Rajeev Bhargava, and Ravi Sundaram, eds., *Multiculturalism, Liberalism, and Democracy* (Oxford: Oxford University Press, 2001).

15. Of course, it may not always be able to be completely neutral regarding it since such asecularism may sometimes threaten the neutrality.

16. I am going directly from talk of "reasons" to talk of "truth." This is a deliberate collapsing of epistemological and metaphysical notions on my part. Some may want to keep epistemological and metaphysical issues apart and say that a principled failure to find *reasons* against a position one is in moral or political disagreement with does not yet show that position to be *true*. It still might not be true, even though one can't establish that to be so. If someone insists on making this sharp distinction between reasons and truth, the relativism I am discussing is a relativism regarding *the former only*. There would have to be *another* kind of relativism regarding truth, in that case, that someone may wish to argue for. Having expressed this caveat, I will continue to talk of the relativist as saying that various positions in disagreement with one another each have the "truth" on their side—and will ask the reader who wishes to make that sharp distinction to simply read my use of *truth* in the text differently from the way it is read when keeping epistemology and metaphysics sharply distinct. Two related caveats. First, I myself have distinguished sharply between questions of the meaning of "secularism" and questions of justifying secularism. But that is a quite different distinction than the one that I am collapsing in this note. All I am doing in this note is saying that I want to formulate a relativism that is generated by a *principled* failure on one's part to provide internal reasons for another position that one is in disagreement with in order to get them to change their mind and come around to one's own position. And I am asking the reader's indulgence in allowing me to calibrate the use of "true" and "false" along these lines, allowing me, that is, to say, of a position against which one in principle cannot provide internal reasons, that it is *true*. The second caveat has to do with the fact that some may think that questions of "truth" and "falsity" don't arise when it comes to morals and politics—they should be restricted only to questions of science and matters approximating science, where value elements are (more or less) missing. I find this view to be quite wrong, but I don't need to argue that here. I need simply only ask once again for terminological latitude on the part of the reader, i.e., ask the reader who has a qualm about using *true* and *false* for political and moral positions to substitute some other words for my use of *true* or *false* (*right* or *wrong* or just *x* and *y* would be fine).

17. It is important to understand what role this evaluative stance, which carries a certain form of humanism with it, is playing in the dialectic of this chapter. It is *not* something that is being wheeled in against relativism *directly*. It is not a matter of saying, "I take an evaluative stance that my position is right and not merely one right position among others." That would be glib and utterly unconvincing, a way of avoiding wrestling seriously with the specter of relativism created (prima facie) by the stress on internal reasons and the denial of external reasons. Rather, the evaluative stance has been wheeled in on the coattails of the Hegelian argument against relativism that invokes the subject-in-history. It props up *that* argument, which is the primary argument against relativism. The evaluative stance is

merely a stance taken on the question of how to interpret history and the prospects it holds out for the possibility of the introduction of conflicts into the psychological economies of those with whom one is in political or moral conflict. It is a stance that gives one the right to take a certain default position on that question.

18. I repeat that, as it happens, of course, the exception was granted only to Muslims, so this is not a good example of the neutralist ideal that Taylor favors, but that is just what I am putting aside from consideration for the purposes of giving this relativistic reading to the Muslims being granted an exception.
19. I think, in fact, that the concession to Muslim personal laws was exactly such a Hegelian moment in the Indian constitution. But I do want to say something to clarify this position, since it is poised to be misunderstood. In the two essays mentioned in note 11, I argue at length how the *state itself* may play a role in helping religious groups and communities to come to devise and see these internal reasons and then to play the role of implementing those changes via reform of laws and customs and so on. Therefore, the idea of *internal reasons for reform* is not to be confused with *internal reform* of a religion. The point of the latter is that the state has no role to play in changes within a religious standpoint. That is not the point at all of this chapter's argument. The point is rather to give religious groups a voice in the processes, in the fraternal spirit that Taylor urges, by allowing them to see and articulate their own internal reasons for any change in their position. It is not to insist that the groups must carry out their own internal changes without any role for the state to play. Sumit Sarkar conflates and confuses this distinction between internal reasons and internal reform in equating my view of these matters with Partha Chatterjee's in his paper, "The Anti-Secularist Critique of Hindutva: Problems of a Shared Discursive Space" in *Germinal* 1 (1994).
20. I must confess to having written an essay about twenty years ago called "Two Concepts of Secularism" (see note 12), in which I discussed how a secularism based on internal reasons is one concept of secularism and another one based on external reasons is a second concept. This is what I am saying in this chapter is a mistake. There is only one concept of secularism, and there are two different paths of justification for them. And even in that early essay, where I did make a contrast between two concepts of secularism in the title, I was very clear in the details of what I had said that I was not really *defining* secularism differently in each, but merely saying that it makes a big difference to politics, in particular a politics that avoids some of the subtle coercions that secularism can be party to, if we take internal and external reasons as different *justifications* seriously and stress the former over the latter. If, in that essay, I was not always as careful to be *explicit* about this distinction between issues of definition, on the one hand, and justification and basis of implementation, on the other, the present essay can be seen as a detailed corrective to such a lapse.

HALF-TOLERATION

Concordia and the Limits of Dialogue

NADIA URBINATI

THE PLACE OF God in the constitution has been one of the most sensitive issues in the debate on the constitutional treaty of the European Union, and this has influenced the process of ratification.[1] In the five decades since the Treaty of Rome was signed in 1957, European leaders have tried to build a united Europe on a *secular* foundation of treaties and economic regulations. These no longer seem to be adequate to the task. Lately, efforts have been made to include another factor—*religion*. In 2006 Chancellor Merkel spoke in favor of a *reference to God* in the European constitution; her views were opposed by secularist France and received with warm support by Spain, Italy, Ireland, Slovakia, and Poland.[2]

The debate on the EU treaty occurs in a time of religious renaissance and testifies to the transformation of the liberal culture from a project of ideological secularization to one that is willing to encourage the encounter between the secular and the religious.[3] In Jürgen Habermas's words, "Western culture has witnessed a transformation of religious consciousness since the Reformation and the Enlightenment" that can be described as a "modernization" of religious discourse; it has also witnessed a parallel transformation of secular consciousness from an intransigent secularism to a "respectful sensibility for the possible existential significance of religion."[4] This comprehensive transformation was facilitated by the liberal framework of modern democratic societies, which has encouraged a renaissance of social concord on a new terrain, one in which the sacred and the profane are no longer estranged from each other but equal participants in the making of a more inclusive and unified public sphere. It is accurate to say that the ideal of Concordia is the *koiné* of contemporary secular Europe.[5]

Preceding the secular transformation of the state and liberal toleration, the humanist ideal of Concordia relied on the premise that religion was the leading feature of Europe's collective identity and the foundation of its political order; it prompted the belief that "discord on religious issues would engender the worst possible disorders and the gravest enmities among men."[6] This ideal engaged Christian philosophers like Erasmus of Rotterdam and politicians like Catherine de' Medici and was steered by the conviction that public dialogue among representatives of opposite Christian denominations would be possible and, in addition, would allow them to overcome their divisions, reach a deeper unity, and secure a perpetual peace. Sixteenth-century Concordia thus meant "harmony and unison of minds and hearts"; its opposite was error and discord, conflict of ideas and between minds and hearts. The art of eloquence and the strategy of dialogue upon which the humanists relied presumed such a consensus of values.

In this chapter I propose a critical examination of this ideal and inquire as to what went wrong with it. My purpose is to spread some grain of skepticism toward the enthusiastic welcome of religions in the public sphere of contemporary democratic societies and call attention instead to the limits of dialogue, rational scrutiny, and persuasion, when issues that involve religious creeds are at stake, and the role of pluralism in the preservation of individual freedom of conscience and social peace. I shall revisit the humanist project of Concordia and the reasons that made its theorists and believers unable to fulfill the promise of fostering the "spiritual unity" of Europe. Christian humanists thought it possible to achieve dialogic cooperation for truth seeking without removing theological dogmas from public forum. But, as we shall see in the analysis of the exemplary case of the Colloquy of Poissy (1560–61), that assumption produced the opposite: it jeopardized the humanists' irenic goal, radicalized religious disagreements, and opened the door to the wars of religions.

I first briefly reconstruct the historical-political context within which preliberal tolerance emerged and the humanist ideal of Christian Concord acquired the meaning of a spiritual and political *koiné* to be achieved through rational conviction in frank and open dialogue; next I elucidate the differences between that rendering of dialogue and tolerance of dissent and its classical background, namely, Cicero's philosophy of universal concord. This will allow me to set the contextual and theoretical premises for analyzing the case of the colloquy for reconciliation of religious disagreements that was held in Poissy a few years before the massacre of the Huguenots. It will appear that the acceptance of pluralism, which is the necessary premise of both freedom of religion and social peace, in fact requires a skeptical attitude and demands a suspension of dialogue and the acceptance of the other, without an attempt to overcome divisions or differences. The recognition of the boundaries that separate persuasion from proselytism intersects with the awareness of the limits of dialogue. This was the insight coming from Jean Bodin, who maintained, as we shall see by the end of the chapter, that religions can hardly be conducive of social unity and harmony when and if their truths are thrown in the public arena as criteria for making decisions on right and wrong.

SUFFERING DIFFERENCE, PERMITTING PLURALISM

CUIUS REGIO, EIUS RELIGIO

Religious pluralism was Christian Europe's most arduous achievement. Its de facto recognition came from the secular authority for reasons that were, strictly speaking, mundane and pertained to the preservation of civil peace and the regulation of social interactions among Catholics and Protestants. Beginning with the Peace of Augsburg (1555), the formula *cuius regio, eius religio* symbolized the attempt to reestablish domestic and international peace after the schism. In the course of several national councils that took place in the German territories and in France a few years after Martin Luther's break (1517), that formula was later on rendered as "one faith, one law, one king," a doctrine that reached its apogee at the end of the wars of religions with the Treaty of Westphalia (1648).[7] It was revered at least until the revolutionary turn prompted by the First Amendment to the U.S. Constitution. The politics of rights and the doctrine of the wall between church and state put an end to both toleration as state politics and the humanist ideal of Concordia Christiana as a political project.[8]

Cuius regio, eius religio had a huge impact in the debates on the authority of the civil power in religious issues and on the destiny of Christian concord. It was meant to give secular authorities the power to contain social unrests by regulating contention over religious practices (yet not dogmas) that the geographical proximity of Catholics and Protestants provoked. It was conceived as a temporarily valid remedy, though. The long-term and ideal solution was that of restoring Concordia Christiana, a goal that enjoyed strong support among theologians, philosophers, and politicians in the early stage of the Reformation.[9]

Clearly, the formula *cuius regio, eius religio* had implications that were unequivocally antipluralistic at the state level (territorialization of each religion), but pluralistic at the continental level (territorialization of state sovereignty). Predictably, therefore, it was met with opposition by medieval cosmopolitan institutions like the Church of Rome ("How dare one nation alter the Church's ordinances?") and the empire (Charles V opposed it in the name of "universal monarchy").[10] Concordia was the political and theological response against that formula. It was meant to provide an ultimate solution to the two challenges for which that *statist* formula was devised: the exigency of social peace and the given fact of pluralism of faiths. Thus it made room for realistic prudence in cases in which dogmatic principles (the so-called fundamentals of faith) were not at stake, but faced religious pluralism with hostility, as a scandal to be stopped or a sin to be repaired. Supporters of Concordia opposed their idea of unity against models of empire that were based on religious pluralism, like the Ottoman Empire or the old Roman Empire.[11]

Yet doubts about the likelihood of the renewal of religious concord surfaced very soon. For instance, in a meeting that the Estates General of Orleans held in the winter 1560–61 to deal with the civil unrest caused by conflicts between Catholics and Calvinists, Michel de L'Hospital, a remarkable humanist, chancellor of Catherina de' Medici (the regent of the French crown), and leader of the "Politique" party in the conflict between Catholics and Protestants, defended the formula *cuius regio, eius religio* as a strategy for peace: "La division des langues ne fait la séparation des royaumes, mais celle de la religion et des lois, qui d'un royaume en fait deux. De là sort le vieil proverb, Une foy, une loy, un roy. Et est difficile que les hommes étant en telle diversité et contrariété d'opinions, se puissent contenir de venir aux armes: car la guerre, comme dit le poète, suit de près, et accompagne discorde et débat."[12] Yet although L'Hospital's words enjoyed wide support in the meeting, some of the delegates were skeptical about the overcoming of pluralism in a new Christian concord. To the Abby Jacques Bienassis, the general vicar of Tours, no alternative seemed feasible in the short term to the fact that France was "to suffer [the presence of] two religions" and any political answer to such a division should start from this basic recognition.[13] *Suffering* religious difference, *permitting* pluralism—this was the very first step toward the recognition of religious freedom and pluralism. In the following section I will examine that early appearance of toleration within Concordia, which I propose to call toleration before liberal toleration.

TOLERATION BEFORE LIBERAL TOLERATION

Toleration developed well before its liberal codification. It made its appearance in a cultural milieu that was opposite of religious indifference and in which spiritual unity was regarded as a supreme good for individuals and communities. Toleration before liberal toleration was a composite phenomenon whose meaning and practices were rooted in antiquity (and Stoicism in particular) and the Middle Ages.[14] The advent of the Reformation, and the traumatic experience of the wars of religion, contributed to changing both its meaning and practice. But in the sixteenth century, before it became an indication of individual liberty of conscience—as in John Locke's formulation—toleration consisted in state policy and a social practice and in both cases was perceived as provisional acceptance of religious difference. *Toleration* consisted in a politics of edicts of "clemency" by civil authorities; *tolerance* was a virtue that allowed for a practice of dialogue among believers.

Toleration acquired a legal meaning as "approbation" of the practice of a minority religion by civil authority with the view of managing conflicts between communities of believers. In sixteenth-century France, for instance, "until" the monarch did not give his approval, a minority confession was temporarily tolerated in the sense that the state suspended its coercive interference with it. As an anticipation of negative liberty, preliberal toleration designated a sphere of human actions that was legally "indifferent" and in this sense free because the state ignored it. This noninterference would cease at the sovereign's discretion whenever it was accompanied by social intolerance and unrest. Toleration was a state policy and, moreover, a "provisional freedom of religion" (*liberté provisoire de religion*) that the state accorded in order to allow believers "to live in peace . . . while waiting for the council."[15] But by the time the Council of Trent ended (1563), hopes for reconciliation had faded away, and at that point pluralism was a reality the politics of toleration registered and justified without trying to overcome—liberal toleration as modus vivendi may be understood to start then.

Tolerance denoted the individual's moral and psychological disposition toward benevolence and respect, virtues essential for dialogue. As a social practice, it was professed and performed in the numerous councils that were held by elite representatives of the various Christian denominations in order to overcome their divisions (the Colloquy of Poissy was an example). This kind of tolerance too was foreign to the spirit of what would later on characterize liberal toleration because it made theological discussion and thus "suffering" of dissent, "a means to a higher end: religious reconciliations."[16] It was not obtained by taking theology out of public dialogue, or making religion a personal or private business, but was intended to be an appreciation of theology as a communal grammar for achieving agreement: the dialogue it promoted was meant to be epistemic since its goal was to demonstrate divine truth with logical discussion and in this way put an end to disagreement on fundamentals of faith.

To conclude, the aim of toleration before liberal toleration was dual: the attainment of social peace by imposing state authority over religious communities and the practice of benevolence toward, although not acceptance of, religious difference.[17] This made it the opposite of a secularist project, as for instance, toleration during the Enlightenment, but also not naturally disposed toward liberal toleration as an art of separation of spheres because it was inspired by an ideal of community rather than individual freedom of conscience. Toleration before liberal toleration was internal to religious discourse and conceived not as a process that would help the differentiation of the spheres of life, but as one that was meant to promote an articulation of those spheres within a unitary horizon of meaning and value that was profoundly religious. Toleration as a state practice was thus not necessarily followed by a practice of tolerance by the believers.[18] In fact, its endorsement by the state or civil authority meant that subjects holding different religious faiths did not tolerate each other, because they did not accept disagreement on issues of faith. When that acceptance finally became a given fact, religious concord as a political project faded away.

DOCTRINAL FLUIDITY

Catholic authorities (the empire and the Church of Rome) dealt with religious pluralism by means of a complex strategy that was simultaneously against *external* threats of division (Protestant churches) and against *internal* ones (heresies, the target of an old battle within Catholicism to be revived in the years of Reformation).[19] It is worth stressing however that while pluralism was opposed at the doctrinal level, realistic prudence and accommodation, particularly in the domain of jurisprudence and municipal administration, played an important role as an avenue toward a permitted practice of tolerance in civil relations. Historians have thus spoken of "fluidity and uncertainty" when describing the status of intolerance and relations among Christian denominations in the years that preceded the wars of religion. For instance, in the case of imperial authority, on some important occasions the implementation of its decisions at the local level was left to the discretion of civil magistrates; this could, and actually did, entail the possibility of moderate decisions and even tolerance of non-Catholic practices.[20]

The practice of "prudence" reflected the condition of social and religious "fluidity," which was testified by an interesting and far from uncommon phenomenon: the conversions or the changing of denominations by Catholics and Protestants alike, which was partly the result of a sincere renewal in spiritual searching and partly the effect of a reasonable difficulty for believers to have a reliable knowledge of the various new Christian confessions and their specificities. But the implications of fluidity were predictable in light of the two above-mentioned approaches by secular and religious authorities. On the one hand, changing denomination was in conflict with the dogmatic identification of religions as well as with the formula *cuius regio, eius religio*, but, on the other hand, it encouraged the idea that the rebirth of Christian unity was possible and close at hand. In addition, such complexity and fluidity was testified by another important phenomenon that characterized the early stage of Reformation and overlapped with the philosophy of Concordia: Nicodemism.

With the official intention of reconciling Christian theologies, some radical ecumenists started practicing a strategy of "programmed religious simulation," a move that acquired very soon the character of a philosophical project of radical humanism rather than religious concord. Reformers were particularly worried by what they saw as an infiltration among their believers of libertines and rationalists whose philosophical disquisitions of religious texts were seen as attempts against religion in and of itself, although played in the name of universalism and harmony. As historians have shown, the dogmatic rigidity of John Calvin (who in 1544 published his *Excuse à Messieurs les Nicodemites*) in matters of ritual, ceremony, and what he himself had once denounced as a Catholic cult for externality was a reaction against precisely that condition of philosophical fluidity.[21] Reformed Christians propelled and necessarily practiced a "politics of identity" that could not be reconciled with Concordia, which they endorsed more as an honorable ideal than as a desired project. The politics of dialogue, which inspired the several councils for religious reconciliation and began in the first half of the sixteenth century, was therefore a failure from the start because, if successful, it would entail the overcoming of dogmatic pluralism (and Reformed churches). Indeed, as we shall see, those dialogues were meant to achieve not merely the "mutual edification" of a common religion but moreover the "demonstration" and acceptance of some fundamental principles of faith in relation to which only temporary forbearance was granted.[22] Dialogues were for the sake of conviction, more than simply conversation, because differences were conceived and treated as indications of error and imperfection.

RELIGIOUS HUMANISM

In a study on religious simulation in the sixteenth century, Carlo Ginzburg has demonstrated that starting from the perspective of spirituality as the true mark of religious faith regardless of rituals and dogmas it would not be hard to dissolve Christianity in a natural religion. This radical irenicism would destroy all positive religions and lead the believers beyond the distinction of confessions and toward a view of the divine that would be purely philosophical, a conclusion that Christian humanists (certainly Erasmus) foresaw and rejected.[23] Secular humanism and Christian humanism competed on the terrain of Concordia, the one by advancing a pantheist perspective and the other by reaffirming a transcendent one; of the two, the latter played certainly a much more prominent role in shaping the destiny of modern Europe. To it we should pay attention if we want to understand the politics of theological dialogue for reconciliation and its failure, at the eve of the wars of religion.

The doctrine of Concordia Christiana acquired momentum after the movement of conciliarism. Whereas the latter represented a request of participation in the government of the Church, the former was meant to be a remedy to the risk of the Church's dismemberment. In political terminology we might say that conciliarism embodied a request for democracy and concord one of sovereign authority.[24] The philosophy of concord built on the Neoplatonic ideal of a polyphonic unity of believers and regarded Christians' accord as the supreme good that alone could keep society in peace. Irenicism was the best product of the Renaissance's ideal of the unity of the world—"*Pax philosophiae* and *Pax fidei*"—and was embedded in the universalism of such quattrocento personalities as Pico della Mirandola and, above all, Nicholas of Cusa.[25]

Nicholas of Cusa, writing in the context of the Council of Basel (1433), thus before the Reform, regarded *concordantia* as a restoration of a divine harmony in the Church, the overcoming of the reasons of discord that followed the dual papacy (Avignon and Rome) and resided in the mixing of temporal and spiritual power: on the one hand, the contestation of pontifical and clerical officials for raising taxes to support the curia and the clergy, on the other, the tension between the Roman center and the localities when bishops had to be appointed. Cusa depicted discord as a lack of consent between the Church's highest hierarchy and the members of the religious communities. Concordia was then a quest of preservation of unity through a regaining of legitimacy. Hence Cusa stated three principles of *concordantia*: harmony; consensus; acceptance. Harmony was the inspiring principle, consensus through dialogue the means to acquire it, and acceptance of the truth the celebration of the restored authority. These spiritual and theological features were rooted in the Christian Neoplatonist idea of harmony as a divine work of creation that humans could grasp through faith (and a reason that was enlightened by faith). "There can be only one wisdom. For if it were possible for there to be plural wisdoms, they would have to derive from one wisdom, for before all plurality is unity."[26] In this divine work, variety of forms was a manifestation of the divine, complementary to the good of the whole. Concordia held for nature as well as for the Church, which was also made of a gradation and diversification of functions (hierarchy) for the good of the general (on this idea the distinction between fundamentals and nonfundamentals of faith rested). The analogy with marriage (*agape*) was paradigmatic: men and wife created a *consensus communis* within which the good of the whole came first and as a result of their components' responsible participation.[27] These were, in brief, the foundations of the philosophical view that inspired the councils for reconciliation after the Reformation, that is to say, when the schism was an incontrovertible fact and the unity of Christianity broken.

Within this new scenario, differences among Christians became an obstacle to be overcome when they pertained to ideas and practices that would contradict the "essentials of faith." Differences were accepted as manifestations of local traditions and rituals, practical variations within a common doctrinal system. They were an enrichment of the divine unity of Christianity if conceived and practiced as complementary to the good of the whole. *Adiaphora*—or "things that make no difference"—was the name for those nonfundamentals of faith that were taken to be not decisive in the moral and religious life of an individual and could thus be tolerated and openly practiced.[28] They were "external" to doctrinal theology and for this reason indifferent to the main goal of doctrinal unity. Actually, Cusa, who was also one of the earliest proponents of a hermeneutical approach to religious texts, interpreted *concordantia* of the essentials of faith as appreciation of theology beyond Christianity itself (although not monotheism). To him, for instance, the Qur'an was not merely a moral and ethical code of a people, but first of all a "book of doctrines" that should be appreciated as such by all believers.

Cusa's humanism was as much unitary as Erasmus's since it did not contain any invitation to secularize religious discourse and pluralize loyalties; the message it conveyed was that of "finding the presence of the Gospel in all other religions," of seeing all religions as expressions of humans' longing for transcendence.[29] This was also the main inspiration of Erasmus's work, which became the most authoritative source of catholicity in the age of the councils for reconciliation. "The sum and substance of our religion," Erasmus wrote in 1523, "is peace and concord. This can hardly remain the case unless we define as few matters as possible and leave each individual's judgment free on many questions."[30]

> Only men, who above all other species should agree with one another and who need mutual understanding most of all, cannot be united in mutual love *by nature* (so powerful everywhere else), nor by training, nor by all the advantages to be anticipated from concord, nor even by awareness of the many evils resulting from war. Only this one animal is capable of speech, and the best reconciler of conflicting needs; he has also been granted the seeds of science and virtue, an intelligence which is gentle in itself and naturally inclines him to benevolence. Just look at all the ways in which nature herself persuades us toward agreement. Not content with the allurements of mutual benevolence, she makes harmonious relations not only convenient but necessary. Thus she divided up the gifts of body and mind in such a way that nobody has them all, or so many that he may not some time need help from another, however insignificant. In all these different ways, nature teaches us peace and concord.[31]

In these words by Erasmus (a premonition of Immanuel Kant's perpetual peace) are contained the main ingredients of humanist Concordia operating in the sixteenth century: a) the idea that the condition of the unity of mankind is written within human nature (human beings are members of one common species); b) the idea that differences among human beings are varieties that develop from within their commonality as an enrichment of it, not a reason for divorce; c) the idea that the arts of language along with reason and the virtues of civility and benevolence are qualities that the moderns should take from the ancients; d) the idea that peace as harmony is the destiny of mankind; and e) the idea that religion is a road to harmony, not to conflicts and divisions. The first four of these aspects testified to the humanists' belonging in the Latin tradition of civil eloquence, the latter was instead what most characterized Christian humanism's Concordia and also, as we shall see, the reason for its failure.

The Latin tradition of eloquence, in particular Cicero's and Quintilian's, was consistently based on Hellenistic universalism and the philosophy of natural equality of human beings as creatures that were able to understand justice and interact by speech, thus naturally disposed toward peace and dialogue, two goals that civil government had the duty to promote or not hinder.[32] It was also ingrained in a moderate skeptical approach that allowed probability and the acceptance of approximations of the truth rather than dogmatic assertions of it. Verisimilitude was the Ciceronian attitude toward achieving truth. Concordia and dialogue or harmony via open discourse were two crucial and intertwined ideals that the ancients bequeathed to the humanists. Let us examine them.

CLASSICAL AND HUMANIST CONCORDIA

Concordia entailed an ideal of peace that was not identical with the kind of peace that states or strangers could reach. In the ancient world, where the *poleis* were in permanent conflict with only temporary intervals of peace, war was an ever present feature of relations between them, a constant and mutual disposition to destroy the enemy or at least weaken it. The logic of relations between states was the law of the strongest, which made peace an always precarious truce among equal partners. But domestic society was not supposed to follow that logic, because conflicts between neighbors could easily degenerate into brutal and radical violence. Concord (*homonoia*), then, was not seen as international peace (*eirene*), but as peace within the city. Indeed the unity of the city required a much more robust peace than that entailed by a truce between previous enemies; the reason was that of avoiding fratricidal wars that would tear apart the polis and decree its death.

In classical times this terrifying possibility was frequently invoked to justify exceptional political measures, as in the case of the Thirty Tyrants who justified their coup d'état in 403 BC as a necessary means to put an end to conflicts that divided the Athenians or, as in the case of the Romans who resorted to the supreme good of concord (*salus rei publicae*) to justify the institution of dictatorship. Dialogue was the strategy to solve disagreements among citizens or members of the same state, a method that relied only on the force of reason and persuasion. In extreme cases of divisions, other strategies besides dialogue were also adopted for restoring concord, like amnesty and oblivion. Finally, in situations of devastating conflicts, when concord was lost, harmony could become the name of a myth or even a utopia. For instance, in the bloody century that preceded the end of the Roman republic, *concordia ordinum* converted into the myth that gave Augustus's empire a moral legitimacy.[33] Likewise, whereas before the Reformation *concordantia* was a feasible goal (Cusa thought it was), once the wars of religion buried Concordia Christiana, harmony persisted as a myth to reemerge under various features, religious or secular, from the Enlightenment idea of a perpetual peace to the unity of Europe and the ecumenism of the Second Vatican Council in the twentieth century.

The Christian humanists' source of inspiration was Rome and, moreover, the philosophy of Cicero, who spoke of *civitas* as a "spirit of harmony and tastes" that existed when "the interests of all [were] the same" because "discord arises from conflicting interests" (*ex utilititatis varietatibus, cum aliis aliud expediat, nasci discordias*).[34] Cicero did not intend to say that all citizens must be perfectly equal in order for the city to enjoy Concordia. He thought instead that inequalities of social status and public honors were variations essential to the making of a just and harmonious society. But inequalities should stir recognition and emulation, not envy or resentment.[35] In sum, Republican Concordia entailed not identical status or sameness but some identity of values or an ethical unity that would make all the citizens *feel* justly treated regardless of their different social condition and inequality. *Concordia animi* is the right way of reading Cicero's appeal to unity.

Clearly, Concordia was a project to be continuously reinforced through civic education or by instilling communal values, relying upon the historical memories of the republic, and constructing exemplary models of virtuous citizens.[36] Cicero rendered harmony as love, or *caritas*, or the condition for civic tranquillity and a life without fear that could exist *only among citizens*, not with the barbarians or the foreigners because it presumed a commonalty of language and laws, of traditions and ethical values, conditions without which dialogue could not take place, but only violence and war.[37] As with conversation among friends, dialogue among citizens was meant to prepare for and cultivate peace as harmony.

Sixteenth-century humanists applied Cicero's ideas to Christianity and endorsed his maxim of *struggle against the factions* as necessary premise for avoiding the dilacerations of the *Res publica Christiana*. Christians fighting against Christians, wrote Erasmus, is equivalent to "fratricide" within the republic. Like civil war, religious war "creates its own priests, bishops, and even cardinals," thinkers and activists who perpetrate hatred, hostility, and division. Thus concord was meant to counter both actual seditious and doctrinal disagreements and to create peace among equals by overcoming disagreements and reinforcing rather than questioning the "spiritual unity" of European Christians.[38] As a consequence, religious toleration was acceptable only as a means for theological and ethical reunification; in fact, to some scholars it was "a choice for the lesser of two evils."[39] To understand the reasons for Concordia's failure we have to turn to its practical component, namely, the role of dialogue in the handling of disagreement.

DIALOGUE AND THE CONSTRAIN OF TIME

Cicero dealt with disagreement in relation to disputes within philosophical schools and among philosophers, not within religious churches and among theologians. This difference is paramount, as we shall see in this section. Cicero argued that when agreement was not possible the individual participant in a philosophical debate (*sermo*) could freely decide to follow his own judgment, if his philosophical school did not offer him any secure guidance on how to solve the conflict between basic assumptions. "But let everyone defend his views, for judgment is free: I shall cling to my rule and without being tied to the laws of any single school of thought which I feel bound to obey, shall always search for the most probable solution in every problem."[40] Cicero did not, of course, intend to say that philosophers should be free in all their opinions or tolerant of all beliefs. His theory of disagreement and the distinction between truth and probability relied upon a basic agreement on what human reasonability (or republican values) was, as we said earlier.

Yet the rules of eloquence were dictated by prudence (*decorum*), which contended that the orator should accommodate himself to the character of the audience and avoid imposing a standard of certainty on materials that had do with conviction and persuasion. Cicero's philosophical school was the Academy, whose basic moderate skepticism was equally distant from Pyrrhonism or absolute skepticism on the one hand and Platonism on the other. Probability instead of total suspension of judgment and arguing *in utramque partem* instead of dogmatic assertiveness were the basic rules of the Academy and civil eloquence.[41] A moderate skepticism was for Cicero the key to the continuation of dialogue: "The philosophers of the Academy have been wise in withholding their consent from any proposition that has not been proved. There is nothing worse than a hasty judgment, and nothing could be more unworthy of the dignity and integrity of a philosopher than to adopt a false opinion or to maintain as certain some theory which has not been fully explored and understood."[42]

Let us now consider the rules of rhetoric. Notice the difference in Cicero's theory between oratory in contestation environments (like a court or a political assembly) in which decisions must be made within a certain time and do not require necessarily unanimity and conversation (*sermo*) in "social gatherings, in informal discussions, and in intercourse with friends," which could go on forever and whose aim is consensus.[43] The former were the site of oratory (judicial and deliberative) while the latter was the site of dialogue or conversation to deal with philosophical questions that were ungraspable by ordinary persons and not to be dealt with by strategic persuasion or resolved by a vote.[44] Moreover, the appropriate places for oratory were large gatherings, but dialogue occurred in small symposia. Whereas rhetoric fits the masses, conversation is for the few. In the case of the humanists, colloquies or councils were the places in which dialogue was performed; it excluded rhetoric and was meant to be a frank and rational discussion among competent theologians to achieve a consensus that was comprehensive and thorough. Finally, as Cicero distinguished between genres of oratory and discussion, he also distinguished between what was fundamental and what was nonfundamental or open to toleration; humanists based theological dialogue on a prior distinction between fundamentals of faith and nonfundamentals of faith. Regarding the former, agreement should go unquestioned, while in the latter disagreement could be accepted and tolerance was not an issue. Dialogues were held in order to restore agreement on the former. In a word, humanists applied Cicero's rules and maxims of philosophical dialogue to theological disputations.[45]

Sixteenth-century humanists were "men of faith" who regarded Concordia as an ideal toward which human life must tend as toward its supreme good, as with the ideal marriage, it was never a given but always a goal, a tendency, and a permanent process of faith renewal; the relationship among believers was supposed to follow the same logic. The moral justification of tolerance within Concordia was that of a *permanent effort* "of ratifications, subtractions, additions, and accommodations."[46] Its Ciceronian equivalent was indeed *sermo*, or the informal discussion between friends or philosophical interlocutors. Yet adaptation and accommodation were not for the sake of combination or syncretism, as with Cicero. Humanists like Erasmus were repelled by oxymoronic and hybrid unions as well as by indifferentism. All these were examples of monstrosities, like the ancient myths of the Centaur, Chiron, or the Chimera; negative myths that Erasmus used to represent the inconstant and fickle individual as opposed to the virtuous one who practiced the ethics of coherence.[47] In sum, the humanists' revision and adaptation of Cicero's philosophy to make it fit theology entailed a departure from classical Hellenism and became the main source of problems in the colloquies between Catholic and Protestant theologians. "This is the difference between the searching of a person of faith and of a philosopher: the former searches that which he has already found, the latter does not sometime find even that which he had intensely searched."[48]

In their attempt to distinguish between humanist toleration and liberal toleration and rescue the former from oblivion and misunderstanding, Gary Remer and Cary Nederman have stressed the link between the classical tradition and the humanist culture of dialogue and singled out three common characteristics: a) proposing "persuasion over force" (which meant that the practice of dialogue was more important than the very adhesion to some principles), b) endorsing a moderate skepticism on nonessentials of faith and thus making toleration ethically superior to a blind adhesion to both dogmas and traditions, and, c) finally, stressing decorum or the civility and propriety in arguing both sides of an issue and thus keeping dialogue always open.[49] In their reinterpretation Remer and Nederman argue that the humanists adapted Cicero's moderate skepticism and Concordia to religious issues so as to achieve the same *minimal* consensus as Cicero's, even if the object of benevolence toward disagreement pertained to theological creeds rather than philosophical schools. "Cicero had believed that *decorum* of *sermo*, determined by *sermo*'s goal of truth, required that the participants be allowed to debate their ideas freely. Erasmus thought that the same *decorum*, with its attendant respect and civility for all participants, demanded toleration for many of the period's theological debates."[50] The problem with this perspicacious and compelling reinterpretation is that it obfuscates what was distinctive about Christian Concordia: portraying as minor or secondary that which was instead major and determinant, a distinction that will emerge in the analysis of the Colloquy of Poissy.

When Cicero discussed the place and the limits of disagreement, he referred to philosophical doctrines, not religious dogmas; he did not presume that natural reason would be in need of the light of religious faith or of the authority of a Church. He thought that "in every inquiry the unanimity of the races of the world must be regarded as a law of nature."[51] Philosophical dialogue was not all inclusive thus, because, to enter it, the interlocutors had to accept the assumption that reasoned speech was the means for conviction, not authority, force, and not even rhetorical stratagems. Cicero could not have contemplated limitless toleration since this would clearly entail a defeat of philosophy itself.

When humanists applied Cicero's rules of *sermo* to theological disputations, they changed the context of dialogue. Indeed, whereas Cicero declared conversation to be philosophical rather than rhetorical because it accepted the minimal premise of reason as a condition of unrestricted investigation, Christian humanists, by making religious dogmas (like the Eucharist, as we shall see) into fundamentals on which participants in the dialogue could not disagree, turned away from *sermo* and were forced to adopt rhetoric and finally interrupt the colloquy. The outcome was that whereas Cicero's fundamentals of reason could not be an object of toleration for the simple reason that this would imply tolerating the wrong, Christian humanists could not make the same assumption on fundamentals of faith, which had to be tolerated precisely because they could not be agreed upon by reason alone or through a frank and an unrestricted dialogue. Were this agreement possible, all Christian denominations would be diluted in one religion with no substantial distinctions; an outcome that was confronted by Christian theologians with anxiety and certainly not desired, either because it could mean a new Catholic hegemony or because it could mean a rationalist rendering of universality with the erasure of all transcendence (as we saw, Calvin's attack against Nicodemism foresaw the antireligious danger contained in the myth of concord). When the difference between Ciceronian dialogue and their religious dialogue emerged during the Colloquy of Poissy, the recognition that Christian Concordia could no longer exist became fatal. As that point, dialogue gave way to rhetoric and the search for unity translated into (or was seen as) a project of conversion or proselytism.

Remer and Nederman stressed the continuity between classical eloquence and Christian humanists' eloquence on their common habit of the mind as reluctance to exclude the possibility of achieving consensus. This would explain the humanists' "reluctance to condemn others for heresy," because condemnation would eventually result in the recognition that division among Christians had won over concord.[52] Moreover, since faith was a process of spiritual search and perfection that was never concluded and belief was always malleable, none could actually decree at what point a person was in the wrong or a heretic, unless one assumed that faith was a status rather than a spiritual condition of searching; unless one assumed that there were as many denominations as individual citadels—according to Locke's principle

Christians thought that reconciliation was feasible or even desirable. Theodore Beza, the representative sent by John Calvin, and the Cardinal de Lorrain were the leading protagonists of the theological discussions.

Deliberative procedures were defined and conceived to establish a dialogue that would allow all the participants to feel secure, free, and respected. Although the host was a Catholic king, Protestants "were to be received kindly and to be instructed with no force save persuasion."[56] The representative of Calvin was given the task of opening the colloquy. In his oration, Beza, anything but a moderate and conciliatory man of faith, perorated the noble cause of Concordia by indicating two things they should avoid, as Nugent comments: "the denial of any substantial differences between the two faiths and the assertion that there were no similarities. Neither was the way to concord."[57] Beza then went on to classify differences within their creeds as "matters of interpretations; and unnecessary accretions" and thereby hoped to clear the floor of useless disquisitions.

But it appeared very soon that the nonfundamentals of faith (rituals, prayers, symbols, community, or local traditions, etc.) did not attract the attention and interest of the participants, who started disagreeing precisely on issues that were supposed to be unanimously accepted. Indeed, moving to discuss sacraments, Beza gave the Eucharist a definition that provoked the first blow of radical dissent: he denied that that sacrament entailed a miraculous change in substance from bread and wine into the body and blood of Christ. Not only did Beza deny the dogma of transubstantiation but moreover he attempted a definition of sacraments that was primed to broaden disagreement by asserting the incompatibility between sacrament and dogma.[58] In claiming that a dogma was "directly contrary" to the symbolic nature of a sacrament, Beza, from the start, jeopardized not only a possible convergence of ideas but above all the possibility of a common denominator for dialogue, that is to say, the Ciceronian premises of *sermo*. "He held that the signs are, as it were, the substance of the sacrament; if they are transformed, the sacrament is abolished. This is the firm distinction between the sign and the thing signified."[59] Beza's "unfortunate error" was to start his oration with an *interpretation*; this move would hardly allow the dialogue to proceed and people to remain open to the possibility of changing their mind.[60] Nugent, commenting on this "error," argued that Beza's contradictory intentions—concord on the one hand and dogmatic assertiveness on the other—epitomized the "illogical" goal of Concordia as a strategy of unity to be achieved on theological issues, that is to say, without admitting toleration of pluralism.

The failure of Poissy was exemplified by the two "illogical" things Beza's inaugural speech wanted to keep together: a) *the denial* of any substantial difference and the declaration that some fundamentals of faith were necessary, wherein it is clear that differences existed precisely on those fundamentals whose interpretation was supposed to be shared by all; and b) *the assertion* that Calvinists and Catholics were different and there were actually few similarities between them. Given his incipit on the value and goal of Concordia, these two assertions were illogical. Rather than bowing to the ritualistic speech of concord and the rhetoric of dialogue, Beza would help the dialogue by acknowledging from the start, rather than concealing, the fact that their reasons for disagreement were substantive and pertained to fundamentals of faiths. Yet the ideal of Concordia was the source of the problem because its philosophy could not allow this move since it did not entertain the idea of an accord that was only instrumental and for sake of mere coexistence. For the colloquy to continue and produce some good results, *agreement* should have been the goal instead of *spiritual unity*, that is to say, *eirene* instead of *homonoia*.

The fact is that had Beza explicitly recognized the differences between Calvinists and Catholics he would have left no room for the kind of dialogue that Concordia prized and to restore which he was sent to Poissy. The paradox was that insincerity was at the same time the condition for a dialogue to persist and the obstacle of a meaningful dialogue. Beza could not openly admit that the age of Concordia was over and pluralism was a reality if the colloquy were to continue. Nevertheless, it was not credible that he or Calvin were truly ready to give up proselytism and accept cohabitation with their direct adversaries.[61] Hence the "illogical" incipit of Beza's introduction: he declared, on the one hand, that differences were secondary and, on the other, that they were fundamental.

That contradiction poisoned the colloquy because the interlocutors were de facto unable or unwilling to declare openly which fundamentals of faith they shared and which they did not. All of them praised Concordia but were unable to tell openly in what Concordia consisted. As soon as they tried to clarify this point they plunged into a panoply of contradictions that made their disagreements even worse than before the colloquy started. As Mario Turchetti noticed, the room for compromise was broader when Christians did not know each other's positions well.[62] Thus, contrary to Erasmus's hope, which was a theoretical inspiration for both Catholics and Calvinists, the fundamentals, rather than the nonfundamentals, of faith became the source of discord. The colloquy exemplified a phenomenon that social scientists have in recent years tested experimentally: the result of deliberation among groups whose members share definite beliefs tends to radicalize their respective loyalties rather than weaken them. "It is the persuasive content of arguments which causes polarization rather than comparisons between oneself and others."[63] The result of discussion is in this case primed to consolidate homogeneity within each group and sharpen divisions with others.[64]

The disagreement over the Eucharist became so intractable that a decision was made to have a few theologians debate it behind closed doors. Thus the original plan and ideal of a public colloquy, with a large audience made of laics and religious representatives of the nobility, the clergy and ordinary people, was renounced. It soon became clear that *publicity could not bear disagreements* because religious pluralism could not be publicly manifested and accepted (a frightening anticipation of the ensuing wars).[65] Moreover, it also became clear that the "experts" or theologians to whom Erasmus had acknowledged toleration, because of their devotion to reason, did not facilitate concord; their disputations and disquisitions actually strengthened divisions (the ethics of coherence strengthened their logical rigidity and promoted intolerance).[66] Finally, it became clear that dialogue would grow vacuously rhetorical, for the most part, because none of the participants was ready to compromise on his faith, confess his disagreement, or listen to what was epitomized as a heretical interpretation of fundamentals of faith. Given all this, not only was the Erasmian ideal of dialogue as a means for the continuation of dialogue abandoned. More fatally, the experience of dialogue actually blocked that ideal and convinced interlocutors that force was perhaps inevitable. The colloquy persuaded the Calvinists and Catholics that the human quality of speech and the virtues associated by humanists with eloquence were not the only means to solve radical disagreement. "Sixteenth century dialogue was just a shade short of war."[67]

WHAT SHOULD BE LEFT OUT?

The failure of Poissy proves what we have said previously: the humanists' adaptation of Cicero's Concordia to a revealed religion ruled by authorized interpreters and structured according to dogmas could not work. In ancient religion there was no distinction between doctrine/nondoctrine (fundamentals and nonfundamentals of faith) because religion was a system of rituals and cults that relied upon ceremonial habits. Pagan religion meant codification of certain practices rather than sincerity of the heart or adhesion to an authoritative declaration of doctrinal validity.[68] So in Cicero's work the distinction between fundamentals and nonfundamentals, as a distinction between those things that could be or could not be tolerated, had no sense because it would amount to a call for tolerating the wrong or an incorrect theory. To Cicero, thus, moderate skepticism and dialogue were for the sake of *achieving clarity of knowledge*: tolerance was not tolerance at all, but suspension of judgment until truth was gained, discovered, or achieved. The contradiction that characterized the ecumenical goal of Christian humanists was that in order to apply Cicero's maxims of eloquence to disputation among doctrines of faith they had to introduce a distinction that would make those maxims unusable: that between the domain in which reason (or dialogue) can operate and the domain of faith in which reason is hardly effective, because of course decisions on the fundamentals of faith could not be made in the name of reason alone and according to the rules of eloquence, although reason and the rules of eloquence were employed by theologians in order to make their case. Humanists applied the maxims of what today we would call reasonable deliberation (ancient eloquence) to an environment that was structurally dualistic and not wholly malleable by philosophical reason. As we have seen, for Christians Concordia was not to be confused with syncretism (Nicodemism was a vice to be avoided as much as religious pluralism).

In consequence, whereas the ancients could take into account the possibility of persuasion to solve those disagreements that civil laws or local traditions left unresolved, Christians had first to delimit the space within which dialogue was not admitted in order to start the dialogue. The paradox was that this preventive limitation could not be made through dialogue because it pertained to dogmas of faith that no rational argument could help explain, as Beza's failed attempt to define a sacrament showed. The preventive separation of what could or could not be discussed could only be made in a dogmatic manner, yet this precluded the possibility of not only finding an accord, but, much more radically, of pursuing it in the dialogue itself. The Colloquy of Poissy proved that a discursive approach to the Eucharist was out of place and could not be made.

As a matter of fact, the choice of having the Eucharist as a fundamental of faith had to be taken as a given in the sense that each Christian had to assume it with no disputation. Differences of opinion could not be allowed as a matter of principle (and not even suspension of judgment in the wait for an ensuing clarification), according to Cicero's notion of the limits of disagreement. In a word, a decision that could not be the result of an open deliberation was needed—it had to be made through an act of authority or through faith, but not through dialogical reasoning. The only possibility was a renunciation of talk and a stop on discussion, publicly or totally.[69]

Dialogue proved to be out of place because the views that caused disagreement could not be made the object of rational discussion (Hans Kelsen was to develop from this his theory that democracy cannot operate with dogmatic creeds).[70] Concordia turned out to be an untenable myth. Moreover, it was counterproductive because any attempt to convince the interlocutor was inevitably experienced as proselytism, a perception that was primed to unleash animosity and disagreement rather than help peace and accord. In sum, the colloquy compromised the very assumption of Concordia Cristiana—the idea that it was not necessary to take theological issues out of dialogue to continue the dialogue and live in peace. Finally, it proved that not all issues can become an object of dialogue and that not all dialogue is a vehicle for peace.[71]

MISTAKE OR DIVERSITY?

From Nugent's reconstruction of the Colloquy of Poissy it appears that by the time the council met, in late summer 1651, the Protestants had already evolved into a form of scholasticism, and their early enthusiasm for *Renovatio Christiana* had crystallized in separate bodies of dogmatic assumptions. Room for dialogue narrowed along with the passage of time, while timing is, as scholars have abundantly shown, a crucial factor in the success or failure of a process of reconciliation.[72] This seemed to disprove Christian humanists' belief that continuation of dialogue was even more important than achieving an agreement. Indeed, if achieving unity is the goal, time delay might not be a good strategy. It is true that in the trial of separation before the final divorce (as before religious divorce), a delay in the process of reconciliation might allow passions to calm down. Yet, in this case, delay is intended to help configure the prospect of accepting and managing divorce, not reconciliation.[73]

When the delegates met in Poissy, the conditions for divorce were there and hardly revisable. Variations in theological interpretation had already hardened into ideological loyalties defining friends and enemies, like irreducible partisanships in cold war–style parties. Language's malleability, which Cicero's rules of *sermo* presumed and Christian humanists prized as pivotal for solving disagreements, could work insofar as and only while beliefs were also malleable. Divisions, on the other hand, went together with antidialogical emotions like resentment and mistrust. But these emotions, which were present in Poissy, made words correspond to unchangeable beliefs, rather than malleable tools of mediation among transformable ideas.

It is reasonable to think that the passage of time and escalation of violence that had, meanwhile, started in many European countries between opposing Christian denominations were not secondary factors in the failure of the colloquy and Concordia more generally. The level of reciprocal prejudices that participants in Poissy showed was insurmountable, so that words compromised dialogue rather than helped it because they were not received with trust but rather as signs of manipulating intentions.[74] Rhetoric came to be seen as sophistry, not eloquence in Cicero's style, and words served to escalate divisions and disagreements instead of helping unity and agreement. (It might be interesting to mention that the decline of Concordia was accompanied by a deep reaction against eloquence and rhetoric, which were accused of helping discord and civil war—this opinion was equally shared by Thomas Hobbes and John Locke).[75] It is fair to say that dialogic concord presumes a concord of values that cannot create itself. Concordia must exist as a viable promise in order for dialogue to occur and for reconciliation to be perceived as a reasonable goal.

This brings me back to the question with which I started this chapter, on whether religious toleration and religious pluralism are feasible within the ideal framework or *koiné* of Concordia. If we recall the view of tolerance that the humanists praised we can say that, despite their assertion to the contrary, they (and in particular Erasmus) regarded toleration as instrumental to dialogue for achieving the unification of faiths, not syncretism as diluting of differences in a kind of natural or minimalist religion.[76] Indeed, in order for their differences to merge, both Catholics and Protestants should have necessarily gone through a process of transformation of their respective creeds: this was actually the goal that justified the continuation of dialogue. This means that a sincere dialogue for conviction would probably have risked making them change their minds and converging unanimously toward some fundamentals of faith that were not necessarily similar to their own. Dialogue within Concord was supposed to deradicalize disagreement and make differences look like variations within one religion, a solution that would translate into reconstituting a catholic perspective and overcoming both Protestant and Catholic creeds.

This ecumenical outcome would perhaps be in agreement with Cicero's goal of a philosophical dialogue and its injunction to suspend judgment when disagreement occurred in order to keep the door open to the possibility of changing one's mind (the Second Vatican Council relaunched the project of ecumenism on this pluralistic premise and significantly emended the sixteenth-century unitary view of concord). But none of the interlocutors who gathered in Poissy wanted to suspend their judgment on their reciprocal interpretations of the fundamentals of faith because none of them questioned the validity of their own creeds. Neither side wanted to become anything other than what they already were. They discussed in order to convince the other without being willing to be convinced by them. This means that their mental habit was radically inimical to reciprocity (on which dialogue needs to rest) and naturally disposed to proselytism. Thus, if dialogue had to continue, it would have to concern nonfundamentals of faith, as actually happened when radical conflict and the wars forced European peoples to practice toleration as an art of negotiating between their different beliefs and abandoning ambitions to overcome their differences.

Within the ideal scenario of a transformative function of dialogue, tolerance would actually be not tolerance of errors but more appropriately a time delay or the suspension of any decision in order to allow more time for persuasion. As we have seen, this would give more of a chance to dialogue in view of a superior stage in which consensus would no longer be questioned. Christian humanists were the representatives of this *transitory view of toleration*. They were the first scholars to face a schism within European Christianity and invoke toleration as a means of conjugating up differences within a substantial religious unity. Their distinction between fundamentals and nonfundamentals of faith defined the threshold of both pluralism and freedom of dissent. It revealed the failure of the goal of unity and the impossibility of applying the Ciceronian philosophy of dialogue in a domain in which specific doctrinal premises needed to be removed from dialogue because they could not be made an object of transformation. The outcome of Concordia would be either instrumental agreement for reason of stability (peace as agreement, rather than harmony) or war. In both cases the two conditions of Concordia would evanesce (as they did): harmony within a unified spiritual community and absence of religious pluralism.

The failure of the several colloquies and councils inspired by the humanist philosophy of Concordia, from that of Ratisbon (1541) to that of Poissy (1561), indicates that it was precisely the translation of Cicero's *Concordia Philosophia* into *Concordia Theologia* that failed, and *pour cause*. Its failure proves that dialogue and deliberative rationality cannot hold when they are applied to religious creeds (unless we do not take the latter to be as prerational manifestations of ideas that rational dialogue can allow to fully illuminate and revolve, as in Hegel's philosophy and, so it seems, Habermas's).[77] That failure proves, first, how improbable the goal was of the humanists who wanted to practice toleration while remaining within a single system of faith or truth (since they did not recognize other religions, save those emerging from within Christianity). Second, it proves that Concordia through frank dialogue cannot be conceived as unanimous conviction but has to make room for pluralism. To be successful and stable over time, toleration must presume and respect pluralism of both creeds and the interpretations of common religious texts on which creeds rely. It must presume, and respect, resistance against changing or refusal to change one's creeds.

Yet not to have a transformative dialogue of this kind does not mean not having any dialogue or not being able to reach a "negotiated" outcome or some reasonable convergence in respect to people's creeds or "fundamentals of faith."[78] As the historical development of the role of secular actors and institutions shows, the failure of the philosophy and practice of Concordia Christiana contributed to strengthening the practice of agreement on nonfundamentals of faith or externalities (*adiaphora*) such as laws and regulations on matters of rituals and social and economic relations among people of different creeds. As it were, Concordia moved from inward to outward; it ended with pertaining to strategies and methods that could make different people coexist within the same geopolitical space, without being requested to change their beliefs or treat them as "mistakes."

PLURALISM AND THE LIMITS OF DIALOGUE

The difference between variations internal to a faith and pluralism of faiths was brilliantly illustrated by Jean Bodin, perhaps the most acute theorist of religious pluralism in the age of Concordia, that is to say, prior to liberal toleration. In his *Colloquium heptaplomeres de rerum sublimium arcanis abditis* (Colloquium of the Seven about Secrets of the Sublime, written between 1593 and 1596, published in 1857), a basic treatise on religious concord-discord, Bodin wrote that without diversity of religions, or with only two dominant and rival religions, political society lacks a constraint that is effective enough to curb the instrumentalist use of public authority by factions of religious citizens and churches without the need for state repression.[79] Moreover, it misses the opportunity to make religions express their richness, an opportunity that only a pluralistic environment can provide. "Otherwise, if one opposite were joined to another opposite with no middle ground between, there would necessarily be continual battle."[80] In a word, civil law was the medium—the common grammar that all must accept—thanks to which religious pluralism and freedom of religion could exist.[81]

Much less worried about pluralism than Locke, Bodin included all positions in his claim for pluralism—Catholics, Calvinists, Muslims, Lutherans, Jews, proto-Deists, Skeptics (though not professed atheists)—and reached the conclusion that friendship among political subjects, as among friends, *can* exist if people share radically different ideas on important issues. He made this claim after having demonstrated that no religion is able to prove itself to be the true one. Bodin's argument for toleration was based not on indifference or Pyrrhonian skepticism but on opposition to conflict among believers in the name of the acceptance of doctrinal diversity with no attempt to convince. His position was not too different from Locke's in that both of them "based their opposition to religious intolerance on the assumption that *their* practices (whoever they be assuming belief in God) are probably no more mistaken than *ours*."[82] Yet Bodin's conclusion on pluralism seemed to be more generous than Locke's: not only would believers have no rational arguments for persuading each other on the truthfulness of their religion (since no religion could make epistemic claims that all would accept on rational grounds), but religion could not be "the subject for discursive argument."[83] The strategy was that of minimizing the doctrinal content of religion and in this way deflating the ethics of coherence and strengthening that of respect.[84] But, after almost four hundred pages of dialogue between representatives of those seven faiths, Bodin concluded with a confession of coexistence among decidedly different faiths:

> Coronaeus bade me to summon the boys to whom he offered the song: "Lo, how good and pleasing it is for brothers to live in unity, arranged not in common diatonics or chromatics, but in enharmonics with a certain, more divine modulation." All were most sweetly delighted with this song, and they withdrew, having embraced each other in mutual love. Henceforth, they nourished their piety in remarkable harmony and their integrity of life in common pursuits and intimacy. However, afterwards they held no other conversation about religions, although each one defended his own religion with the supreme sanctity of his life.[85]

Theological disputations left Bodin's interlocutors with the same religious beliefs as they had at the beginning of the dialogue. Moreover, it left them with the conviction that they should be free to practice their faith while also dropping any ambition to convince others or overcome their disagreements or merge differences on issues of religion. Toleration was, more than with Locke, a politics of difference, one in which religions not only could, but would coexist if they abandoned their respective presumption of truth; indeed, by coexisting they would have the chance to express their differences more completely than if they lived segregated and separated. Pluralism of religions worked as a checks-and-balance mechanism (concord-discord) that would help stability and peace. Bodin's outcome was an argument in favor of diversity and pluralism, while clearly separating civil law and religious law. Without acknowledging this dual source of behavior—the one inspiring piety and the other inspiring truth— it would have been hard to achieve both religious peace and liberty of religious beliefs. Bodin's restraint in welcoming religions' participation in public debate over their fundamentals was, of course, marked by the tragic experience of the massacre of the Huguenots and the wars of religion, which led him to conclude that monarchical sovereignty (the state) was the only secure form of Concordia and thereby civil, not religious.[86]

We do not need to embrace Bodin's doctrine of absolute monarchy to appreciate his insight that however prepared we are to cooperate in a "reconstructive work" of dialogue that is primed to free both religions and philosophies of their respective rigidity, we should not want public dialogue to make us overcome the dualism of faith and reason or their interpretations or finally religious pluralism—in other words, we should not want to fully pursue the "reconstructive work" that dialogue for reconciliation is to encourage if performed sincerely and thoroughly. A nonperfectionist regime of toleration does not demand that all citizens have an equal degree of virtue of toleration or that the attitude toward toleration is the same for all.[87] It does not, above all, demand that toleration be identified with religious concord on the fundamentals of faith because it considers toleration an invitation not to overcome differences but to respect them. In Bodin's rendering, toleration teaches us how to live with substantive differences and renounce transforming them into mere variations of tonality within a harmonious unity.

The analysis of the character and decline of the ideal of Concordia Christiana on the eve of the wars of religion shows us that toleration emerged as a peaceful acceptance of different faiths when government and church leaders as well as believers started considering it as a complex set of practices of peaceful coexistence situated between two extreme and persistent possibilities of either violent conflict or spiritual homogeneity. Seen from the perspective of this tension, toleration acquires the character of a practical habit of respect for each individual, the recognition that in each of us there is something inviolable and unreachable to respect, in which the interruption of dialogue on what we regard as a matter of fundamentals (of faith) may be indispensable. To paraphrase Bodin, the moral of respect rests on the recognition of difference with no attempt to persuade.

The seven protagonists of his dialogue resolved to have peaceful conversation after each of them abandoned all attempts to advance their points of view as prerogatives of true religion. Conversation among believers of different religions could thus continue because and insofar as it was, so to speak, a purposeless or, more correctly, not driven by the goal of solving dissent and embracing consensus. Exchanging disagreement for difference, error for pluralism, was a remarkable transformation that brought Concordia Christiana to an end and opened the door to a perspective that was more audacious than Locke's principle of privatization of creeds because it was more consistently pluralist, since faiths were not simply allowed to exist but invited to interact and respect each other. Bodin dissociated benevolence from the goal of persuasion, linking it to an acceptance of diversity and made it a civic virtue. The motor of dialogue was not the emendation of errors, because consent could not be the goal of a discourse that had no truth as its object. The motor was, instead, the recognition that social harmony requires the ability to make dissonances coexist: thanks to their coexistence, the intermediary tones that make polyphony possible and agreeable can be found. Bodin was not the only one who thought that a state with two religions was not more secure for peace than a state having one religion. Moreover, he thought that the more numerous religions in a society the more each of them could give the better of itself without jeopardizing civil peace because it was too weak to cultivate the ambition of achieving total power.

Besides reasons of prudence and stability, a sincere and irreducible plurality was to Bodin the condition for a cultural environment that respected the particularity of each believer because it was better disposed to facilitate median and mediating positions. The interlocutors of his dialogue, while unable and unwilling to achieve a comprehensive consensus on their fundamentals of faith, were, however, able and willing to find local consent on specific issues under discussion. Within each religion, Bodin believed, there was at least one principle that could be bridged with at least one principle of another, so that all faiths could, at the end, contribute to making a network of relations. Interreligious relations looked like a constellation of partial overlapping. If the Ciceronian idea of a *natura communis* was to be consistently pursued, then a consensus achieved by overcoming pluralism would not be the goal. Instead, the coexistence of differences through the creation of chains of relations that did not command either absolute communication (dialogue until the resolution of disagreement), monadic isolation, or the refusal of any form of dialogue would be strived for.

NOTES

I would like to thank the participants of the seminar on toleration at Columbia University with whom I discussed prior versions of this chapter. Moreover, I would like to express my profound debt of gratitude to Carlo Invernizzi Accetti and Luke MacInnis, whose critical observations have been important in the completion of this chapter.

1. Supports of the motion to have explicit reference to God in the Treaty of Lisbon (2007) were particularly strong in Ireland, which rejected the treaty in 2008 along with France and Holland (a second Irish referendum in October 2009 allowed ratification).
2. "I underlined my opinion that we need a European identity in the form of a constitutional treaty and I think it should be connected to Christianity and God, as Christianity has forged Europe in a decisive way"; Chancellor Merkel's words cited in euobserver.com, August 29, 2006.
3. This transformation seems to correspond to what Charles Taylor has defined as "secularity" or the passage from a secularist ideology to a secular age in *A Secular Age* (Cambridge: Belknap, 2007); see in particular the introduction.
4. Jürgen Habermas, "Religion in the Public Sphere: Cognitive Presuppositions for the 'Public Use of Reason' by Religious and Secular Citizens," in *Between Naturalism and Religion,* trans. Ciaran Cronin (London: Polity, 2008), pp. 136–38.

5. In the course of the debate, delegates and politicians from Germany, Italy, Poland, and Slovakia lobbied for a phrase in the treaty, adapted from the Polish constitution, which would argue that "the Union's values include the values of those who believe in God as the source of truth, justice, good and beauty as well as those who do not share such a belief but respect these universal values arising from other sources." On December 17, 2007, the preamble of the treaty was amended as follows: "Drawing inspiration from the cultural, religious and humanist inheritance of Europe, from which have developed the universal values of the inviolable and inalienable rights of the human person, freedom, democracy, equality and the rule of law."
6. Joseph Lecler, *Histoire de la tolérance au siècle de la Réforme*, 2 vols. (Aubier: Montaigne, 1955), 2:40. Yet this view persisted beyond humanism; see, for instance, Charles Louis de Secondat, Baron de Montesquieu, *The Spirit of the Laws* (1748), trans. Anne M. Choler, Basia Carolyn Miller, and Harold Samuel Stone (New York: Cambridge University Press, 1989), bk. 25, chs. 9 and 10.
7. Cf. Joseph Lecler, "Les origins et le sens de la formule: *Cujus Regio, Ejus Religio*," in *Recherches de Science religieuse* 38 (1951): 119–31, and *Histoire de la tolérance,* 2:36–43.
8. It is interesting to notice that Habermas criticizes John Rawls for being too close to classical liberalism precisely because he is too faithful to the dualism implied in classical liberalism. Habermas, "Religion in the Public Sphere," pp. 119–28. "With the establishment of modern liberal states . . . the state is expected to be neutral rather than restrained in its treatment of conflicts of value or religions. . . . Equality before the law and respect for the rights of individuals and minority groups tend to make toleration politically redundant." David Heyd, "Is Toleration a Political Virtue?" in Melissa S. Williams and Jeremy Waldron, eds., *Nomos XLVIII: Toleration and Its Limits* (New York: New York University Press, 2008), p. 175.
9. Mario Turchetti, *Concordia o Tolleranza? François Bauduin (1520–1573) e i "Moyenneurs"* (Milan: Franco Angeli 1984), pp. 102–8.
10. Donald Nugent, *Ecumenism in the Age of the Reformation: The Colloquy of Poissy*, (Cambridge: Harvard University Press, 1974), p. 8.
11. This position was shaped by Catholics and Protestants alike; on models of empire that were based on religious pluralism, see Joseph Lecler, "Liberté de Conscience: Origins et sens divers de l'expression," *Recherches de Science religieuse* 54 (1966): 394; and Turchetti, *Concordia o Tolleranza?* pp. 418–25.
12. Michel de L'Hospital, "Discours pronouncé à l'ouverture de la session des Etats-généraux assemblés à Orléans, le 13 décembre 1560," in *Discours Politiques 1560–1568* (Paris: Paleo, 2001), p. 40. In his *Le but de la guerre et de la paix* (1570), L'Hospital strongly defended the Catholic view of Concordia along with, however, an orderly and peaceful government (pp. 143–69). The novelty of his position consisted in that, contrary to other concordataires, he proposed to pursue not the former at the expense of the latter, but rather the latter first; cf. Lecler, *Histoire de la tolérance,* 2:45–46.
13. Cited in Lecler, *Histoire de la tolérance*, 2:41–42. A few months later, the anonymous author of a very important pamphlet, *Exhortation aux Princes . . . pour obvier aux seditions qui sem-*

blent nous menace pour le fait de la religion (1561), was even more explicit: "il n'y a point de moyen plus prompt et plus expdéditif que *de permettre en votre république deux Eglises*: l'une des Romains et l'autre des Protestants" (p. 44).

14. In antiquity "*tolerantia* stood for the bearing of anything which was a burden" to the human body and the mind. In early Christianity that meaning was given a religious connotation and was associated with "*patientia*" (as in St. Paul's Letter to the Corinthians). In the Middle Ages *tolerantia* was also a social and political concept that denoted "forbearance of bad people" or bad habits by some people. It pertained to the practice of "a powerful collectivity that could destroy the tolerated people." Thus *tolerantia* came to mean "self-restraint of political power" or abstinence from the use of destructive force. The two main collections in which the practices of *tolerantia* were made into precepts of prudent behavior were the *Decretum Gratiani* (circa 1140) and the *Decretals* of Gregory IX (1234), the former a private compilation of authoritative texts and the Bible, and the latter an official text of the Church; István Bejczy, "*Tolerantia*: A Medieval Concept," *Journal of the History of Ideas* 58 (1997): 367; see also Georges Chantraine, "La doctrine catholique de la tolérance au xvi siècle," in Université de Montpellier III (Paul Valery), *Naissance et affirmation de l'idée de tolérance, XVI et XVIII siècle. Bicentenaire de l'Edit des non catholiques (Novembre 1787), Actes du Vème Colloque Jean Boisset,* ed. Michel Peronnet (Montpellier: Editas, 1988), pp. 1–18.
15. Lecler, *Histoire de la Tolérance,* p. 43.
16. Nugent, *Ecumenism in the Age of Reformation,* p. 11. Free speech among the "experts" because they were guardians of the truth was invoked by Erasmus: Manfred Hoffmann, "Language and Reconciliation: Erasmus' Ecumenical Attitude," in *Erasmus of Rotterdam Society Yearbook Fifteenth* (1995): 78–79.
17. Differences between humanists' toleration and both liberal toleration and enlightenment toleration can be detected for instance in the works of John Locke and Pierre Bayle, the former a theorist of toleration as a right-based argument of religious liberty, and the latter a skeptical defender of religious toleration on the ground of freedom of conscience; cf. Gary Remer, *Humanism and the Rhetoric of Toleration* (University Park: Pennsylvania State University Press, 1996), in particular the introduction; and Pierre Forst, "Pierre Bayle's Reflexive Theory of Toleration," in *Nomos XLVIII*, pp. 78–113.
18. Mario Turchetti, "Religious Concord and Political Tolerance in Sixteenth and Seventeenth-Century France," in *Sixteenth-Century Journal* 22 (1991): 18–19; Anna Elisabetta Galeotti, *Toleration as Recognition* (Cambridge: Cambridge University Press, 2002), pp. 1–3.
19. The Third Lateran Council (1179) intended to restore ecclesiastic discipline and in view of this goal stated both a new method for the election of the pope (the "two-thirds majority" instead of either unanimity or simple majority) and the excommunication of heretics (Canon 27); see the translated canons in Rev. H. J. Schroeder, O.P., *Disciplinary Decrees of the General Councils: Texts, Translations, and Commentary* (St. Louis, MO: Herder, 1937), pp. 214–35.
20. Hence, for instance, the edict against the heretics by the Emperor Charles V in 1535 gave local magistrates a certain "discretion" in adapting the norm to the "heresies committed by the bourgeoises" (or nonreligious subjects). This pragmatic behavior made possible that

a heretic like François Bauduin enjoyed a relative freedom in the early ten years of his theological activity (1535–45) in France and the Low Countries; see Turchetti, *Concordia o Tolleranza?* pp. 49–56.

21. Cfr. Delio Cantimori, "Nicodemismo e speranze conciliari nel Cinquencento italiano," in *Quaderni di Belfagor* 1 (1848): 12–23; Carlo Ginzburg, *Il nicodemismo. Simulazione e dissimulazione religiosa nell'Europa del '500* (Turin: Einaudi, 1970); Eugéne Droz, *Chemins de l'hérésie: Textes et documents*, 4 vols. (Geneva: Slatkine, 1970–1976), 1:131–271; and Carlos M. Eire, "Calvin and Nicodemisme: A Reappraisal," in *Sixteenth-Century Journal* 10 (1979): 45–69.
22. "Dialogues of mutual edification," as Newman wrote, entailed "talking with men of other faith, by being prepared to learn from them." Jay Newman, *Foundations of Religious Tolerance* (Toronto: Toronto University Press, 1982), p. 107. These kinds of dialogues existed when interlocutors abandoned the goal of achieving one religious truth by intellectual means ("dialogues of demonstration"), but this was not how theologians, Catholic and Protestants, practiced dialogue in the councils of the sixteenth century, as we will explain. For a "dialogue of mutual edification" to exist, plurality of faiths must be assumed by the interlocutors; this was the important contribution of Jean Bodin, who, as we shall see at the end, concluded for this reason the age of Concordia Christiana and its practice of "dialogues of demonstration." For the different interpretations of dialogue in the humanist age of Concordia, see Cary J. Nederman, *Worlds of Difference: European Discourses of Toleration, c. 1100–c. 1550* (University Park: Pennsylvania State University Press, 2000), ch. 1.
23. Ginzburg, *Il nicodemismo*, pp. 119–50; but see also pp. 14–15 where Ginzburg analyzes the negative reaction of Erasmus against early proponents of simulation (who were Protestants).
24. Scholars of early humanism have linked early church conciliarism with republican ideals in Florence and interpreted the transition from conciliarim to Concordia catholica as the parallel of that from the republicanism of libertas and the republicanism of the common good. "Just as the *via concilii* gave way to the *concordantia catholica*, and republican *libertas* to *il bene commune*, so, in the Florentine church, did corporatism yield to hierarchy." Gerald Christianson, "Cusanus, Cesarini and the Crisis of Conciliarism," in Inigo Bocken, ed., *Conflict and Reconciliation: Perspectives on Nicholas of Cusa* (Boston: Brill, 2004), p. 94.
25. Nugent, *Ecumenism in the Age of the Reformation*, p. 4; for an analysis of the main ideas of the Middle Age and early humanist philosophers on Concordia and peace, see the rich study of Nederman, *Worlds of Difference.*
26. Nicholas of Cusa, "On the Peace of Faith," in *On Religious Harmony, Text, Concordance and Translation of De Pace Fidei,* ed. James E. Biechler and H. Lawrence Bond (Lewiston: Edwin Mellen, 1990), 4:11.
27. Anton G. Weiler, "Nicholas of Cusa on Harmony, Concordance, Consensus and Acceptance as Categories of Reform in the Church, in *De concordantia catholica*," in Bocken, *Conflict and Reconciliation.*
28. *Adiaphora* were "externals" in relation to what the Mosaic Law commanded; they were indifferent in relation to the New Law (or Christ's revelations) and pertained to the practical or ethical life, as, for example, marriage or property or even rituals. Bernard J. Verkamp, *The*

Indifferent Mean: Adiaphorism in the English Reformation to 1554 (Athens: Ohio University Press and Detroit: Wayne State University Press, 1977), pp. 20–25.

29. Joseph Hopkins, "The Role of *Pia Interpretatio* in Nicholas of Cusa's Hermeneutical Approach of the Koran," in Gregorio Piaia, ed., *Concordia discors: Studi su Niccolò Cusano e l'umanesimo europeo offerti a Giovanni Santinello* (Padova: Antenore, 1993), p. 272. All monotheistic religions, Cusa implied, converged in the desire of spiritual nourishment, or "the food of intellectual life," even when, as in the case of the Qur'an, they promised "a Paradise where there are rivers of wine and honey." Cusa proposed to thus go beyond a literary interpretation of the holy texts (all of them) and read words "figuratively": the attainment of immortality was the supreme good on which all believers would concord; Cusa, *On Religious Harmony*, 50–53 (pp. 47–50).
30. Erasmus to Jean de Carondelet, January 5, 1523, in *Collected Works of Erasmus* (Toronto: University of Toronto Press, 1974), 9:252, 232–34. The Catholic Erasmus was criticized by the Catholics because of the latitude of his adiaphorism; cf. Erika Rummel, *Erasmus and His Catholic Critics*, 2 vols. (Nieuwkoop: De Graaf, 1989), in particular 2:40–41. On the other hand, Erasmus's position was judged weak by the Reformers because of its ecumenical vocation in an age in which religion was hardly separable from politics; cf. Johan Huizinga, *Erasmus* (New York: Scribner's, 1954), pp. 239–43 (who describes Erasmus as "centrist"). On the contrast between Erasmus's conception of peace and the theologians of his time, Protestant and Catholic, see Ross Dealy, "The Dynamics of Erasmus' Thought on War, " in *Erasmus of Rotterdam Society Yearbook Four* (1984): 53–67.
31. Desiderius Ersamus, "The Complaint of Peace" (1517), in *The Praise of Folly and Other Writings*, ed. Robert M. Adams (New York: Norton, 1989), pp. 90–91.
32. Searching for the "sources" of the "principles of fellowship and society," Cicero found them in what connected "all the members of the human race," namely, "reason and speech, which by the processes of teaching and learning, of communicating, discussing, and reasoning associate men together and unite them in a sort of natural fraternity." Cicero, *De Officiis*, trans. Walter Miller (Cambridge: Harvard University Press, 1990), pp. 53–55.
33. The ideal of concord materialized in architecture in order to remember past revolutions or celebrate recovered harmony; in ancient Athens *homonoia* was made into a statue for public veneration; in Rome the temple of Concord stood central in the forum and was the most venerated; finally, in Paris, Place de la Concorde was named after the Revolution.
34. Cicero, *The Republic*, trans. Clinton Walker Keyes (Cambridge: Harvard University Press, 2006), pp. 74–75.
35. Cicero, *De Officiis*, pp. 253–55.
36. "For just as in the music of harps and flutes or in the voices of singers a certain harmony of the different tones must be preserved, the interruption or violation of which is intolerable to trained ears, and as this perfect agreement and harmony is produced by the proportionate blending of unlike tones, so also is a State made harmonious by agreement among dissimilar elements, brought about by a fair and reasonable blending together of the upper, middle, and lower classes, just as if they were musical tones." Cicero, *The Republic*, pp. 181–83.

37. Cicero, *De Officiis*, p. 193.
38. Erasmus, "The Complaint of Peace," p. 104–5.
39. Bejczy, "*Tolerantia*," p. 376.
40. Cicero, *Tusculan Disputations*, trans. J. E. King (Cambridge: Harvard University Press, 1945), p. 335.
41. Cf. Remer, *Humanism and the Rhetoric of Toleration*, pp. 16–26.
42. Cicero, *De natura deorum*, ed. Arthur Stanley Pease (Cambridge: Harvard University Press, 1955–1958), I.1.
43. Cicero, *De Officiis*, p. 135.
44. For an excellent analysis of the difference between persuasion and conviction in classical and modern rhetoric, see Chaim Perelman and L. Olbrechts-Tyteca, *The New Rhetoric: A Treatise on Argumentation,* trans. John Wilkinson and Purcell Weaver (Notre Dame: University of Notre Dame Press, 1971), in particular part 1.
45. Cf. the excellent study of Remer, *Humanism and the Rhetoric of Toleration.*
46. Jean-Claude Margolin, "Sur un paradoxe bien tempéré de la Renaissance: Concordia discors," in Piaia, *Concordia discors*, p. 428.
47. Ibid., pp. 421–32.
48. Norberto Bobbio, "Veritá e libertá" (1960), in *Elogio della mitezza e altri scritti morali* (Milan: Linea d'Ombra, 1994), p. 61.
49. Cfr. Remer, *Humanism and the Rhetoric of Toleration*; Nederman, *Worlds of Difference.*
50. Remer, *Humanism and the Rhetoric of Toleration,* p. 41.
51. Cicero, *Tusculan Disputations,* p. 37.
52. Nederman, *Worlds of Difference,* p. 3.
53. Hence Pierre Bayle transferred the condition for an encounter among people of different creeds from theology to morals and human reasonability, which he regarded as connatural to human nature; this was the main topic of his work, *Philosophical Commentary on These Words of the Gospel, Luke XIV.23 'Compel them to come in, that my House may be full,'* 2 vols. (London: Darby, 1708), now in a new edition edited by John Kilcullen and Chandran Kukathas (Indianapolis: Liberty Fund, 2005).
54. Unsigned review of Nugent's doctoral dissertation in *Church History* 35 (1966): 354.
55. In 1651 two distinctive assemblies were convoked to solve the problem of toleration of an extra religion: the assembly of the clergy in Poissy, to overcome theological controversies, and the assembly of the laiques in Pontoise (the nobility and the third estate), to discuss the financial crisis, thus fiscal and political issues. In theory the goal was that of preparing the French delegation for the ecumenical council that, it was announced, would meet in Trento. But the political party, namely, Catherina with the support of L'Hospital, dreamed of transforming it into a colloquy of religious reconciliation in France. Catherina thus invited a prominent delegation of non-Catholics, that is to say, Huguenots' representatives, by sending an invitation to England (Peter Martyr Vermigli, the first Regius Professor at Oxford and an enormously respected spiritual leader and theologian of Reformed Christianity), Geneva (Théodore de Bèze or Theodore Beza, second in leadership only to Calvin), and the Palatinate (Francis Naudouin and George Cassander). In his prefatory remarks,

L'Hospital used the language of Concordia and compared the tasks of the conveners to that of a doctor who "tries all means in order to cure the sick person." Lecler, *Histoire de la tolérance,* 2:49. The National Synod was open to public attendance of both the religious and laymen, and among the public was the philosopher Peter Ramus. Nugent, *Ecumenism in the Age of Reformation,* p. 94.

56. Nugent, *Ecumenism in the Age of Reformation,* p. 95.
57. Ibid., p. 97.
58. The idea of "transubstantiation" received ecclesiastical sanction in Canon 1 of the Fourth Lateran Council (1215). Scholars surmise that the idea of Christ's flesh and blood materializing in communion may be traceable in the twelfth century and was used for the first time by Hildebert of Tour and later on by the future pope, Alexander III. Canonization occurred at the same council in which excommunication of heresies was launched, and particularly of the Albigenses, the Cathari, and the Waldensians, who rejected the Trinity and claimed the dual nature of Good (Father and Son). Schroeder, *Disciplinary Decrees of the General Councils,* pp. 236–44.
59. Nugent, *Ecumenism in the Age of Reformation,* p. 99.
60. Beza did not seem to realize that at the same time that he was making claims for toleration (before the colloquy met, he had negotiated with the French monarch the toleration of his cult so as, de facto, to legalize pluralism) his appeal to concord was untenable: Turchetti, *Concordia o Tolleranza?* p. 409.
61. Turchetti, *Concordia o Tolleranza?* pp. 410–11.
62. In the early stage of the Reformation, when believers did not have a clear knowledge of their differences, the behavior of "religiously motivated simulation" was practiced: dissenters participated in the Catholic rituals in order not to be exposed to persecution because they thought that the core of their faith would not be compromised by an external practice; cf. Ginzburg, *Il nicodemismo*, pp. 119–20. Applying the distinction between exteriority and interiority, positions of moderation and tolerance proliferated; they paved the way to the distinction between civil and sacred, as one can see with François Bauduin: "We have to prudently and religiously discern between divine and human law, spiritual and civil, sacrosanct and profane; because their functions and goals are distinct." Turchetti, *Concordia o Tolleranza?* p. 54.
63. Rupert Brown, *Group Process* (Oxford: Blackwell, 2000), p. 204.
64. See the report of the cases of failure of deliberating groups in Cass R. Sunstein, *Infotopia: How Many Minds Produces Knowledge* (Oxford: Oxford University Press, 2006), ch. 2. But the phenomenon of the radicalization of differences per effect of the vicinity of two opposite creeds was already detected by Pierre Bayle, *A Philosophical Commentary* (New York: Peter Lang, 1987), p. 484.
65. On the absence of an audience as a determining factor in the pursuit of dialogue when a bargaining condition is difficult, see Jon Elster, "Deliberation and Constitution Making," in Jon Elster, ed., *Deliberative Democracy* (Cambridge: Cambridge University Press, 1998), pp. 109–10.

66. In later councils the role of theologians declined while legal experts and bishops acquired more power; at that point, however, the meetings discussed nonfundamentals of faiths or practical problems of coexistence. Nelson H. Minnich, *Councils of the Catholic Reformation: Pisa I (1409) to Trent (1545–63)* (Burlington: Ashgate Variorum, 2008), pp. 435–40.
67. Nugent, *Ecumenism in the Age of Reformation,* p. 145.
68. Peter Garnesy, "Religious Toleration in Classical Antiquity," in W. J. Shiels, ed., *Persecution and Toleration* (Oxford: Blackwell, 1984), pp. 8–9; and J. A. North, "Religious Toleration in Republican Rome," *Proceedings of the Cambridge Society* 25 (1979): 86; Remer, *Humanism and the Rhetoric of Toleration,* p. 41.
69. In the course of the colloquy it was decided to have meetings with a select few behind closed doors in order to discourage the possibility of conflicts and altercations between opposing factions.
70. Hans Kelsen, "Absolutism and Relativism in Philosophy and Politics," in *American Political Science Review* 42 (1948): 906–14.
71. The outcome of the disagreement on fundamentals had the consequence of stiffening positions; it transformed into dogmas that which could not be objects of speculation because they could not be objects of disagreement: "Because Luther considered transubstantiation an inadmissible speculation, the Council [of Trento] declared it an article of faith." Remer, *Humanism and the Rhetoric of Toleration,* p. 106.
72. Nugent, *Ecumenism in the Age of Reformation,* pp. 220–21; Lecler, *Histoire de la tolérance,* 2:57. Jon Elster's analysis of argumentation in contexts of reconciliation may be of some help: "Strategic Use of Argument," in Kenneth Arrow, ed., *Barriers to the Negotiated Resolution of Conflict* (New York: Norton, 1995), pp. 236–57.
73. Jon Elster, *Ulysses Unbound* (Cambridge: Cambridge University Press, 2000), p. 13.
74. Nugent, *Ecumenism in the Age of Reformation,* p. 93.
75. Quentin Skinner, "Moral Ambiguity and the Renaissance Art of Eloquence," in *Visions of Politics,* 3 vols. (Cambridge: Cambridge University Press, 2002), 2:264–85.
76. This can be also said of John Stuart Mill's notion of pluralism, which is somehow part of the ideal of Concordia's reconciliation under one truth, although it refers of course to philosophical truth, not religious truth. Carey J. Nederman, "Toleration, Skepticism, and the 'Clash of Ideas,'" in John Christian Laursen and Carey J. Nederman, eds., *Beyond the Persecuting Society* (Philadelphia: University of Pennsylvania Press, 1998), pp. 66–67.
77. Habermas, "Religion in the Public Sphere," pp. 14–43.
78. I thank Akeel Bilgrami for suggesting that I think of negotiation as a viable outcome whose attainment does not require a dialogical disposition as with the humanist ideal of Concordia.
79. "CURTIUS: Nothing is more destructive in a state than for citizens to be split into two factions, whether the conflict is about laws, honors, or religion. If, however, there are many factions, there is no danger of civil war, since the groups, each acting as a check on the other, protect the stability and harmony of the state." Jean Bodin, *Colloquium of the Seven About Secrets of the Sublime* (1588), ed. and trans. Marion Leather Kuntz (University Park: Pennsylvania State University Press,), p. 151 (IV, 117). For an excellent analysis of Bodin's

theory of religious pluralism as condition for negotiation, see Andrea Suggi, *Sovranitá e Armonia. La tolleranza religiosa nel 'Colloquium Heptaplomeres' di Jean Bodin* (Rome: Storia e Letteratura, 2005), in particular ch. 5.

80. Bodin, *Colloquium of the Seven,* p. 148 (IV, 116).
81. In effect, an important and unsolved question within the tradition of Concordia was precisely which of the two powers, the spiritual and the temporal, should be held responsible for preserving Concordia. In Erasmus's Republica Christiana, Christ was the center of gravitation or the actor of Concordia; while in Bauduin it was instead the prince or the secular authority; cf. Turchetti, *Concordia o Tolleranza?* pp. 114–18.
82. Preston King, *Toleration* (London: Allen and Unwin, 1976), p. 87.
83. Quentin Skinner, *The Foundations of Modern Political Thought,* vol. 2 (Cambridge: Cambridge University Press, 1978), p. 249.
84. The association of "strongly held beliefs" with intolerance and, vice versa, of a more skeptical outlook with toleration is widely echoed in contemporary analysis: Skinner, *The Foundations of Modern Political Thought,* 2:244–54; King, *Toleration,* pp. 122–31; for a critical reading that stresses instead the "treacherous" and relativist implication of skepticism, see Richard Tuck, "Scepticism and Toleration in the Seventieth Century," in *Justifying Toleration: Conceptual and Historical Perspectives* (Cambridge: Cambridge University Press, 2009), pp. 21–35; for a challenge of the "modernist" assumption that links toleration to skepticism, see Nederman, "Toleration, Skepticism, and the 'Clash of Ideas.'"
85. Bodin, *Colloquium of the Seven,* p. 471 (VI, 471). An illuminating interpretation of Bodin's strategy of toleration within pluralism has been achieved by Antonio Gramsci, *Quaderni dal carcere,* ed. Valentino Gerratana (Turin: Einaudi, 1975), pp. 1573–74.
86. Kuntz used Bodin's case to prove that toleration developed from within Concordia; see Marion D. Kuntz, "The Concept of Toleration in the Colloquium Heptaplomeres of Jean Bodin," in Laursen and Nederman, *Beyond the Persecuting Society*; yet the kind of Concordia Bodin seemed to achieve at the end of his dialogue was that of civil law rather than spiritual or religious culture.
87. Michael Walzer, *On Toleration* (New Haven: Yale University Press, 1997), pp. 8–13. The recognition of toleration by the Catholic Church was fully achieved with the Second Vatican Council, and, in particular, the document *Dignitatis Humanae,* in which toleration was directly associated with religious freedom and freedom of conscience, the implied assumption being that "genuine religious toleration is achieved when people hold their religion as so important, so absolute, that to part from it is to die." George Carey, "Tolerating Religion," in Susan Mendus, ed., *The Politics of Toleration in Modern Life* (Durham: Duke University Press, 2000), p. 52. Wherein it must be implied that the limits of dialogue define the respect of difference and, consequentially, the renunciation by any religion to persuade or proselytize.

2

BEFORE AND BEYOND CLASSICAL APPROACHES TO TOLERATION

BEYOND TOLERATION

Civility and Principled Coexistence in Asokan Edicts

RAJEEV BHARGAVA

SECULAR NATIONALISM DEVELOPED in India with its own myths and legends. In his self-transformative, nationalist classic, *The Discovery of India,* Jawaharlal Nehru quotes H. G. Wells: "Amidst the tens of thousands of names of monarchs that crowd the columns of history . . . the name of Asoka shines, and shines almost alone, a star. . . . More living men cherish his memory today than have ever heard of Constantine or Charlemagne."[1] In another work, *Glimpses of World History,* Nehru writes,

> Men of religion have seldom, very seldom, been as tolerant as Ashoka. In order to convert people to their own faith they have seldom scrupled to use force and terrorism and fraud. The whole of history is full of religious persecution and religious wars, and in the name of religion and of Gods perhaps more blood has been shed than in any other name. It is good therefore to remember how a great son of India, intensely religious, and the head of a powerful empire, behaved in order to convert people to his ways of thought. It is strange that any one should be so foolish as to think that religion and faith can be thrust down a person's throat at the point of the sword or a bayonet.[2]

In the mythology of secular nationalism, Asoka is the tolerant king par excellence. It was only a matter of time before a step was taken within the nationalist narrative to move from tolerance to secularism. It was claimed that Ancient India, particularly in Asoka's time (304–232 B.C.E.) and because of his initiative, formulated a conception of the proto-secular state in India.[3] Asoka's tolerance toward all religions was the forerunner of the policy of religious neutrality associated with secularism. The clear implication of this was that this new attempt would not have been possible without something akin to a secular state in the Indian tradition.

This view has been vigorously challenged in India, particularly for its inexcusable anachronism—it reads too much of the present into the past. Obviously at issue here is not the term *secular.* The anachronism is not due to the extrapolation of a currently used term to an entity in the past. The absence of a suitable translation of *secular* in any Indian language is only a small piece of evidence in the overall argument, not its conclusion. Even the absence of a clear concept points only to the low level of articulacy of secular orientation, not to the lack of it. The crux of the matter is the availability of a conceptual resource. But let me not confuse the reader by introducing the distinction between a concept and a conceptual resource. Assume that some scholars have claimed that a full-fledged attempt, regardless of its success then or in the future, was made by Asoka to formulate a conception of what we now call the secular state. A few years ago I would have ridiculed this claim on the ground that ideas presuppose specific contexts and these contexts are not reproduced from time to time. However, today I am only cautiously critical because I see that these scholars were trying to put their finger on something important, even though they were making obvious mistakes in doing so.

In order to rescue the claim, we need to formulate it differently: at crucial junctures in Indian history, certain conceptual spaces were opened up that, under certain conditions, and provided we build an appropriate narrative, can be seen to contribute to the growth of modern secularism. I have used the phrase *conceptual spaces* in the plural. I mean here that some spaces open up simultaneously or over time, which enable multiple historical agents to imagine new concepts, provided they have the motivation to do so. A conceptual space may open up and may remain wholly unutilized for long periods of time, sometimes so long that it may entirely recede out of our background, totally forgotten. Or else, it may get filled up by concepts, though these concepts may be in different stages of articulacy, some clearly formed, others only half done, still others barely born. Some concepts in the space may have a very short life—they get made, are used and destroyed; others have a much longer period of gestation. Most are revived, modified, recast, recycled, reappropriated. Some are even mutated. The important thing is they are available in the conceptual stock as a resource, for use, dissemination, and, under certain conditions, for mobilization.

A reasonably articulated and complex concept draws elements from multiple conceptual spaces, provided there are agents with the motivation to do so. This usually happens over long periods of time. This conceptual work is never fully finished, and frequently the elements are never fully related to one another. So one may find different concepts generated over different periods of time that retrospectively belong to one family or strongly resemble one another. Seen teleologically, some older conceptual elements may even be seen as evolving into something that is now well formed. At key moments in the history of a society, all these elements drawn from different periods of history, and therefore from different conceptual spaces, may be forged together to form a broad conception. Such a conception may even crystallize around a single word. Often the same word is used as the foci of the crystallization of many related conceptions. One can trace their different trajectories and offer a narrative of the different sources of a concept and a term associated with it (or many concepts and a term or one concept with many terms associated with it).

Now, I wish to argue that one such space was opened up in the third century B.C.E. by Asokan edicts and filled by the conception of Dhamma, and this partly explains its crucial importance to modern India's secular project. But Asoka's Dhamma can be easily misunderstood. Official Indian ideology, encouraged by modern scholarly commentators, have frequently associated it with the idea of toleration. This is misleading, particularly if we don't grasp the background context in which *Dhamma* emerges. Dhamma, I argue, was a major attempt to introduce norms of civility among rival followers of major systems of beliefs and practices, to forge an order where potentially conflicting religious and philosophical groups could enjoy principled coexistence.

TWO EDICTS ON INTERGROUP RELATIONS

Asoka's edicts, rediscovered between the late eighteenth century and the mid-twentieth century, lie scattered in more than thirty places throughout India, Nepal, Bangladesh, Pakistan, and Afghanistan. Most of them are written in Brahmi script, from which all Indian scripts and many of those used in Southeast Asia later developed. The language used in the edicts found in the eastern part of the subcontinent is Prakrit, associated with the people of Magadh; the one used in edicts found in the western part of India is closer to Sanskrit, using the Kharoshthi script; one extract of edict 13 is in Greek and one bilingual edict in Kandahar, Afghanistan is written in Greek and Aramaic. Asoka's edicts, the earliest decipherable corpus of written documents from India, have survived throughout the centuries because they are written on rocks, cave walls, and stone pillars. These edicts were decodified by British archaeologist and historian, James Prinsep.

The location of the rock edicts, often governed by the availability of suitable rocks, are found along the borders of the empire; the edicts on pillars were largely in specific cities and along roads within the empire. Some, like the Lumbini pillar, mark the Buddha's birthplace, while its inscriptions commemorate Asoka's pilgrimage to that place. Others are to be found wherever there was sufficient concentration of populations so that they could reach as many people as possible. These edicts appear to be in Asoka's own words rather than the more formal language in which royal edicts or proclamations in the ancient world were usually written. At the core of these edicts are a set of precepts about how to lead a good individual and collective life. For the purposes of this essay, however, I focus on two major rock edicts, no. 7 and no. 12.

What do these edicts tell us? The seventh edict begins, "The beloved of the gods wishes that "all Pashandas[4] must dwell everywhere, in every part of his kingdom."[5] This seems like a simple, quite inconsequential statement and has been treated as such by commentators who have a rather sanguine view of social and religious conditions in Asoka's India. Thus Vincent Smith claims that

> the Dharma which he preached and propagated unceasingly with amazing faith in the power of sermonizing, had few, if any, distinctive features. The doctrine was essentially common to all religions. When we apply to Asoka's policy the word "toleration" with its modern connotation and justly applaud the liberality of his sentiments, another qualification is needed, and we must remember that in his days no really diverse religions existed in India. Buddhism and Jainism both were originally mere sects of Hinduism—or rather schools of philosophy founded by Hindu reformers—which in course of time gathered an accretion of mythology around the original speculative nucleus, and developed into religions.[6]

The same sentiment is echoed by Radha Kumud Mookerjee, who says, "It is to be remembered that Asoka's toleration was easy enough among the different denominations of the time, which were all but offshoots of the same central faith and did not differ among themselves so completely as the religions of Jesus, Zoroaster, or Mahomet introduced later into the country. Thus it was not difficult for the emperor, with due credit to the liberality of his views, to discern 'the essence of the matter in all sects' and honour it duly."[7]

To be sure, some commentators recognized what might have been at stake that compelled the inscription of some Asokan edicts.[8] For instance, D. R. Bhandarkar says that people in Asoka's times had lost sight of the essentials of their faith and begun to focus excessively on rituals and theology. In these matters there was unending acrimonious wrangling. Therefore, "When Asoka lived and preached, religious fanaticism and sectarian spirit were rampant."[9] Yet even he seems not to make the connection between Asoka's wish to have different religious groups cohabit to the rampant sectarianism of that time. Bhandarkar does not seem to recognize the real import of Asoka's wish. What plausibly was the thick context in which he was compelled to *say* this? Why should Asoka have said this? What could the context be in which he is compelled to *say* this? We get no sense of this from existing literature.[10] At any rate, it is not clear what form this strife took. Were sects expelling one another from territories where each was dominant? Had they segregated one another? Was something akin to what we now call "ethnic or religious cleansing" attempted in that period? But if intense sectarian strife existed, there must at least have been some violence between sects, even if it was not purely motivated by doctrine. It is again difficult to tell unless we try and imagine vividly what the background conditions were to some of these key edicts.

The twelfth edict implores that all pashandas restrain their speech, a specification of a more general self-restraint, *samyama,* mentioned in the seventh edict. This is seen as a virtue, even a civic virtue. But why restrain only speech? Why is this the core, the saara of all pashandas? Why burden it with so much importance? What is the link between restraint on speech and co-existence? Does speech have the power to disrupt coexistence? We all know that it can but under what conditions is it so acutely significant as to become one of the central problems of a society and the chief concern of its royal edicts? Does speech have the power to push everyone over the edge, or are people already so much on the edge that even speech can push them over it? Surely it is easy for a reasonable person to tolerate people with whom she has minor differences. The difficulty of tolerance arises only when people with major, virtually irreconcilable differences encounter one another. What then is the context in which speech is virtually the sole carrier of deeply uncomfortable, major differences?

BACKGROUND: PRE-AXIAL CONFLICTS IN INDIA

The sixth century B.C.E. was a period of great social ferment. Karl Jaspers has famously termed this extraordinary period in world history the Axial Age. Jasper's own formulation is deeply problematic, yet it does point to something of huge importance in every major civilization.[11] Among Indian historians, Romila Thapar came quite close to making much the same point. She describes this period as a "century of questioning." There was vigorous debate and discussion among multiple sects concerned both with "religious belief and philosophical speculation." Among these Thapar singles out the uncompromising materialism of the early Charvakas, the metaphysical subtleties of the Upanishadic thinkers, and the dominant ritualism of the Vedic brahmins. It seems that for her local, internal critiques had by this period given way to a more general and accentuated social critique, hence the term the "century of questioning." I do not dispute this, but quite clearly the term *axiality* refers to something deeper, signaling that something extraordinarily new was now at stake. Thapar's description of this ferment does not quite get here.

I believe that, despite all its problems, the term *axiality* is not entirely inappropriate for this period, for something new and very radical begins to take shape, changing the entire intellectual landscape and carrying the potential of an enormous social revolution.[12] In order to better grasp what I have in mind, I would try to offer a quasi-phenomenological account of this period.

Pre-Buddhist India was dominated by the Vedas. The Rg Veda, the first and most important of these, contains hymns first meant only to be recited and much later written down. The hymns were essentially for the kshatriyas and the brahmins and reflected the beliefs and practices of these two upper castes. The hymns centered around sacrificial rituals (*yajnas*) performed for wealth, good health, sons, and a long life for the *yajamana*—all constituents of a this-worldly conception of human flourishing. Some sacrifices were simple, domestic affairs, performed by the householder. Others involved animal sacrifice in order to procure horses, cows, land, and more riches, for which the participation of ritual specialists was requisite.

Ritual sacrifice was also seen to be propitiating gods: powerful, mostly benevolent beings who could be persuaded by these offerings to intervene in the world of men. Dharma in the Rg Veda refers to ritual sacrifice—"sacrifice as the power supporting the cosmos and sustaining life and, socio-economically, as the law men must act upon."[13] Because it refers to something other than and, in some sense, beyond human beings, it is not anthropocentric. Yet as it largely involves a transaction between self and the world, it would not be inappropriate to call it an ethic of self-realization. To attain all this-worldly goods, ritual sacrifice must be performed and gods propitiated so that they can intervene in this world to facilitate self-realization.

Two interesting developments within this worldview must also be noted. First, sacrificial rituals increasingly became longer, elaborate, and complicated, sometimes necessitating the simultaneous involvement of several Brahmanas.[14] This meant the deployment of massive wealth to perform the ritual and to offer *dakshinas* (donation, fee, or reward) to the Brahmanas. Second, as these rituals became more complex and expensive, they appeared to enhance the intrinsic worth of the ritual, as if a magical quality inhered in the sacrifice itself and its performance was sufficient to yield all goals of human flourishing. All attention began to be paid to the precision with which the elaborate ritual was performed, down to its minutest detail. The slightest deviation could result in the frustration of the desired objective. The more sacrifice was regarded as possessing a mystical potency superior even to the gods, the more the propitiation of gods became redundant or at best secondary. As Surendranath Dasgupta puts it, "If performed to perfection, it was capable of fulfilling the desired objective independent even of the gods"[15]

Another question to be addressed is this: how must we reconcile the assertion that the entire purpose of sacrifice was for this-worldly human flourishing with the claim that one of the purposes of rituals was to yield benefits beyond this life and that the world was not only for humans but also included gods? A couple of points should help resolve this apparent contradiction. First, a distinction between the terrestrial and the celestial is compatible with both spheres existing in the same cosmos. Gods were immortal and moved constantly between the terrestrial and the celestial, but this mobility was very much a part of this cosmic world, quite like movement of birds and planes, no matter how high they soar, is a part of the same world. Second, the cessation of life on earth meant a flight to another *loka—swargaloka* or *narkaloka—* depending upon the quantum of spiritual merit acquired.[16] However these lokas too were a part of the same cosmos, not radically otherworldly. Some of them were inhabited by gods, some by demons, and others by ancestral spirits. Life after death was life in another of these lokas, very much in this cosmic world conceived more widely. Indeed, there is more than a hint in several texts of that period where *amratva* ("immortality") means simply the endless duration of one's life in this world of sensuous enjoyment, a notion far closer to *samsara* than to anything resembling *moksa.*

We already have here indications of several sources of potential conflict between followers of different weltanschauungs as well as among those with a similar worldview: an internal conflict within followers of Vedic teachings, first, between those who indulged in expensive and elaborate rituals and those who found this baroque quality entirely unnecessary, wasteful, and distracting from their primary objectives; second, between those who believed in the necessity of propitiating gods and those who gradually moved away from this view and felt that the only significant action (*karma*) was the sacrifice (*yajna*) itself.

A third conflict also existed. Several commentators attest to the presence of pre-Aryan people in India. One such group was probably called Munis, a wandering group of sparsely clad ascetics, deeply skeptical about the idea of a creator of the universe, believing that the world in which they lived was real and that salvation in this world was possible by exacting practical discipline.[17] They were generally pessimistic about other forms of liberation in this world and had little conception of any other world. The Munis are infrequently mentioned in the Vedas, but that is probably due to their radical difference with the Vedic tradition and their consequent marginalization. It does not mean that their existence in this period was rare.[18] Thus a third major conflict existed between the Vedics and the pre-Vedic Munis, one ritualistic, believers in gods, seeking this-worldly goods and pleasures, and very largely materialist, the other renouncing this-worldly pleasures and rituals, rejecting beliefs in gods, and seeking liberation deep in the forests through rigorous practical discipline.

THE BACKGROUND: CONFLICT BETWEEN PRE-AXIAL AND AXIAL RELIGIONS

I believe we now possess a richer understanding of the background to Asoka's Dhamma, but are still nowhere near capturing the deeper and perhaps more central conflicts of that period. A new cosmology, born out of the confluence of existing Vedic and pre-Vedic traditions but radically opposed to them, illustrates the first of these.[19]

The key difference lies in the birth of the idea of radical transcendence and therefore of a duality between this world (*samsara*) and *Brahman* or *Atman*, the ultimate reality pervading the whole universe or our deepest inner, imperishable selves. Samsara is radically separated from Brahmana or Atman in that the latter can be achieved only by totally negating the former. Liberation (*moksha*, *mukti*) from the cycle of *samsara* could be achieved only through *jnana*, knowledge that could not be obtained through mere intellectual exertion. *Jnana* was knowledge of an inner, intuitive, experiential kind that could only come upon the seeker as a sort of revelation that would transform him instantaneously. Against Vedic ritual sacrifice, we find, in the *Chhandogya Upanishad* (3.8.11), Yagnavalkya tell Gargi that moksha cannot be attained by performing sacrifices. Nor could moksha be obtained, contra the Muni and early Jain tradition, by physical austerities even for thousands of years. Offerings (*dana*), sacrifices, recitations of Vedas, and performance of austerities may earn merit, but only steadfastness in pursuit of the knowledge of Brahman would help us achieve moksha or true immortality.[20]

Both Brahman and Atman are wholly outside the given, immanent, and mundane world and manifest a point from which one can, to use Benjamin Schwartz's phrase, "stand back and look beyond" and contemplate it. Hence the appropriateness of the term *radical transcendence.* Hence also the aptness of the use of axiality. The Upanishads provide the axial turn in Indian civilization. Here we have the birth of a major potential conflict between vastly different weltanschauungs. For nothing that the Vedic peoples or the Munis think to be significant is truly or ultimately important for Upanishadic thinkers. Indeed, what is of great value to one worldview might be of least value to the other.

Nonetheless, there is one sense in which the break between the pre-Vedic/Vedic and the Upanishadic followers may not have been total. This has to do with the necessary place of others in an ethic of self-realization. What follows are very tentative remarks, the principal import of which is that higher-order other-related values or principles (let's call this morality higher, separate, and transcendental) are negligible or secondary in pre-Buddhist thought in the Indian subcontinent. Allow me to elaborate. For Vedic Brahmanism, Dharma has less to do with what we owe one another. Neither sacrificial rituals nor gods are invoked for the good of the generalized others, say for the Munis. In both its individual or collective forms, this is a self-focused ethic of fulfillment or realization. The content of this ethic does not change with the introduction of the idea of radical transcendence. The early moment of the axial turn in Indian civilization does not appear to make the generalized other central to its ethic of individual or collective self. To be sure, notions of justice, right, and wrong exist, but these are probably in the hands of the kshatriya king, matters decided in any given context by his will or judgment. Dharma in its Vedic or post-Vedic Upanishadic senses has very little to do with what we, by some transcendental necessity, owe one another.

All this begins to change with developments in later Upanishadic thought and more clearly with the Buddha. With Buddha's teachings, the transcendental point, to use Gananath Obeyesekhre's phrase is "ethicised" (in my terminology, one might say moralized).[21] From now on, judgments of the rightness or wrongness of action are "mediated and delayed." They may even be enunciated after one's death. This is the birth of transcendental morality—a transcendental evaluation of the rightness or wrongness of action in relation to others that affects a person's life not in this world alone but his destiny after death, outside this world. This also entails a shift in the meaning of Dharma. Dharma from now on also begins to mean this radically transcendental morality. Quite clearly, there must have been not only a conflict between ancient ethics and this new ethic inspired by Buddha but also a contest over the meaning of key terms, such as *Dharma.* We now have two radically differing notions of dharma, one a particular ethic of a single-cosmos oriented (this-worldly) self-realization and the other, a transcendental morality for all concerned with right interpersonal conduct. Indeed, even the term *interpersonal* is not quite correct, because the conduct in question includes how human beings behave toward nonhuman animals. "All" means all humans and animals, virtually all living species. The protest over ritual sacrifice was perhaps more against the sacrificial killings of animals. This made eminent economic sense, but is not reducible to it. For the kshatriyas, war had become a mode of life, and perhaps the greatest benefit yielded by yajna sacrifice was success in war. The kshatriyas needed animals, which they stole from ordinary pastoralists. War, on the other hand, meant not only the arbitrary killing of humans and animals but also the destruction of people's livelihood. Thus both pastoralists and small farmers may have risen in protest against war and sacrificial killing.[22] Buddha's teachings thus instantiate a major transvaluation of Vedic values, a "dynamic best captured in Assmann's notion of normative inversion whereby one group's rights and responsibilties are turned by another group into prohibitions and scandals."[23]

A thicker description of the multiple sources of manifold conflicts in Asoka's times is now clearly available. In addition to the three conflicts mentioned earlier, in this section I have provided an account of at least two conflicts that probably go much deeper: between pre-Vedic and Vedic immanentists and transcendentalists who developed the Upanishads and evolved the notion of the radical distinction between samsara and Brahman/Atman. A second, even deeper conflict exists between two different ethics, one Upanishadic, which has a transcendental metaphysics but no (or perhaps a weak) conception of transcendental morality, and the other that opposes transcendental orders of the real outer or inner world, but develops a strong idea of transcendental morality that allows judgments from outside any this-worldly point on the actions of every subject, both self- and other-related—i.e., related to one's kith and kin, one's community (*jati*), and even those entirely outside one's fold. The social ramifications of this conflict can hardly be overestimated.

I hope to have shown the deeply mistaken character of the view that religious interaction in Asoka's period of rule was relatively trouble free and that he must have had an easy time finding common ground among followers of different schools of thought. It is well known that shared philosophical and cultural assumptions provide no immunity against intense conflicts. The assumption that offshoots of an entity conflict weakly with their parent is even more untenable. Buddhism may have been an offshoot of "Hinduism" but conflicted with it at many levels, on many issues. As for Jaina philospphy, it is not even entirely clear what epistemic gain ensues in seeing it simply as an offshoot of Hinduism. Thus, Vincent Smith and Radha Kumud Mookerjee clearly underestimate the depth of conflict in Asokan times. Thapar and Bhandarkar are right that this was a period of intense and bitter sectarian conflict. However, in my view, even they are unable to home in on the novelty of what was at stake in Asoka's period. By vividly representing the central conflicts of those times, this account now gives an entirely different gloss on Romila Thapar's remarks that this is a period of intense sectarian struggles and to her claim that the sixth century B.C.E. was "the century of universal questioning."[24] It also helps us to see the real issues at stake in those struggles—a conflict between notions of weak and radical transcendence as well as between immanent and transcendental moralities. The sixth century B.C.E. must have been a century of massive intellectual and emotional turmoil with gigantic social implications, the like of which had never been witnessed earlier. It appears that the need of the times was a political morality that could arbitrate between multiple, radically different, often incommensurable rival conceptions so that each could coexist and learn from one another.[25]

THE REAL SIGNIFICANCE OF THE SEVENTH EDICT

I hope by now we also possess a much better understanding of what exactly is so novel about the harmless-looking statement in the seventh edict. Given the many-layered, incrementally deep conflicts involving several different groups and the necessity imposed by trade and urban conditions for them to cohabit, Asoka had to evolve some way to hold them together. Buddha's teachings had provided him with conceptual resources to imagine something that would be more than ad hoc and tactical, something long-lasting and endorsable from within each pashanda's perspective.[26] They had given him the hope in the development of public norms from below and the redundancy of orders from above. One of them was that all pashandas must dwell everywhere in his empire.

Among historians, only D. D. Kosambi appears to have grasped the true importance of this statement. Kosambi believes that the edict is meant to communicate primarily to leaders of each pashanda rather than directly to pashandas themselves. Through the seventh edict, Asoka effectively grants these leaders permission to travel freely everywhere in the kingdom to provide them an opportunity to teach and convert each other. Asoka impartially grants this privilege to religious teachers of all pashandas. It is likely that the edict became necessary because mutual interaction and the attempt to preach once own ethics to others had begun to cause severe friction, leading to the birth of local rules forbidding one pashanda from communicating with or, worse, entering into the territory of another pashanda—something akin to what Sudipta Kaviraj in a different context has called back-to-back neighborliness. Instead of perpetuating mutual exclusion and the resulting homogenization of each settlement, Asoka, it seems, gives assurances to the leader of each pashanda that they must feel secure everywhere and encourages free interaction and dialogue amongst them, albeit now regulated by moral norms.

As mentioned earlier, he is able to do so by virtue of a major conceptual transformation, facilitated by a change in the background conditions, perhaps even in the social imaginary. A new form of society, far more heterogeneous than the original simple tribe community, had come into being. Living together here was terribly different, but, at the same time, no longer an optional extra, but inevitable, a natural part of one's environment. To respond to the crisis generated by radical heterogeneity, a new legitimating ethic became necessary. Buddha's teachings made possible a different conception of Dharma. It needed a great leap of imagination to arrive at the view that what we call dharma can be used not only for personal self-fulfillment or the fulfillment of the needs of specific groups, but rather to ease the newly emergent problems of a form of society that simply could not do without diverse groups. It is a discovery of the first magnitude that dharma or religion can be used to ease the difficulties of early society, to make the common life of diverse elements of society easier. It necessitated that a collective ethic substitute correct ritual by good deeds for the sake of others.

Moreover, Buddha's teachings opened up the possibility of the radical sociopolitical restructuring of the world and the self by politico-moral action from above. Buddha's ethic included the pivotal importance of moral action. Once one stands outside the whole cosmos and is able to see its limitations, and once the transcendental point from which one examines the cosmos is viewed as emanating a moral vision, it becomes possible to imagine a profound restructuring of society and polity in accordance with that vision. Once again, D .D. Kosambi is imaginatively on to this point when he says that, more than a personal conversion of the emperor, there appears to have taken place in Asokan times a deeper conversion of the whole previous state apparatus. The king not only preaches a new morality but is able to launch radically new political and administrative measures that include public morality as an essential ingredient and provide a framework within which radically differing ethics can coexist and nourish one another.[27]

Also emerging at this time in India is the idea of the Cakravartin, the wheel turner. The wheel that these great rulers turn is the wheel of Dharma. Whereas the Buddha turned the wheel of the Dharma in the religious sphere, the cakravartin turns it in the political sphere. The cakravartin conquers other kingdoms not by physical force but by moral appeal.[28] Wherever he travels he is welcomed, and people voluntarily submit to his rule out of respect for his adherence to the principles of Dharma. The cakravartin represents the Buddhist political ideal of the just ruler or universal monarch who brings peace and prosperity to his subjects.[29] "The normative king, it seems, is intrinsic to the social and moral order of the world."[30]

Given the birth of the idea of a moral ruler or the "normative king," a third interpretation of the statement in the seventh edict is also possible. Here the focus is less on what leaders or followers do to one another and more on the relationship between the king and pashandas. It is safe to assume that throughout the pre-Asokan period the king could expel Brahmanas and *sramanas* from his territorial domain. Through the seventh edict, Asoka attempted to prevent this. Given that right and wrong actions were determined by the king himself, there must have been arbitrary exercise of power. The law must not have been applied in a consistent or legitimate manner but in a highly personal and arbitrary one. Thus *raja*s are often depicted as rewarding or punishing according to the way their personal interests were served.[31] Thus the seventh edict was an attempt to tame the institution of kingship and to contain the absolute exercise of power by the application of the principle of dhamma. Indeed, the reconceptualization of dhamma may also be viewed as an attempt to transform power into authority by infusing it with certain norms. Dhamma was an immutable moral principle that was above the king, the raja of the raja.

SEARCH FOR A COMMON GROUND

What, despite profound differences in worldviews, could the basis of such coexistence be? For a start, the possibility of coexistence depended on toleration, the capacity to put up with the practices of others despite deep moral disagreement. Better still, it needed mutual adjustment and accommodation. Vedic, Brahmanical ethics needed to be moralized, to some degree; the shramanic worldview, the worldview of Buddhists, Nirgranthis, and Ajivikas needed to accept some value in rituals and rites. This could hardly have been easy, given the shramanic contempt for rituals and the brahmanic distaste for antiritualistic, transcendental morality. The edicts encourage partial reconciliation. They note that rituals play an important role in the daily lives of people. They are also significant on occasions of birth or marriage of sons and daughters, journey, sickness, and death.[32]

This concession to rituals is subtly though not totally offset by welfare measures mentioned in the edicts, presumably something all good kings must undertake. Asoka speaks of the importance of planting banyan and mango trees, digging water wells, building rest houses, and securing varieties of medicinal herbs, hinting that it is the duty of the king to provide a healthy life and physical comfort to his subjects. This is echoed elsewhere in Buddhist texts. "After the *cakkavatti* had brought the entire universe under his umbrella, he must proceed to ensure that his people live in comparative comfort, in a world where destitution has been wiped out. Instead of only punishing offenders, which would merely ensure the stability of the social order but not make for moral order, the normative king first had to provide the poor and deprived with the essentials of existence."[33] The *dhammikodhammaraja* must not merely be concerned with upholding the property and family rights of people in society, but go beyond these minimum obligations and also ensure that everyone's basic needs are met.[34]

Several edicts mention, however, the limited value of rituals and ceremonies. They may be appropriate in certain contexts, but "bear little fruit" and are of "doubtful value."[35] More importantly, rituals do not address one of the most burning moral issues of the times: interpashandic disagreement and conflict. Hence, edict 12 says, "The beloved of the Gods does not wish to overvalue gifs and sacrifice. More important than these is the reverence one's faith commands or the number of its followers or its core ethical values. Even more important than these ethical values are the essentials of all faiths and pashandas. It is these essentials that constitute the common ground of these seemingly conflicting conceptions."[36]

What then is the common ground among rival conceptions? For Asoka, dhamma constitutes the all-important common ground, the essentials, of all pashandas. What then are these essentials? Interpreters here give differing answers: Dhamma is sometimes seen as virtue, religious truth, or simply piety. But the most convincing answer, consistent with what has been mentioned previously and substantiated by Obeyesekre and Tambiah, is that dhamma is akin to transcendental morality. If so, it is fair to say that for Asoka rites and rituals have no meaning unless embedded within an ethical perspective, and the ethical import of these gifts is overridden by their lack of moral significance. This is why they may be offered only *as long as they are not injurious to anyone* (humans as well as nonhumans). No animal may be killed in order to be sacrificed. Nor should there be any *samaja* ("assembly") for such a purpose, implying that other kinds of assemblies, especially the *sangha*, are permissible.[37]

What then is the content of dhamma? The fundamental principle of dhamma is *vacaguti*, variously interpreted as "restraint on speech" or "control on tongue." It is significant that the edicts recommend that there be restraint on speech, but have little to say on restraining actions. Its almost as if the spoken word is not only more important than the written word but also more significant than physical action. Here again it is crucial to retrieve the surrounding context of Asokan edicts.

THE TWELFTHTH EDICT: RESTRAINT ON SPEECH

We can't recover that world, but we can imagine one where virtually nothing is written or read. Writing and reading have not yet taken possession of our psyche.[38] Speech has no visual presence; it can't be seen. Every word is spoken. Language is rooted and resides almost entirely in sound. Text, meaning something strung together, is also only spoken and heard. Everything is thought aloud and communicated. The spoken word carries the entire burden of our emotional life, all that uplifts or gets us down, brings us together or pulls us apart. The entire complex of art, philosophy, and religion—poetry, our deepest metaphysical thoughts, acts to honor gods and goddesses are all spoken, recited, sung, chanted, and heard. All these are composed, transmitted, stored, reproduced, and enriched orally. One might even say then that life itself is lived in sound. And, perhaps, destroyed in sound too.

Not only life but also public life is lived and extinguished in sound. Indeed, the public domain is constituted almost entirely by the spoken word and can therefore be disassembled by it too. After all, when words flow off the tongue effortlessly, they also tumble out inadvertently and, what is worse, carelessly. But then, words that matter must be enunciated with great care and even greater thought, for once uttered they can't be withdrawn. It is important in such cultures to differentiate such unguarded speech from one that carries weight or is valued. If they are to perform all the functions that the written word serves for us now, such treasures must be stored and remembered in memorable forms. To be remembered without being written and to be effective, this speech must be crafted with great economy and be crisp, rhythmic and rendered with great power. Only thus will it transform into a powerful mode of action. Words in oral cultures have always had enormous power. They can beckon gods to help us tide over problems, create something out of nothing, empower or disempower others, turn them into stone, even kill them. Words can be weapons or an elixir. They can soothe or cause grievous hurt. In oral cultures, words have magical potency.

One can hardly overestimate the immediacy and vibrancy of social interaction and, more pertinently, the agonistic energies in predominantly oral societies and its publics. Verbal duels, speech fights, word wars, verbal tongue lashings of adversaries in intellectual combats—all these are commonly found in societies largely unaffected by writing. Moreover, vitriolic reciprocal name-calling exists frequently, with fulsome expression of self-praise and excessive bragging about one's own prowess.

Given this context, one can now understand why oral speech acts appear to have more weight than all other forms of action. It is almost as if the greatest harm that might be inflicted on the other is through speech rather than physical action. It is not clear from the edict what the level of physical violence in that society was, if social interaction was already civil enough for people to even conceive that they could injure or kill one another over philosophical or religious differences. At any rate, either "hate speech" was considerably more significant than physical violence or else physical violence was largely confined to the territorial aggression and politics among the kshatriyas. Quite certainly the antagonistic energy in speech was unmatched even by physical violence. Generally people knew how to do things with spoken words. They poked fun, ridiculed, abused, cursed, mocked, scoffed at, were satirical and sarcastic, belittled and humiliated others—all by subtle manipulation of the spoken word.

Madhav Deshpande provides an extremely interesting example of the oral skills of ancient Indians.[39] The term *devanaampriya* literally means beloved of the gods. In the edicts the word is used extensively as an honoric adjective for Emperor Asoka. This is a bit odd, because the edicts were written after Asoka had turned Buddhist, and in this early period of Buddhism the existence of gods was frequently denied. The Vedics frequently refer to followers of Buddhism and Jainism as *devadvis,* i.e., haters of god. Deshpande recounts an interesting passage from the *Skanda Purana* in which Vishnu is reincarnated as Buddha in order to first lure the *asura* Mauryans. The *shudras,* Vedics believed, had wrongly usurped the rule of the earth into abandoning the Vedic dharma, making sacrifices redundant and denying the existence of gods and then destroying them in a battle between *devas* and *asuras.* In a battle between good and evil, the real lovers of the gods, the Vedic people had to defeat all those who were haters of gods. In short, *devanaampriya* could be used as an honoric title only for Vedic kings. How then could Asoka, a ruler who was not from the kshatriya caste and who is widely believed to deny the existence of gods, refer to himself as *devanaampriya?* From Asoka's point of view to follow his ancestors in using this term was perfectly valid politically and morally. He wished to support and get support from all pashandas, not only from fellow Buddhists, Ajivikas, and Nirgranthis but also from followers of Vedic dharma, those who believed in gods and in the value of ritual sacrifice for their propitiation. But from the Vedic point of view this usage must have been entirely inappropriate. However, instead of trying to reappropriate it, the Vedics began to use the term as one of abuse and contempt. Even Upanashadic philosophers might have used the term in the same manner, implying a fool (*moorkha*), i.e., devoid of the knowledge of the Brahma. *Devanaampriya* became a synonym of *devadvis. Devanaampriya* now begins to have a negative valance because a once-positive term is being used sarcastically. In short, they fiercely contested the legitimacy of Asoka's use of the term for himself by first disassociating, then renouncing, and finally denouncing the term.

TWO FORMS OF SELF-RESTRAINT

We do not have much evidence of the verbal battles and hate speech of that period, but the edicts imply that verbal wars in that period were intense and brutal. They simply had to be reined in. But what kind of speech must be curbed? Edict 12 says that speech that without reason disparages other pashandas must be restrained. Speech critical of others may be freely enunciated only if we have good reasons to do so. However, even when we have good reasons to be critical, one may do so only on appropriate occasions and even when the occasion is appropriate one must never be immoderate. Critique should never belittle or humiliate others. Thus there is a multilayered, ever deepening restraint on one's verbal speech against others. Let us call it *other-related self-restraint*. However, the edicts do not stop at this. They go on to say that one must not extols one's own pashanda without good reason. Undue praise of one's own pashanda is as morally objectionable as unmerited criticism of the faith of others. Moreover, the edicts add that even when there is good reason to praise one's own pashanda, it too should be done only on appropriate occasions and never immoderately. Undue or excessive self-glorification is also a way to make others feel small. For Asoka, blaming other pashandas out of devotion to one's own pashandas and unreflective, uncritical, effulgent self-praise can only damage one's pashanda. By offending and thereby estranging others, it undermines one's capacity for mutual interaction and possible influence. Thus there must equally be multitextured, ever deepening restraint for oneself. Let this be *self-related self-restraint*.

Elsewhere, in the seventh edict, Asoka emphasizes the need not only for self-restraint, *samyama*, but also *bhaavshuddhi,* again a self-oriented act. *Bhaavashuddhi* is frequently interpreted as self-purification, purity of mind. However, this term is ambiguous between self-purification within an ethic of individual self-realization or one that at least includes cleansing one's self of ill-will toward others. My own view is that, in the context of the relevant edicts, the moral feeling of goodwill toward others or at least an absence of ill will toward others must be a constitutive feature of what is meant by *bhaavshuddhi*. Self-restraint and self-purification are not just matters of etiquette or prudence. They have moral significance.

Given all this, and in order to advance mutual understanding and mutual appreciation, it is better, the edict says, to have *samovaya*, concourse, an assembly of pashandas where they can hear one another out, communicate with one another. They may then become *bahushruta*, i.e., one who listens to all, the perfect listener, and open-minded. This way they will not only have *atmapashandavraddhi*, the growth in the self-understanding of one's own pashanda, but also the growth of the essentials of all. The edicts here imply that the ethical self-understanding of pashandas is not static but constantly evolving, and such growth is crucially dependent on mutual communication and dialogue with one another. Blaming others without good reason or immoderately disrupts this process and, apart from damaging dhamma, diminishes mutual growth.

The edicts add that no matter how generous you are with gifts and how sincere your devotion to rituals, if you lack *samyama*, *bhaavshuddhi*, and the quality of *bahushruta*, then all the liberality in the world is in vain. Conversely, one who is unable to offer gifts but possess the aforementioned virtues lives a dhammic life. Thus one whose speech disrespects no one, who has no ill will toward others, and who does no violence to living beings is truly dharmic. Dharma is realized not by sacrifice but by right speech and conduct.

IS THIS TOLERATION?

Thapar says, "the 7th edict is pleading for toleration among all sects."[40] Likewise, the term *religious tolerance* is also used by Tambiah.[41] Is the term *toleration* or *tolerance* appropriate in this context? In the classical seventeenth-century meaning of the term, to tolerate is to refrain from interference in the activities of others, although one finds them morally disagreeable, even repugnant, and despite the fact that one has the power to do so.[42] Here one puts up with, even suffers, the morally reprehensible activities of others. The powerless other escapes interference of the powerful because the latter shows mercy toward them, a virtue in the powerful exercised in relation to those who do not really deserve it. Let's call this a hierarchical notion of toleration, given the asymmetry of power between the two groups and the attitude of superiority that one has toward the other. A second conception exists: Two groups, equally powerful, may also tolerate one another. Each has power to interfere in the activities of others and each finds the other morally repugnant, but both refrain from doing so because the mutual costs are too high. This is modus vivendi toleration. Clearly the Asokan case does not fall within either of these two conceptions.

A third conception is also nonhierarchical. Here A and B refrain from interfering in each other's activities out of indifference and because they don't particularly believe that one is more powerful than the other. True, they do not heartily approve of each other. The acceptance of one another may be somewhat grudging, more out of resignation than enthusiasm. It may also be true that this new disposition is a result of the dilution of the perceived power of the larger group, softened by the force of principles or reason or commerce or due to the disuse of collective power in matters concerning ultimate ideals. Neither really cares for another, as long each keeps out of the other's way. This is live-and-let-live attitude, one that is found in postindustrial, individualist, liberal societies. Everyone, in this conception, has a right to be, as long as he causes no harm to others. I may disapprove of what you do, but as long you do it in your privacy and not in my face I don't really care. The Asokan case does not fall under this conception either. If none of these conceptions is able to cover the Asokan case, then why use the term?

The basic idea of toleration is that A does not accept B's views or practices, but still refrains from interfering in it, even though one has the power to do so. A fourth conception may not violate this basic idea and yet be distinct from the other three conceptions. Parents often put up with the blemishes of their children that they would not suffer in others. We choose to overlook a fault in our lover, even in our close friends, that we would not excuse in anyone else. We might endure deep difference in worldviews in fellow citizens because we value fraternity. In all such cases we put up with dislikeable states of doing or being in others, even if we have some power to do something about them, simply because we have love or loving feelings for them. Here one tolerates not despite hate but rather because one loves the other. A mixture of love, friendliness, and fellow feeling is in the background or becomes the ground of a different conception of toleration.

Unlike other conceptions, which presupposes the idea that oneness with significant others as well as God is achieved by abolishing/ignoring/belittling the radical other, i.e., by eliminating plurality, here, in the second conception, oneness is attained by accepting all radical others as equally significant because they variously manifest one supreme being or concept. Thus to tolerate is to refrain from interfering in the life of others not despite our hatred for them, nor because we are indifferent to them, but because we love them as alternative manifestations of our own selves or some basic norm common to all of us. We may not be able to do or be what they are, we may even dislike some of their beliefs and practices, but we recognize that they are translations of our own selves or of gods within each of us. This binds us together in a relationship of lasting affection.

So suppose that A accepts the value of many though not all of B's beliefs and practices, but recognizes that beliefs and practices he does not accept follow from some of those he does or that some beliefs and practices he is unable to endorse follow inescapably from B's different background, then, out of respect for some of his beliefs and practices, A would put up rather than interfere with those with which he disagrees. Asoka's views, I believe to have shown, fall broadly within this fourth conception. If so, one might use the term *toleration* in this context, as long as one is careful not to confuse it with the other three, more standard conceptions.

But in the end it is perhaps better to avoid using the term *toleration*. No matter what its surrounding context, toleration focuses solely on a set of other-related self-restraints. But Asokan edicts clearly go beyond this by also making it necessary to observe a set of self-related self-restraints. In mutual toleration, each observes identical forms of self-restraint: I don't interfere in your beliefs and practices and you don't in mine. But the edicts speak instead of what we might call correlative self-restraints. One is not asked to refrain from excessively criticizing others and oneself. Instead, one is asked not to immoderately, and without good reason, be critical of others or indulge in the correlative practice of self-praise, quite a different thing altogether. It is by simultaneously observing both forms of self-restraint that one completes a moral act. It is better to say then that the edicts outline original norms of civility and principled coexistence among radically differing pashandas in a deeply heterogeneous society.

The distinction between the two forms of self-restraint is important because it helps us to more clearly see why Asoka's political morality is not reducible to but goes beyond toleration in every sense of the term. An example here from our own time might illustrate my point. India is a country where a majority of its people either call themselves or are taken to be Hindus. Though not entirely, the ethos of many of India's social and political institutions is saturated by one or the other strand of "Hinduism." So, regardless of our evaluative judgment, it would not be entirely incorrect to say these institutions are somewhat Hinduized or wear a Hindu look. Yet India also has Muslims, Christians, Parsees, Buddhists, Jains, Sikhs, atheists, and people with many other not so easily definable outlooks. Sections of Hindus may find their practices disagreeable, morally discomforting, or just downright strange, but they tolerate them. They may collectively have power to interfere in them, even banish them, but they refrain from doing so. Indeed, legally they have no other option. These religious communities have rights not to be interfered with in their religious and cultural practices. But the minorities will not be able to effectively exercise their rights if Hindus do not possess the capacity for other-related self-restraint. Most Hindus do, as a matter of fact, exercise such restraint. But is this sufficient for a morally justified coexistence between Hindus and minority communities? Suppose then that community-specific rights of minorities are respected, but Hindu self-assertion becomes more pronounced. Let us say they build new temples around every corner, ensure that these are mightier in size than mosques and churches, fund new radio and television channels that stream Hindu teachings and no other, introduce textbooks that speak largely of and glorify Hindu gods and goddesses, change national and state symbols in order to make them explicitly and exclusively Hindu, and so on. What would the impact be on the psyche of the minorities? Most likely, it will increase their sense of social and cultural alienation. It will force them to feel left out of many public domains. It might even lower their self-esteem. Alternatively, Hindus can show some self-related self-restraint, so as not to show off, to not always wear their religion and culture on their sleeve, to not always advertise their wares. Indeed, to persistently announce in public that you are the boss in your own country might be a sure sign of deep-rooted insecurities and anxieties, one that is both potentially damaging to others and to oneself. Abandoning this self-related self-restraint might then adversely affect everyone and destroy the very fabric of contemporary Indian society.

I have argued that Asoka's conception and policy of dhamma cannot be properly understood unless we vividly imagine the background conditions within which it emerged. The ambition of a new public morality widely endorsed by all affected groups could not have been possible without the pressing need to come up with a novel initiative in conditions of acute conflict among rival worldviews. At the center of these struggles were bitter disputations between predominantly one-world-oriented practioners of ritual sacrifice and those who opposed such violent rituals and sought a transcendental, world-negating morality for all. The availability of new conceptual resources forged during these disputes made it possible to devise a policy that, though not guaranteed to succeed, gave hope for a durable principled coexistence between groups engaged in fierce verbal disputes. This new political morality placed at the center a series of self- and other-related restraints. Only the simultaneous exercise of these new voluntary constraints could ensure amicable collective living. This policy might be called toleration, but only with a massive change in its dominant meaning. On standard interpretations, toleration involves the privatization of ill will or hatred. Both must be neutralized, if not expunged. However, this new notion implies no such thing. Quite the contrary, for it presupposes in the background something closer to goodwill and respect. But, in the end, even this might not be appropriate. Till we discover a suitable prakrit, pali or sanskrit term, it is best to call it civil.

APPENDIX: THE TWO ROCK EDICTS IN TRANSLATION

ROCK EDICT VII

His Sacred and Gracious majesty desires that in all places should reside people of diverse sects (pashandas). For they all desire restraint of passions [*samyama*] and purity of heart [*bhava-'sudhi*]. But men are of various inclinations and of various passions. They may thus perform the whole or a part (of their duties). But of him whose liberality is, too, not great, restraint of passion, inner purity, gratitude and constancy of devotion should be indispensable and commendable.

Translated by Radha Kumud Mookerjee, *Asoka* (New York: McMillan, 1928), pp. 149–50.

ROCK EDICT XII

King Priyadarsi honours men of all faiths, members of religious orders and laymen alike, with gifts and various marks of esteem. Yet he does not value either gifts or honors as much as growth in the qualities essential [*sàra-vadhi*] to men of all faiths. This growth could take many forms, but its root is in guarding one's speech [*vachi-gutì*] to avoid extolling one's own faith and disparaging the faith of others improperly or, when the occasion is appropriate, immoderately.[43]

The faiths of others all deserve to be honored for one reason or another. By honoring them, one exalts one's own faith and at the same time performs a service to the faith of others. By acting otherwise, one injures one's own faith and also does disservice to that of others. For if a man extols his own faith and disparages another because of devotion to his own and because he wants to glorify it, he seriously injures his own faith.

Therefore concord (samavàyo or samanvaya) alone is commendable, for through concord men may learn and respect the conception of Dharma accepted by others. King Priyadarsi desires men of all faiths to know each other's doctrines and to acquire sound doctrines.[44] Those who are attached to their particular faiths should be told that King Priyadarsi does not value gifts and hours as much as the growth in the qualities essential to religion in men of all faiths. Many officials are assigned to tasks bearing on this purpose—the officers in charge of spreading Dharma, the superintendents of women in the royal household, the inspectors of cattle and pasture lands, and other officials. The objective of these measures is the promotion of each man's particular faith and the glorification of Dharma.

Translated by N. A. Nikam and Richard McKeon, *The Edicts of Asoka* (Chicago: Chicago University Press, 1962), pp. 58–59.

NOTES

1. J. L. Nehru, *The Discovery of India* (Delhi: Oxford University Press, 1989 [1946]), p. 135.
2. J. L. Nehru, *Glimpses of World History* (Delhi: Oxford University Press, 1989), pp. 62–63.
3. For example, Lorenzen says, "The appeal to the religious tolerance of Asoka and Akbar as important premodern and precolonial precedents for the policies of religious tolerance and legal equality common (virtually by definition) to modern secular states seems to me to be quite appropriate and useful, even if the claims sometimes sound a little anachronistic." See David N. Lorenzen, *Kabir and the Secular State*, Colegio de México, p. 7. Available at http://ceaa.colmex.mx/profesores/paginalorenzen/imagespaglorenzen/KabirSecPia2.pdf; accessed January 3, 2012.
4. This is one of the most difficult terms to translate. Its standard meaning is "heretic," but clearly Asoka does not use it in this sense. The standard translation is "sect," which is unsatisfactory because of its Christian association. There is an imaginative suggestion, now rejected, that it might be linked to *prasha,* a term in *avestha* and similar to *prashna* in Sanskrit, meaning "question." An imaginative translation could then have been a group of questioners or enquirers. But there is no strong evidence to support this view. Radha Kumud Mookerjee links it to *parishad,* meaning "assembly." But that too is not accepted by everyone. Perhaps the best translation would be "followers of a school of thought or teachings." I here use it to mean this and will continue to use the prakrit word *Pashanda* in the main text.
5. The identification of King Priya-darshi with Asoka was confirmed by an inscription discovered in 1837.
6. Vincent Smith, *Asoka, Buddhist King of India* (Delhi: Oxford University Press, 1920), p. 61.
7. Radha. Kumud Mookerjee, *Asoka* (London: McMillan, 1928), p. 66.
8. D. R. Bhandarkar, *Ashoka* (Asia, 2000 [1925]), pp. 111–12.
9. Ibid., pp. 111–13.
10. There is virtual consensus that this was a period of bitter sectarian strife. Bhandarkar says "It is plain that there was friction and bitter spirit between these (Ajivikas, Nirgranthas and Buddhists) sects" and 'When Asoka lived religious fanaticism and sectariarianism was rampant." See D. R. Bhandarkar, *Asoka* (Calcutta: Asian Educational Services, 1925), p. 112.
11. On problems in the idea of axial age, particularly in its application to the Indian context, see the articles of David Schulman, "Axial Grammer" and Sheldon Pollock, "Axialism and

Empire" in Johann Arnason, S. N. Eisenstadt, and Bjorn Wittrock, eds., *Axial Civilizations and World History* (Boston: Brill, 2005), pp. 369–96 and pp. 398–450.

12. It has been argued, especially by Pollock, that many features here described as prior to and definitive of the Vedic culture may in fact have developed in response to the threat posed by Buddhism. But he agrees that such proclivities were always present within it. See Pollock, "Axialism and Empire," ibid., p. 410.
13. See Joel P. Brereton, "Dharman in the Rg Veda," *Journal of Indian Philosophy*:32 (2004): 485; and Albrecht Wezler, "Dharma in the Vedas and the Dharmasastras," *Journal of Indian Philosophy* 32 (2004): 647.
14. See, among others, S. M. Jamison and Michael Witzel, *Vedic Hinduism*, available on www.people.fas.harvard.edu/-witzel/vedica.pdf (1992), p. 4.
15. Surendranath Dasgupta, *A History of Indian Philosophy* (Cambridge: Cambridge University Press, 1963), p. 21.
16. Monier Williams's Sanskrit-English dictionary has a long discussion. Among other things, he speaks of "seven worlds described as earth, sky, heaven, middle region, place of re-births, mansion of the blessed, and the abode of truth."
17. See G. C. Pande, *Studies in the Origins of Buddhism* (Delhi: Motilal Banarsidas, 1995 [1957]), pp. 257–62. Also see Edward Fitzpatrick Crangle, *The Origin and Development of Early Indian Contemplative Practices* (Weisbaden: Harrassowitz, 1994), p. 28. Crangle writes, "Early Vedic practices involve, by and large, a worldly attitude whereby the worshipper seeks to appease gods by performing various ritual sacrificial ceremonies. The Rg Veda, however, mentions some opposed to Aryan rituals. . . . These were unbelievers, riteless people. . . . Outstanding in this regard were the Munis. . . . The Rg Vedas offer the earliest literary evidence for the existence of Munis."
18. D. D. Kosambi also mentions the existence of non-Aryan people called Nagas, who were settled in parts of what now are Bihar and UP. They did not speak the Aryan language and appeared not to have any contact with the Aryans. This appears to confirm G. C. Pande's claim that a group of wandering ascetics called Munis, marginal to Vedic life, also existed in the region. D. D. Kosambi, *An Introduction to the Study of Indian History* (Bombay: Popular Prakashan, 1985 [1956]).
19. Dasgupta discusses the ways in which Asvaghosha reinterpreted the teachings of the Buddha by incorporating some of the Upanishadic ideas, but since his time is believed to be after the Mauryan Empire, it is not of much relevance here, except for highlighting the fact that within Buddhism elements of Brahmanical thought were incorporated and vice versa. Dasgupta, *A History of Indian Philosophy,* pp. 88–89.
20. Upinder Singh, *A History of Ancient and Early Medieval India* (New Delhi: Pearson, 2008), pp. 208–9.
21. Gananath Obeyesekere, *Imagining Karma* (Princeton: Princeton University Press, 2002).
22. "There were sound economic reasons for Asoka's change to rule by morality, from the precepts of a book which not even its greatest admirer could accuse of being moral." Kosambi, *An Introduction to the Study of Indian History*, p. 223.
23. See Pollock, "Axialism and Empire," p. 404.

24. Romila Thapar, *Asoka and the Decline of the Mauryas* (Oxford: Oxford University Press, 1961), p. 4.
25. Kosambi proposes that a number of sects with subtle metaphysical differences arose in protest against the "monstrous cancerous growth of sacrificial ritual in the tribal kingdoms." The greatest fruit of the *yajna* sacrifice was success in war; fighting was glorified for its own sake as the natural mode of life for the ksatriyas, while the brahmin's duty and means of livelihood was the performance of vedic sacrifices. Kosambi, *An Introduction to the Study of Indian History*, p. 166.
26. Sadly, this might have been the primary reason why his empire was so brief, ephemeral, and anomalous. Equally, this surely is the only reason why Asoka's Dhamma continues to be remembered more than two thousand years later.
27. Kosambi claims that the statement "King Piyadasi Beloved-of-the-gods desires that all sects may reside everywhere" sounds trivial, having at best been interpreted as permission for people to travel freely. In fact, he argues, this was the most far-reaching concession to the new method of administration by dhamma." He adds that religious teachers who might make converts had previously been forbidden to enter crown villages, which covered the greater part of the countryside. But now Asoka encouraged this transformative interaction, regardless of sect. He further claims that "Asoka is not preaching Buddhism, nor morality in general, but proclaiming the superiority of justice, social ethics, over naked force backing arbitrary laws. This was necessary because the sects, already engaged in heated theological discussion, might disturb the very peace and welfare they were supposed to promote, once state backing made them fashionable." See Kosambi, *An Introduction to the Study of Indian History*, pp. 200–3. Finally the rules governing ordinary people and the ruler himself stemmed from the same moral source. This was quite unlike the statecraft recommended by Chanakya where an entirely amoral ruler committing all kinds of crimes against subjects and neighbors reigned over a morally regulated population.
28. The reference to conquerers by physical force is to those who perform the Brahmanical *asvamedha* rite. In contrast to the *asvemedhi,* rival kings welcome and submit to the *chakravartin* and ask him to teach them (*anusasamaharajati*). Damien Keown and Charles S. Prebish, eds., *Encyclopedia of Buddhism* (New York: Routledge, 2010), p. 273.
29. Ibid., p. 274.
30. Ibid., p. 167.
31. *Samyutta Nikaya*, 3:301–3.
32. Major Rock edict IX.
33. Ibid., p. 165.
34. The ideal king Maha Sudassana, for instance, establishes a perpetual grant (*evarupangdanangpatthapeyyang*) to provide food for the hungry, drink for the thirsty, gold for the poor, money for those in want, as well as wives for those who required them. *Digha Nikaya*, 2:137; *Dialogues of the Buddha*, 2:211. This *dhammikodhammaraja* "patronizes *samanas* and *brahmanas* who are worthy, providing them with all the things necessary to pursue their goals." *Digha Nikaya*, 2:141; *Dialogues of the Buddha*, 2:217.

35. See Rock Edict II in N. A. Nikam and Richard McKeon, *The Edicts of Asoka* (Chicago: Chicago University Press, 1962), p. 44.
36. See Heinrich Zimmer, *Philosophies of India*, ed. Joseph Campbell (Delhi: Motilal Banarsidas, 2000 [1951]), pp. 469–70. "Asoka, rather than trying to uphold one view or the other—and thereby identifying himself with one school or the other—sought to emphasize what he held to be the 'essence' common to all sects and schools. Doing otherwise would have been to encourage a more vociferous conflict of ideas and practices among these sects and schools, thereby compromising the concord and cohesion he was trying to build up within his kingdom."
37. This is clearly implied in the Rock Edict I. See Radha Kumud Mookerjee, *Asoka* (Delhi: Motilal Banarsidas, 1962), pp. 128–29.
38. This is denied by many scholars who wrote early in the twentieth century. Mookerjee writes that literature and culture seem to have filtered down to the masses so as to produce a comparatively large percentage of literacy. Radha Kumud Mookerjee, *Asoka* (New York: McMillan, 1928), p. 102. Vincent Smith points out that the existence of edicts in the vernacular shows mass literacy. Vincent Smith, *Asoka, The Buddhist King* (Oxford: Oxford University Press, 1920), p. 139. Such views are naive. The epigraphic habit had barely begun to form in Asoka's time. The rulers had begun to play with the new technology, no doubt. Asoka can even be credited for having realized the enormous future potential of writing and to have been among the first to have used it for dissemination and "moral conquest." But mass literacy at that time is inconceivable, because there was little need for it. Besides, a large heterogeneous empire dictated that edicts be written in different languages. Nothing about widespread literacy can be inferred from it. To say that the edicts were written in the vernacular would entail that Greek and Armaic were vernacular languages, which is absurd. It is best to go along with Stanley Tambiah on this issue. He writes, "The intellectual milieu in which early science and philosophy advanced was essentially oral, small scale and face to face. If this was true of early Greece, it was emphatically true of India in the Axial Age. See Stanley Tambiah, "Reflexive and Institutional Achievements of Early Buddhism," in Shmuel Noah Eisenstadt, *The Origins and Diversity of Axial Age Civilizations* (Albany: SUNY Press, 1986), p. 461.
39. Madhav Deshpande, "Interpreting the Asokan Epithet Devanampriya," in Patrick Olivelle, ed., *Asoka in History and Historical Memory* (New Delhi: Motilal Banarasidas, 2009), pp. 16–44.
40. Thapar, *Asoka and the Decline of the Mauryas*, p. 139.
41. Stanley Tambiah, *World Conquerer and World Renouncer* (Cambridge: Cambridge University Press), p. 64.
42. See for example, Susan Mendus, *Toleration and the Limits of Liberalism* (London: Macmillan, 1989).
43. In Radha Kumud Mookerji's translation, *Asoka,* the phrase used is "without any ground."
44. This translation crucially excludes one critical term, i.e., *bahu-srutà,* literally meaning "one who has listened to the many," which therefore means one possessed of wide learning.

EMPIRE AND TOLERATION

A Comparative Sociology of Toleration Within Empire

KAREN BARKEY

TOLERATION BY ITSELF has become a contested term. It evokes cultural and social inequality, a solution in multicultural settings when differences cannot be fully accepted or assimilated and toleration remains the next best thing for the management of society without internecine violence. Critics argue that toleration is necessarily embedded in power relations where the powerful make decisions about how to tolerate the "intolerable." Others argue that toleration bypasses judgment on cultural difference, accepts and relativizes, but does not expose culture to criticism. These criticisms remain interesting, but they do not provide us with the tools to construct a different form of ethnic and religious coexistence, especially in the new world order of politicized identities and politicized cultures. The best way to rethink the concept of toleration is to embed it into actual historical circumstances where it was practiced and analyze its sociological dimensions.

A well-known set of historical examples of toleration remains traditional multiethnic and multireligious empires. Here the power of the examples stems from the often simple correlation that is assumed between empire and toleration where empires were seen as tolerant, if only by necessity, given that they acquired an enormous diversity of peoples they could not transform into a homogeneous entity. The comparison was then extended to empires and nation-states, where empires were tolerant political formations and nation-states, with their nationalizing instinct, were often intolerant of diversity. The question remains, however, whether empires as a form of governance have a greater prospect for toleration than nation-states. The answer is remarkably complex and necessitates profound analytic study in the political sociology of empires that both theorizes the conditions for toleration and the circumstances under which such conditions might be altered. Because, as we shall see, the relationship between empire and toleration is complicated by the fact that imperial states are neither always tolerant nor always intolerant; they can tolerate some groups while persecuting others.

In this chapter I will use toleration as a sociological category that needs to be analytically unpacked, historicized, and described in its variations. I then hope to show that we can historically analyze the diverse trajectories of toleration in different empires and contribute to understanding how toleration can become the practice of diversity. I pose here the puzzle of the Ottoman and Habsburg Empires, which started with different policies of toleration, crossed paths in the eighteenth century, and reversed their course of action. The Ottomans began with greater toleration of diversity, the Habsburgs with attempts at confessional absolutism, but during the eighteenth century the Ottomans embarked on a route of intolerance and persecution of the very groups they had gladly tolerated, while the Habsburgs declared the Edict of Tolerance. It is these different initial state understandings of toleration and persecution as well as the changes in each trajectory that I study to show the benefits of sustained sociological analysis of toleration in historical settings.

Toleration, much like Nettl argued decades ago for stateness, is a variable.[1] The important move on Nettl's part was the incorporation of the study of the state into the substance and methodology of the social sciences. In this way he accorded the state an existence in social science as a way to see it as the linking of all kinds of institutions, processes, and projects that varied in time and space. In the same manner that the state was assessed in its structural, ideological, and cultural dimensions, toleration can be as well. This essay attempts to do just that, while historicizing the concept and providing examples. I argue that there are multiple variations of the emergence of toleration—we have to focus on the social organization of societies where toleration becomes possible. Moreover, I argue that toleration is, sociologically speaking, an organizational by-product of relations between public authorities and communities (or individuals) and relations between communities with regard to how to coexist, refrain from violence and persecution of the other, and ensure their livelihood. It emerges from the relational context of networks and institutions, involves both the ideas and strategies of actors and groups, and is shaped by the historical and contextual setting. Looking at toleration as the outcome of social organization, I would like to argue, temporarily disengages us from ideological and cultural critiques, freeing us to understand the parameters of toleration and its variation in all its historicity and complexity.

THE STATE, COMMUNITIES, AND BOUNDARIES: CONCEPTUAL TOOLS OF TOLERATION AND PERSECUTION

I define persecution as violence against a specified people and/or groups. Persecution includes compulsion in matters of religion, as well as forced conversion, mass murder, and expulsion. I define toleration as more or less absence of persecution: the acceptance of a plurality of religions, but not necessarily their acceptance into society as full and welcomed members/communities. Toleration then really means the acceptance of "difference" and a lack of interest beyond the instrumentality to maintain a coherent polity. As Ira Katznelson suggests, "Toleration addresses some of the most difficult and persistent features of human social relations. When hatred combines with hierarchy, individuals and groups are exposed to zealotry and danger. Toleration is an act of bearing and allowing. It is a choice of not doing despite the ability to act."[2] Toleration therefore implies "not acting," which comes from thoughtful or strategic action that causes restraint. It denotes a choice made by public authorities as well as groups within society to use command and moderation. In that sense toleration is still essential to many societies where diversity and difference are the norm, where groups strongly claim their groupness as essentialized identities, and therefore remains a core value of human societies because it cautions us to use restraint.

Persecution and toleration are relational concepts. They both refer to relations between religious and ethnic groups, between religious and secular authorities and their minority/majority populations. We have tended to think of these concepts separately, and most studies of both Western and non-Western cases ignore the deep interdependence between persecution and tolerance. Societies both persecute and tolerate. David Nirenberg, in his work on medieval Aragon, demonstrates the degree to which violence was part of the *convivencia* that most scholars interpret as peaceful coexistence. He shows how the underlying logic of violence helped shape relations between groups. In that sense he urges us to look at the way in which tolerance and intolerance are articulated in everyday life.[3] In many of the premodern empires where toleration was possible, the threat of persecution was also very real. In his work on Reformation Europe, Scribner argues, "there were moments or circumstances in which intensified persecution could be mobilized for various reasons, yet it was not possible for this to be continuous over time or across an entire society."[4] Scribner adds that "persecution which is both extensive and intensive is socially dysfunctional in the long or even medium term, and persecution may be more a matter of short term political conjunctures or expedients."[5] These are different views of the articulation between persecution and toleration. Scribner directs us toward more clearly delineated practices, explosions of persecution that shatter the peace of coexistence before they are remade into another bounded and negotiated settlement. Nirenberg reacts to these sharper delineations, arguing for more fuzzy boundaries between toleration and intolerance.

In the social science literature, often by focusing on the dramatic events of insecurity and violence, we overlook the degree to which groups separated and mingled, cooperated and alienated each other, but, in the long run, persisted. We forget that, for long periods of history, groups defined and bounded by difference lived with each other without escalating into violence.[6] We therefore have to take the relational dynamics of groups and their temporality, seriously, looking at the *longue durée* of relations between groups, searching for the various combinations of toleration and persecution as they emerge in the context of societies with significant diversity.

Attention to temporal dimensions of toleration cannot be unidirectional, however. By focusing on medieval Europe and the Reformation only, we can easily fall into the trap of conceiving one master civilizing process that takes societies from persecution to toleration. While this is also contested in the context of medieval and early modern Europe,[7] it is instructive to study different trajectories. The Ottoman Empire that moved from a form of toleration vis-à-vis religious communities to intolerance and disastrous ethnic and religious conflict in the nineteenth century is a case in point. In this particular case the circumstances of international and imperial transformation altered the nature of state society compacts, moving the state away from its traditional role of imperial management of diversity to that of participant in the strife between competing ethnic and religious groups. The question then becomes how to explain the breakdown of social and political mechanisms that ensured toleration in society. What was toleration based on, and how did it change?

Historical studies are replete with references to persecution or toleration being the result of strong or weak secular or religious actors and institutions. Some, like G. R. Elton, argue that persecution results from a strong church that views tolerance as weakness,[8] others focus on individuals such as strong local bishops and magistrates who protected groups from persecution and weak ones who could not.[9] At another level, discussions regarding the natural proclivity of the masses to oppress and the tendency of the authorities to protect have not been resolved either. Is it strong or weak authority? Is it secular or religious authority? Or is it popular or literate classes? Such questions demonstrate the need to historicize toleration and persecution, understanding the relations and structures that lead to their emergence. Focusing solely on actors rather than relations across boundaries leads us astray and into contradiction. To understand toleration we have to embed social actors in the networks of relations and institutions of the time that provide the context and the meaning within which they act. State authorities often arrive at their calculus of toleration or persecution within the ambit of institutions of the time, themselves the outcomes of sets of historical and structural relations between states and social groups.

Finally, we have to deal with various types of explanations, especially the contrast between explanations of toleration based on ideological changes and the more utilitarian models of strategic necessity.[10] In Western European thought the ideological argument evolved from collective mentalities to an internal organic germination of tolerance resulting from the thought of Christian humanists. Therefore ideas of tolerance, developed from the seventeenth to the nineteenth century to allow for the possibility of peaceful pluralism, inspired people to practice it in their daily lives, spreading it across society. In the second view, social and political exigencies rather than philosophical commitment led groups to find ways to live together, and therefore lived experience led to toleration. Such arguments emphasize that states were always involved in political compromise, handing out privileges and protection for those deemed to be of use to the crown.

A more boldly economic view originated with the work of Henry Kamen, where the rise of toleration was the product of free trade rather then the ideas of the reformers.[11] Though Kamen spelled it out more generally, historians—based on small case studies—started demonstrating that economic and political exigencies made cities, localities, regions, societies, or even empires tolerate minorities, since state leaders well understood the need for toleration to maintain peace, develop their realm, and take advantage of the rich variety of resources different groups offered. The 1781 Edict of Toleration issued by Joseph II of the Habsburg monarchy was one such example of an economically motivated act of toleration.

Toleration in historical circumstances has arisen as well from the religious and political exhaustion of contesting parties where a precarious balance was carved between different groups to provide breathing room, such as with the Peace of Augsburg in 1555 or with the Edict of Nantes in 1598. But, as Zagorin argues, since Catholics and Protestants did not really believe in toleration, their truce was temporary and did not bring about permanent peaceful coexistence. In this he stresses that political expediency unaccompanied "by a genuine belief in and commitment to toleration as something inherently good and valuable" is not enough. An ideological and/or theological rationale is as necessary as a political goal.[12] Grell and Scribner succeed at both politicizing and historicizing toleration while providing numerous local examples of how tolerance and intolerance worked themselves out in local contexts.[13] When Scribner identifies many different forms of tolerance, he provides us with a consistent message of pragmatic choice: "in changed circumstances, toleration was a privilege that could be withdrawn; or it was no more than a working political compromise that could be altered if and when circumstances allowed."[14] Toleration, therefore, is of multiple kinds and degrees, as much as it is situational and contingent on the institutional and historical circumstances at play.

Moreover, prior to the development of ideas of toleration in the West, practices and forms of toleration were widespread in many different areas of the world. The edicts of Ashoka, the rule of Akbar in Mughal India, the multiple centuries of Ottoman peaceful diversity are examples of toleration, each requiring to be understood more fully. What were the means of accepting difference, how were societies organized, what did these leaders try to achieve, what was strategic, and what was normative about toleration in these societies? These are questions we still need further answers to. Properly historicized studies of toleration in diverse societies with different rule are certain to provide us with the tools to theorize toleration more deeply and powerfully.

A theoretical framework that works to explain toleration and persecution, as well as the movement in space from one form of intergroup relation to another, needs, first, to explain the existence of a boundary between groups that defines them and shapes relations within and across communities. Boundaries define and delineate difference. Second, in both situations of toleration and persecution, whether weak or strong, the state remains a key actor that scholars have to contend with. Public authorities will accept or reject the plurality of communities, harm or hinder, protect, or surrender religious and ethnic groups. In interethnic episodes of violence that get out of hand the state's actions will determine whether a larger foundation of persecution or tolerance will prevail. Third, and related to the second, we need to consider the manner in which difference is organized in society, the plurality of communities and identities, and the manner in which the relations of power are ordered in systematic ways. Finally, a successful framework needs to explain not only why toleration emerges in some settings and not others but also how toleration can turn into persecution (and vice versa).

A few decades ago Fredrik Barth alerted us to the importance of boundaries in the creation and the reproduction of ethnicity. Boundaries, he elegantly argued, shape and canalize social life and social relations between groups.

What happens at the boundary has a tremendous effect on the self-definition, identification of a group as well as its relations with others.[15] In understanding boundaries, many students of ethnicity have made a sound argument that states, through their actions and policies, can create, define, and manipulate ethnicity, therefore contributing to the marking of boundaries.[16] Joane Nagel, for example, focused on the political organization and operation of the state to clarify conditions under which ethnicity is reinforced. She argued that if the state organizes political access and participation along ethnic lines, then the latter will be reinforced.[17] By contrast, Eugene Weber showed how, by organizing around universal and republican principles, a state can forcefully erase differences between populations based on ethnicity, language, and history.[18] In the study of empires, whether the imperial state organizes around existing ethnic and religious boundaries (social and territorial), or whether it creates new administrative boundaries, it runs the risk of creating, maintaining, and reinforcing ethnicity and religious identification.[19]

Another important insight regarding boundaries and communities is a long-standing sociological one that people associate with others who resemble themselves and have been defined in similar ways.[20] More recently, the insight that communities persist despite the spread of modernity has been addressed by economists Sam Bowles and Herb Gintis, who argue that communities persist because they resolve economic or other collective problems that cannot otherwise be handled by individuals acting alone, markets, or states.[21] This is, I argue, not just a valuable insight for modern and postmodern societies. It remains equally valuable for premodern societies where communities also endured not just because of archaic feelings and intolerance to strangers but because the flow of information, the degree of trust between individuals, tended to be greater among those on the same side of the boundary, rather than across the boundary, facilitating relations and the resolving problems. It is, therefore, important to look at the ways in which communities persist in premodern times as well. As such, the social organization of ethnic and religious communities, their potential for mobilization, their degree of politicization will affect their relations with the dominant state. Such relations will also determine which groups can be tolerated and which cannot be tolerated.

When discussing the role of public authorities, toleration requires a certain basic level of state recognition of plurality of communities and identities, even if groups are not equal vis-à-vis the law. Many different historical and cultural antecedents and legacies, particular alliances the state enters into and the specific configuration of diversity on the ground, will affect this perspective on pluralism. A positive public attitude toward pluralism serves to encourage tolerance between communities, with the state leading by example or by force.

A Barthian perspective, one that underscores the importance of boundaries in the creation and reproduction of ethnicity,[22] helps us understand how boundaries are created: how they maintain themselves, and how interactions at the boundary create, reproduce, and uphold categories of actors. In order to perceive relations across boundaries we need to first think of the nature of boundaries. Boundaries separate, mark categories, and shape and channel social action. They also produce the conceptual distinctions that people overlay onto the objective boundary, thereby creating the restrictions, symbols, practices, and ways of identifying and separating.[23] Boundaries as such, in their conceptual representation, can be understood as rigid and impermeable or as flexible, easily crossed, and function as "mobile markers of difference."[24] That is, state and social actors understand difference to be a fact of social organization, but understand their location and significance to be variable and somewhat open to manipulation. Thus the more rigid the boundary between "us" and "them," the less movement and sharing across the boundary, the higher the degree of intolerance. Furthermore, boundary problems, considered in network terms, add more insight to the problem of toleration and intolerance. Ron Burt, for example, argues that, to the degree that network closure is avoided and brokerage across boundaries is possible, groups will tend to be more open to new ideas, cross-cultural innovation, and therefore, I think, accommodation.[25] The boundary then is the key site of negotiation between groups of different social and cultural organization. What is the negotiation based on?

The work of Charles Tilly on social boundary mechanisms and that of James Fearon and David Laitin on explaining interethnic cooperation can be seen as elaborations of the Barthian perspective and studies of relations at the boundaries.[26] Tilly maintains that both the degree of "localized common knowledge that participants in a transaction deploy" and the extent of "scripting for such a transaction that is already available jointly to the participants" are important to understand the circumstances under which groups tend to engage in transactions across boundaries. Local knowledge includes tacit understandings, such as those about spatial go and no go areas, memories of earlier conversations and interactions. Scripts are models—both normative and practical—for how interaction is supposed to occur, often secured by formal as well as informal rules and institutions backed by sanctions.[27] It is the relationship between scripts and local knowledge that provides the framework within which individuals, groups, and communities interact. The state or religious authorities might impose the script and the local knowledge of the particular community would help alter and shape the script through state society relations. Public authorities might be open to and strongly influenced by local knowledge when they shape their script, or they might ignore relations and traditions on the ground to firmly establish their ruling script.[28]

Political scientists James Fearon and David Laitin are much more interested in understanding the internal communal mechanisms that provide checks and balances regarding intergroup conflict. In their research, while the boundary is certainly a key site of negotiation, the strategies of group actors are decisive to ensure peace and restrain violence from spiraling. The key mechanisms of action to prevent a spiral of violence in which one side punishes the other collectively are patterns of group-to-group interaction largely unmediated by public authority. In such cases the absence of violence is simply a by-product of relations across boundaries and on the ground. Here not only are we asked to conceptualize particular intergroup process in the absence of the state and definite relations of domination across groups, but we are also prompted into a tit-for-tat game in which the actual cultural and social content of relations are insignificant. The calm that emerges from such boundary relations cannot be considered toleration, since toleration, as argued early on, is about suspending action and accepting to live with those who are deemed to be intolerable. However, this interethnic conflict and cooperation argument remains interesting since it provides us with examples of what community leaders will do to keep peace between communities, especially when the state will severely punish transgressions. Therefore, at moments of interboundary conflict, community leaders who engage in cross-boundary policing can maintain the greater toleration of the state.

In addition to these insights, we need to expand the analysis to theorize more effectively about situations where public authority is present or absent. While Bowles and Gintis as well as Fearon and Laitin focus on the communities themselves and the internal mechanisms of community survival and intergroup peace, we can only use their insight by adding the state as an important player in the relational field of ethnic and religious peace.

In understanding the emergence and transformation of toleration as well as persecution, we need to analyze the role of public authorities in the creation, maintenance, and provision of meaning to the boundaries that separate groups. We also need to understand the manner in which scripting by authorities and elites as well as local knowledge set rules for behavior across boundaries, how they set rules and conventions that become practiced by actors on different sides of the boundary. We can apply these insights to the historical trajectories of two empires that were contemporaries and whose historical trajectories were deeply intertwined. Yet their approaches to the management of diversity, to the toleration of religious diversity were often opposite and moving in different directions.

HISTORICAL CASES: A COMPARISON OF OTTOMAN AND HABSBURG TRAJECTORIES OF TOLERATION

The Habsburg and Ottoman Empires have been compared in many different contexts, especially in their nationality policies toward the end of their rule.[29] There has been, however, little work done on a comparison of the two empires along the dimensions of religious and ethnic toleration.[30] This is regrettable, since, at their foundation, the differences between the two empires are straightforward in that the Ottomans emerged as a more inclusive and tolerant polity, whereas the Habsburgs committed themselves to a level of religious orthodoxy that ended in violence against non-Catholic groups. Such differences are widely accepted despite the usual description of the Ottomans as a warfare-conquest-based empire and the Habsburgs as an empire built on marriage alliances. Yet the trajectories of these empires were reversed over the course of the eighteenth and early nineteenth century. At that time commercial development across the European world economy pushed the Habsburg emperors to the implementation of wide-ranging toleration toward their different religious and confessional groups, while economic incorporation had the reverse effect in the Ottoman Empire. The explosion of trade with the Western world and the connected developments in the Ottoman Empire moved a relatively tolerant state toward policies that culminated in the ethnic and religious bloodshed at the end of the empire. Seemingly, then, the same kind of phenomenon, economic development, had opposing effects on contemporary and comparable empires. Both the inquiry into the divergent forms of emergence and the puzzle of the changing policies and paths of toleration are interesting and liable to help us refine the concept of toleration, especially as it applies to premodern polities. It also bears to complicate the simple correlation between empire and toleration.

Though the Habsburg brand of "confessional absolutism" had harnessed a strong Catholic identity into state making, with the persecution and assimilation of Protestants through the sixteenth and especially seventeenth centuries, the eighteenth century spurred the development of mercantilism, state-directed economic growth, together with the realization that economic development necessitated the maintenance of privileges and immunities to diverse merchant groups and many different religious-ethnic groups. Consequently, Maria Theresa and, even more than her, her son Joseph II undertook sweeping social, economic, and educational reforms meant to create a new social order. Joseph's Toleration Patent of 1781, which offered different confessional groups and religious minorities religious, civil, and economic rights, initiated a solid evolutionary trend toward political emancipation, though short of creating its own French Revolution, since the reforms were strictly within the framework of an absolutist regime.

The Ottoman route to political emancipation was different. The Ottoman Empire as a multireligious hybrid empire developed early on a multiconfessional project that brought about early centuries of religious toleration. Not only was Ottoman Islam moderate, and institutionally dependent on the state, but the lack of a critical religious body such as the Catholic Church allowed for an entirely different initial conceptualization of diversity where religious difference was tolerated and the establishment of boundaries between groups helped the state and community leaders maintain a relative degree of inter-religious, interethnic peace. To complicate the historical analysis further, while the Ottomans were keen on being a diverse society, tolerant of non-Muslim communities, they became intolerant of Muslim heterodoxy, pursuing various Sufi orders. The toleration of non-Muslims, however, began to change with the eighteenth-century economic boom, where different European and local actors partook in the boundary production and maintenance functions of the state. Trade and economic development furthered inequalities between groups, and struggles between state-sponsored groups and European-sponsored groups, enhancing divisions within society. To take advantage of trade and economic development, community leaders developed into ethnic entrepreneurs, redefining ethnic and religious boundaries. The result was ethnic and religious competition rather than religious and confessional cooperation and tolerance.

We can use the theoretical framework just presented to understand the various choices of Ottoman and Habsburg elites both at the moments of the emergence of the empires as well as after the onset of economic transformation in the eighteenth century. Taking the role of the state seriously, we can distinguish between two different political authorities embedded in different alliances, with different historical legacies and religious perspectives. Such different political authorities facilitated the construction of rigid versus flexible boundaries between religious groups, crystallizing very different approaches to whether the other should be tolerated or persecuted. At their moments of emergence and early consolidation, the Ottomans were tolerant and the Habsburgs were intolerant of diversity. In this context toleration was the acceptance of diversity, the attempt to refrain from violence against those who were not of the same faith, and ensuring their security and livelihood. Persecution was the refusal to accept diversity, its coercion, and the brutal assimilation of difference into sameness.

Both cases have their narratives of emergence where a cultural script (religious blueprint and institutional knowledge as well as past practices) was confronted with the political and socioeconomic exigencies of the ground. The Ottomans emerged as relatively open-minded, tolerant state builders who brokered across the local groups and religions to construct a hybrid state. The Habsburgs, who became regretful of their initial negotiations with Protestant elites with the coming of the Counter-Reformation, quickly altered their course of action to build a robust "confessional absolutism" with the support of a strong Catholic Church. They chose to persecute instead of effectively brokering across groups. Each of these paths has to be understood in their respective historical context.

In the Ottoman Empire what came to be seen as a form of toleration emerged out of an Islamic approach to rule that accepted Christianity and Judaism as the two other religions, as well as a political Ottoman construction that made Islam a religion organized and strictly dependent on the state. Islam then provided the initial boundaries between Muslims and non-Muslims with instructions on how to run an Islamic state with non-Muslim populations ensconced in their particular religious and ecological niches. As the foundational legal and cultural system of the state, Islamic law and its practice dictated a relationship between a Muslim state and non-Muslim "Peoples of the Book," that is, Jews and Christians. According to this pact, the *dhimmis*, non-Muslims, would be protected, could practice their own religion, preserve their own places of worship, and to a large extent run their own affairs provided they recognized the superiority of Islam. Such was the preliminary script, based on the Pact of Umar, and as such it presented public authorities and communities with the boundaries that defined relations.[31]

Perhaps more significant was the historical and cultural legacy of the origins of the Turkic warriors who were to shape the Ottoman Empire. They came to Anatolia with past experience that combined Islam with their Turkish-Mongolian origins; their history of mixing in the lands they inhabited from China to the Pontic steppes shaped their view of intergroup relations. Later, as they settled in the Anatolian plateau to form the Seldjuk Empire, their patterns of intermarriage, the common appropriation of religious symbols and imagery (for example, the bust of Jesus in relief on Danismend coins), the continual contact across the frontiers with Orthodox Christendom, point toward fluid boundaries in multicultural settings. The fact that, in the early 1300s, Turkic chieftains wore their religion lightly is demonstrated further by their ability to convene meetings of theologians from different religions, letting them preach, but also engage in debates on religion with Muslims.[32] The particular nexus of emergence and early encounters with the "other" remain indispensable to understanding the precise brand of Ottoman "toleration." That early Ottomans were not boundary conscious and, in fact, exhibited a strong syncretic and multivocal religious understanding strongly favored by a heterodox form of Islam was crucial to the structure of opportunities present at the moment. Much of the movement back and forth at the frontiers occurred when the Turkish tribes did not have a strong institutionalized Islamic identity and when religion had not become atrophied into one formal tradition, again fostering openness to a diversity of views. At the same time, there is no doubt that they strategized, since conquering tribes practiced a policy of *istimalet*, that is, an attempt to make the indigenous population look upon them favorably by offering incentives, promising generosity and concessions such as permissions to retain lands and resources. The conditions on the ground were more favorable to an accommodationist strategy. Since the demographic and military advantage was not clearly in the hands of the Turks, this required openness toward Christians, making them allies, warriors in their cause, and incorporating them into the redistribution of resources.[33] Also, the frontier between Orthodox Christianity and Islam was extremely fluid, allowing for alliances and cultural interchange. This fluidity and tolerance was reinforced by the antagonism between Greek Orthodoxy and western Catholicism. The schism that was reinforced by the sack of Constantinople in 1204 would both bring peoples of different religions closer together and provide the conquering Ottoman state with room to maneuver and exploit divisions outside its realm. The Ottoman state emerged as a hybrid state that included Muslim and Orthodox Christian elites as both their religious idiom was syncretic and their experience with the boundaries and communities on the ground necessitated accommodation, brokerage across religious and social networks. The institutional innovation that brought Ottomans to success was toleration as a strategy of incorporation.[34]

This emergent form of accommodation to and toleration of non-Muslims was to get institutionalized further through the threshold of imperialization, with an understanding of diversity as a positive value for society, especially as robustly endorsed by public authorities. The legendary account of Sultan Suleiman the Magnificent's words on this question are evocative. Asked whether Jews should be exterminated from his empire since they were usurers, he responded by asking his councillors to observe the vase of multicolored and shaped flowers, admonishing them that each flower with its own shape and color added to the beauty of the other. He then went on to affirm that "he ruled over many different nations—Turks, Moors, Greeks and others. Each of these nations contributed to the wealth and reputation of his kingdom, and in order to continue this happy situation, he deemed it wise to continue to tolerate those who were already living together under his rule."[35] Often these policies of toleration extended beyond the core Ottoman lands, especially the Hungarian and Habsburg edges where the contentious politics of the post-Reformation played themselves out. The Ottomans eagerly interfered on behalf of the reformed churches, seeing them as more compatible with Islam, but also found anti-Catholicism to be politically and culturally useful. Stephen Fisher-Galati puts it plainly: "the infidel Turk was, in fact, the probable savior of Protestantism in Germany and the ultimate guarantor of Protestant interests in Hungary and Transylvania."[36] Even though this assessment is clearly exaggerated, recent work on the antecedents of John Sigismund's Edict of Torda (1568) shows that about twenty years earlier the pasha of Buda, representative of the sultan, had issued a similar edict of toleration where he stated that "preachers of the faith invented by Luther should be allowed to preach the Gospel everywhere to everybody, whoever wants to hear, freely and without fear, and that all Hungarians and Slavs (who indeed wish to do so) should be able to listen to and receive the word of God without any danger. Because—he said—this is the true Christian faith and religion."[37] Such examples of public authority involvement in the social and cultural relations between communities of different religions are reproduced in various ways across the empire.[38]

The Habsburg pattern was different in that toleration was not the rule, but the exception. Habsburg Christianity no doubt embodied a different perspective of the unity of church and polity, but also was firmly grounded in the belief in the exclusive domination of Christianity. The Habsburg Empire emerged not only from the Holy Roman Empire, but, more generally from a medieval persecuting Christian Europe that had seldom tolerated Jews and had launched the Crusades against the Muslim enemy. The Catholic religion, its institutions and its values, were fully fused with the political order, and the Habsburgs, as descendants of the Holy Roman imperial church, saw themselves as the guardians of all Christendom and the frontiers protecting Christian Europe against Islam. The expansion and consolidation of the Habsburg Empire at the beginning of the early modern period did come about through key marriage alliances, first with Burgundian and Spanish dynasties, then with the king of Hungary and Bohemia, establishing the second Habsburg state in east-central Europe. The first, with Castille as the center, would be where future emperors of the eastern empire were educated and where they learned the lessons of conflict between different Christian confessions. Rudolph II (1576–1612) and Matthias I (1612–1619) both were educated in the court of Philip II where they learned that religious uniformity was necessary for imperial unity.[39] The eastern empire was consolidated and separated from the Spanish counterpart firmly when Ferdinand I was elected and crowned king of Bohemia in 1617, of Hungary in 1618, and then declared emperor in 1619 with the death of Matthias. This was the beginning of a new era for the German branch of the Habsburg dynasty and the beginning of a process of centralization and consolidation of an empire.[40]

With the confessionalization of Western Europe as the Reformation unfolded, the east-central empire, the Habsburgs had included much diversity: a large segment of the German-speaking population of the Austrian, Hungarian, and Bohemian lands and Inner Austria's Slovenes and Upper Hungary's Slovaks and parts of Vienna had become Lutheran. The Magyars of Hungary had become Calvinists, and the Czechs who maintained Catholicism were still practicing anti-Roman Hussite or Utraquist versions, and many Czechs had also become Calvinists. At the Croatian border, Catholic Croatia encountered large numbers of Orthodox Serbians.[41] There were many reasons for this, among them that, during the early establishment of the empire, rulers who were busy fending off other external forces, such as the Turks, chose to allow Protestantism, providing both Catholic and Protestant nobles the right to impose their religion over their subjects. Maximilian and Rudolf both were also tolerant of Judaism, and in 1609 Rudolf officially granted freedom of worship to the Bohemian confession.[42] The three rulers, Maximilian II, Rudolph II, and Matthias I were each faced with political and economic crises during which they agreed to protect the rights of their Protestant nobility.

The emergence of this new confessional map and the proliferation of these Christian churches outside the Catholic Church, with the acquisition of a variety of lands and diverse populations, turned the Habsburg Empire into a veritable confessional mosaic. The dominant religion, Roman Catholicism, was the state religion in tension with other recognized churches, the Protestant, Uniate, and Orthodox. Within Europe the Habsburgs quickly became among the most troubled by the religious conflicts of the Reformation. The Catholic Habsburgs were becoming the minority, and the issue of ruling such confessional diversity became paramount. It was this religious chaos, this lack of clearly defined orthodoxy and structure that the Habsburg state faced. Moreover, as Daniel Nexon explains, the danger was that the Protestant Reformation had created transnational and transregional movements that "crossed social, economic and regional divisions" and "undermined the ways in which European rulers had maintained their authority by dividing and ruling their subjects and holdings."[43]

A powerful process of Catholicization was chosen not just because it was consonant with the historical traditions and ideological legitimacy of the dynasty but also because institutionally the Catholic Church had the means necessary, especially the cadres of Jesuit preachers, teachers, professors, censors, and advisers, and the Catholic Church was eager to work with the state in the project of imposing Catholic confessional uniformity. Among the variety of responses to the process of Catholicization, the Bohemian and Moravian provinces rebelled in 1618 as they feared that they were losing their religious freedom. With the Battle of the White Mountain in November 1620, a deep and violent process of uniformization of religious faith commenced. The result was that, with the reign of Ferdinand II and throughout the Counter-Reformation, persecution became excessive and strident, a policy of the crown intent on consolidation and centralization with religious unification necessary to ensure loyalty. The reimposition of Catholicism as the only state religion proceeded to the detriment especially of the Protestant landed nobility, forcing an important demographic shift in the Czech population of the time. Accordingly, about 150,000 Protestant refugees fled from Bohemia and Moravia, their manors were appropriated by Catholic nobility, and the casualties only grew in numbers in the ensuing Thirty Years War.[44]

The process of imposing Catholic uniformity worked in different ways. In the case of Bohemia and the Hereditary lands of Austria, rebellion and warfare facilitated massive, coercive transformations. Here, in what Bireley calls "confessional absolutism," centralization, the princely dominance over estates, and the advancement of Catholicism was unified into one coherent policy of state making.[45] Different forms of control and reorganization of religious boundaries were established in Hungary and Transylvania. Though diversity and toleration was mainly seen through confessional lenses, there were other groups such as Jews and Muslims who also lived within the confines of the empire. Though Jews fared better overall than Protestants, they remained in a precarious situation, a privileged corporation whose privileges were awarded and withdrawn for political and economic reasons. While they were financially important to the crown, they unintentionally entered the contested terrain between the crown and the nobility, part of a struggle for political jurisdiction. Such a precarious condition led to many local expulsions, with the striking expulsion of Jews from Vienna in 1669.[46] Similarly, in Bohemia and Moravia they were sent into exile or illegality, with ghettoization as the next step in the eighteenth century. The situation for Jews only worsened as the restrictions in their social and legal status increased, with the persecution reaching its height during the reign of Maria Theresa. It is during her reign that Jews were evicted from Prague (1744), only a portion of the greater numbers of Protestants, "heretic" Bohemian and Moravian farmers were sent to Prussian Silesia, and many more revolts were harshly suppressed between 1775 and 1777. Her chancellor, Wenzel Anton von Kaunitz, tried to explain the importance of toleration of Protestants, since she risked losing them to Prussia, but to no avail.[47] It was only under the rule of her son Joseph II that Habsburg policy would start changing.

The Habsburg monarchy then established itself and consolidated its power by persecuting difference as it perceived it to be a threat to state building and

Catholic consolidation. In this case not only the spread of Reformation ideals but also the potential networks of alliance between coreligionists across regional and political boundaries was perceived as a threat to the state and the Catholic Church. The state-making alliance of Habsburg political and religious authorities instead chose to construct rigid boundaries, eliminate diversity that had emerged from the Reformation, while maintaining some restricted compacts with the Jewish or other trading groups in specific locations when this directly served their economic interests.[48]

EIGHTEENTH CENTURY REVERSAL: HABSBURG TOLERATION AND OTTOMAN PERSECUTION

From the eighteenth century on, both empires experienced tremendous economic change that came as development as well as a crisis of resources. Both empires were challenged by outside forces, lost territories, and experienced crises of state finances. In each case state elites reacted to such financial crises by trying to reorganize the fiscal system to better finance the state, but also opened up opportunities for new forms of transformation, temporary relief to state treasuries, new relations between elites and the state, as well as new socioeconomic and political relations across diverse ethnic and religious groups. In each of these cases an established cultural script, one of Catholic dominance and the other of Islamic rule over diversity, was challenged by emerging ideas of the Enlightenment, toleration, as well as ideas of reform. Again, in each case, the particular outcome of toleration or persecution emerged through the combination of exigencies on the ground and negotiations around cultural understandings, long-established, but now freshly contested.

The Habsburg case is a good example of the development of toleration for reasons of economic and trading opportunities. The Habsburgs lost three wars from 1733 to 1748, with important territorial losses. Among the losses, that of Silesia to Prussia during the War of Austrian Succession hit the empire hard. The much discussed tendency toward economic stagnation then became more daunting, since Silesia was an important economic domain that by itself contributed 25 percent of the direct tax revenues of the empire.[49] During the peaceful moments of Charles VI's reign (1711–1740), there was an effort toward industrialization and mercantilist development. However, the question of industrialization, reform, and economic development took on more urgency during the reign of Maria Theresa (1740–1780). Maria Theresa was the first monarch to confront the financial crisis, and her government understood the necessity for administrative and financial reform. On the economic front, government encouragement and promotion of private investment went a long way to promoting proto-industrialization, with many new factories and processes of production. To facilitate production and commerce, the government also worked to remove some impediments to development, such as guild restrictions or discrimination against non-Catholic skilled workers.[50] Many of these changes paid off relatively quickly. By 1754, crown income had doubled from 20 to 40 million florins.[51] A staunch supporter of the Counter-Reformation, Maria Theresa's actions cannot be seen as motivated by religious toleration, but rather by a program of economic development. When she took specific steps to attract Ottoman and other traders into Austrian lands, when she declared Trieste a free maritime city and granted merchants their religious freedom, this was the result of economic expediency. Over time, Greeks, Armenians, and Italians were given burgher status in cities.[52]

The Habsburg Empire in the mid-eighteenth century was certainly experiencing a type of toleration that emerged from economic necessities, where concerted action on the part of state leaders loosened the boundaries between groups to allow for trouble-free trading relations. Maria Theresa was conflicted about religious toleration. She continued to espouse religious uniformity as the key to imperial success, yet she agreed with a few actions that would help free trade restrictions on non-Catholic subjects. Meanwhile, larger moves toward religious toleration were afoot in the empire, and Maria Theresa's son, Joseph II, and her foreign minister, Wenzel Anton von Kaunitz, strongly encouraged her to follow the trend. Kaunitz's views on toleration in particular were genuine, as he had been strongly influenced by the Enlightenment and his readings of Voltaire's *Traite sur la Tolerance* (1763), and had tried to implement his ideas with many actions such as the granting of small communities of Greeks freedom of worship, fighting against a decree on blasphemy in Austria and Bohemia. By the 1760s, various intellectuals and members of the Masonic movement, some of whom were government officials, turned toward policies of toleration, independently reaching the conclusion that confessional toleration was the better solution.[53] Yet the church and society at large were not ready for these changes.

When Joseph II became regent with his mother in 1765 and then emperor in 1780, he was ready to push on a more general and practical form of toleration. He would become the emperor of the Edict of Toleration, but he was primarily a state builder, pragmatist, and cameralist in his thinking, most notably impressed by the ideas of Cesare Beccaria, who preached for government to satisfy "the welfare and happiness" of the greatest number of its people.[54] For Joseph II, the good of the state, the reorganization of society to serve it better, drove ideals of forbearance and accommodation to religious and ethnic difference. His enlightened absolutism brought about the Edict of Toleration for religious minorities in the empire and the Protestant and Orthodox subjects of the monarchy. He understood that "a confessionally even-handed polity asked only for civic loyalty from its citizens and was strengthened by the gratitude of religious minorities."[55] Some of his policies had started with the Jews, as he first gave them educational and vocational opportunities, then proceeded to eliminate the various reprehensible restrictions that Jews had lived with within Habsburg lands. The Patent of 1782 eliminated dress restrictions and opened up some professions to Jews, while keeping restrictions about settlement and population. It is important to understand that the toleration program was not all encompassing and did not apply to every community of non-Catholic persuasion. Even within communities, distinctions were made. Areas of commercial importance were provided with privileges of economic and cultural dimensions, while places such as Galicia, a Jewish province par excellence, was left untouched. In Trieste, which had been a commercial center for a long time where Jews had lived with many long-established privileges, the locals had to petition Joseph II to include ancient privileges with the new ones.[56] In response, Joseph II assured the Jews of Trieste that his intention was to improve their fate and not take their privileges away.

Here we see the coming together of *raison d'état* and mercantilism that dictate a policy of toleration. In his patent, he declares: "for me toleration means, without taking account of religion . . . employ and allow to own lands, enter trades and become citizens, those who are competent and would bring advantage and industry to the Monarchy." In the end, the genteel toleration patent was not enough to heed off antimonarchy nationalist uprisings. That came partly as a result of the other side of the toleration coin, that of enlightened absolutism, the policy that created adversity and upheaval in the monarchy.

In the case of the Ottoman Empire, state leaders were also at the forefront of the response to the economic development and challenges of the eighteenth century. However, unlike the Habsburg monarchy, they were less involved in the redrawing of interreligious and interethnic boundaries. When state reforms came to pass in the nineteenth century, ethnic and religious boundaries had been reaffirmed, antagonism across boundaries was already a fact of life. Very differently from the Habsburg attempts at mercantilist and then cameralist reforms, in the Ottoman Empire, the market developed from within the merchant class in the empire, without direct state support and encouragement. The Ottoman state's economic policies in the eighteenth century, which were still fiscalist, provisionalist, and traditionalist, kept state leaders from investing directly in the market.[57] They attempted to benefit from it only indirectly, through control of trade routes (although diminished) and taxing the profits of their merchants. Yet, as both internal and the external demands expanded, market forces started eroding the command structure of the Ottoman economy, allowing for an unprecedented flow of goods and the development of credit outlets. In many ways then, the economy was flourishing just as the state confronted severe cash flow problems. The solution was an attempt to redirect societal wealth to the state.

Overall, even though markets developed and merchants expanded their wealth, this economic transformation was not altogether beneficial to all members of the Ottoman state and society. First, it developed as the result of Ottoman incorporation into the Western system, becoming much more profitable for the Western nations. The Ottomans ended up in a semicolonized pattern. Second, the economic transition generated bitter competition between social groups for resources and privileges, impacting issues of religious and ethnic difference. Where non-Muslim merchants emerged as key intermediaries between Europe and the Ottoman Empire, and when

Europeans actively used them to carry on their work in the empire and ensured that they acquired a protected status, tensions between communities increased and Europeans interfered more frequently. What ensued was widespread anxiety about the rapid upward mobility of non-Muslim mercantile classes and the natural order of Ottoman society. Given the vagaries of commerce and the insecurity of the intermediate position that many non-Muslims were locked into, they chose to revert to a community based on ethnic and religious ties, familiar local identities tying them to the national discourses available in their Western interactions. Therefore non-Muslims who had spread throughout the empire with trade and finance developed far-reaching networks, started in the eighteenth century, to consolidate their identities around the traditional differences maintained by empire. Muslims, on the other hand, who were locked out of many trading relations because they were not Christian or did not know the European languages, became aware of their newly acquired disadvantage and united in their Muslim identities in resentment. This was a recipe for intercommunal disaster.

The upshot was that toleration based on Muslim hegemony was broken. By the nineteenth century, Ottoman reforms to respond to European pressure and deal with increased ethnic and religious contention led to genuine attempts in 1839 and 1856 to construct an emancipated civil society. The economic advantages of the non-Muslims were now compounded with political equality in the eyes of the Muslim population. These were only some of the ingredients that brought Ottoman society into violent conflict, not to mention the rise of Balkan nationalism, the immigration of Muslims into Ottoman lands from lost territories, and the increased Islamic identity emerging in the empire. The process of economic development initiated by Western trading not adequately controlled and harnessed by the imperial government triggered a reversal of long-standing Ottoman toleration of non-Muslims, reverting to violence in the tragic trajectory from empire to nation-state.

On the road to the dissolution of these empires, their international position, the actions of the imperial states, as well the boundaries that were reformulated in the eighteenth century prepared the ground for explicit forms of religious toleration in the Habsburg Empire while bringing about local massacres and state-led genocide in the Ottoman Empire. While the history of the transitions to nation-states was complex, there is no doubt that part of the difference between the two empires was in the manner in which the imperial states decided to respond to the complicated double act of economic crises and economic opportunities working themselves out in the eighteenth century. Yet the development of mercantilism and the enlightenment ideas that were indigenous to the West were also more beneficial to the Habsburg monarchy, which was accorded a protection in the concert of Europe. This was just the opposite in the Ottoman Empire, which was caught in a moment of weakness, perceived as the "Sick Man of Europe," and possibly only had the choice of being incorporated as a semicolonized entity. Within the latter, toleration was dismantled at the level of the populace, only to be taken up more harshly by a weakened and threatened state.

The comparative analysis of these two cases, which came to maturity in around the same centuries, declining and disappearing at the same time, demonstrates, first, that the positive relationship that has been assumed between empire and toleration is not necessarily the case. Empires have had the potential for toleration and in many circumstances have chosen to incorporate different populations and have refrained from persecution. Yet they have also engaged in serious persecution of minority populations. Such a comparison of toleration also allows us to study the conditions under which toleration can emerge, how it is sustained and becomes institutionalized in society. Toleration then can be examined in its historical, analytical, and cultural dimensions. By historicizing toleration, we understand the variations of the phenomenon and its life cycle, its emergence and persistence, and also its transformation. By looking at its analytic dimension, we can understand the conditions under which toleration emerges, why it emerges, whether for pragmatic or idealist reasons or a combination of the two. Here I argued that toleration was a relational boundary phenomenon and that we needed to understand its various dimensions within this framework. By looking at its cultural dimension, we can both understand how toleration becomes perceived and understood by members of society and how cognition of toleration impacts the actions of individuals.

NOTES

1. J. P. Nettl, "The State as a Conceptual Variable," *World Politics* 20 (1968): 559–92.
2. Ira Katznelson, "Regarding Toleration and Liberalism: Considerations from the Anglo-Jewish Experience," in Ira Katznelson and Gareth Stedman Jones, eds., *Religion and the Political Imagination* (Cambridge: Cambridge University Press, 2010), p. 48.
3. David Nirenberg, *Communities of Violence: Persecution of Minorities in the Middle Ages* (Princeton: Princeton University Press, 1996).
4. Bob Scribner, "Preconditions of Tolerance and Intolerance," in Ole Peter Grell and Bob Scribner, eds., *Tolerance and Intolerance in the European Reformation* (Cambridge: Cambridge University Press, 1996), p. 43.
5. Ibid.
6. James D. Fearon and David D. Laitin, "Explaining Interethnic Cooperation," *American Political Science Review* 90, no. 4 (December 1996): 715–35.
7. See Heiko Oberman, "The Travail of Tolerance: Containing Chaos in Early Modern Europe," in Grell and Scribner, *Tolerance and Intolerance,* p. 1331.
8. G. R. Elton, "Persecution and Toleration in the English Reformation," in W. J. Sheils, ed., *Persecution and Toleration* (Oxford: Oxford University Press, 1984), pp. 163–87.
9. Gavin I. Langmuir, *Toward a Definition of Antisemitism* (Los Angeles: University of California Press, 1990), pp. 63–99.
10. Ira Katznelson calls these evolutionary and realist explanations of toleration. See his "Regarding Toleration and Liberalism: Considerations from the Anglo-Jewish Experience," in Gareth Stedman Jones and Ira Katznelson, eds. *Religion and the Political Imagination* (Cambridge: Cambridge University Press, 2010).
11. Henry Kamen, *The Rise of Toleration* (New York: McGraw Hill, 1967).
12. Perez Zagorin, *How the Idea of Religious Toleration Came to the West* (Princeton: Princeton University Press, 2003), pp. 12–13.
13. Grell and Scribner, *Tolerance and Intolerance.*
14. Scribner, "Preconditions of Tolerance and Intolerance," p. 39.
15. Fredrik Barth, *Ethnic Groups and Boundaries: The Social Organization of Cultural Difference* (Boston: Little Brown, 1969), p. 14.
16. There is no doubt that the literature where this argument has been exposed most clearly is that of the colonial state. For examples, see David Laitin, *Hegemony and Culture: The Politics of Religious Change Among the Yoruba* (Chicago: University of Chicago Press, 1986); Mahmoud Mamdani, *Citizen and Subject: Contemporary Africa and the Legacy of Late Colonialism* (Princeton: Princeton University Press, 1996); Joel Migdal, *Strong Societies and Weak States* (Princeton: Princeton University Press, 1988). These are just some examples from a much longer list of studies of colonial relations.
17. Joane Nagel, "The Political Construction of Ethnicity," in Susan Olzak and Joane Nagel, eds., *Competitive Ethnic Relations,* (Waltham, MA: Academic, 1986) pp. 93–112.
18. Eugen Weber, *Peasants Into Frenchmen: The Modernization of Rural France, 1870–1914* (Palo Alto: Stanford University Press, 1976).

19. The case of the Soviet Union and the creation of the Republics is an excellent example. There is an extensive literature on this, though in sociology Brubaker has made the point most succinctly. See Rogers Brubaker, *Nationalism Reframed: Nationhood and the National Question in the New Europe* (Cambridge: Cambridge University Press, 1996).
20. P. F. Lazarsfeld and Robert K. Merton, "Friendship as a Social Process," in Monroe Berger and Robert Morrison MacIver, eds., *Freedom and Control in Modern Society* (Princeton: Princeton University Press, 1954); George Homans, *Social Behavior: Its Elementary Forms* (New York: Harcourt Brace, 1961).
21. Samuel Bowles and Herbert Gintis, " Social Capital and Community Governance," *Economic Journal* 112 (November 2002): F419–F436; Samuel Bowles and Herbert Gintis, "Persistent Parochialism: Trust and Exclusion in Ethnic Networks," *Journal of Economic Behavior and Organization* 55 (2004): 1–23.
22. Fredrik Barth, ed., *Ethnic Groups and Boundaries: The Social Organization of Cultural Difference* (Boston: Little, Brown, 1969).
23. Michele Lamont and Virag Molnar, "The Study of Boundaries in the Social Sciences," *Annual Review of Sociology* 28 (August 2002): 167–95.
24. Karen Barkey, *Empire of Difference: Ottomans in Comparative Perspective* (Cambridge: Cambridge University Press, 2008).
25. Ronald S. Burt, "Structural Holes and Good Ideas," *American Journal of Sociology* 110 (2004): 349–99.
26. Charles Tilly, *Durable Inequality* (Los Angeles: University of California Press, 1998); Fearon and Laitin, "Explaining Interethnic Cooperation."
27. Tilly, *Durable Inequality.*
28. James Scott, in his book *Seeing Like the State,* similarly deals with the way in which public authorities in the formulation of their high-modernist projects often ignore local knowledge (which he calls metis) and often will fail as a result of such intransigence. See his *Seeing Like a State: How Certain Schemes to Improve the Human Condition Have Failed* (New Haven: Yale University Press, 1998).
29. Solomon Wank, "The Habsburg Empire," in Karen Barkey and Mark von Hagen, eds., *After Empire: Multiethnic Societies and Nation-Building, The Soviet Union and the Russian, Ottoman, and Habsburg Empires* (Boulder: Westview, 1997), and "The Disintegration of the Habsburg and Ottoman Empires: A Comparative Analysis," in Karen Dawisha and Bruce Parrott, eds., *The End of Empires* (New York: Sharpe, 1996), pp. 94–120; Alexander Motyl, "From Imperial Decay to Imperial Collapse: The Fall of the Soviet Empire in Comparative Perspective," in Richard L. Rudolph and David F. Good, eds., *Nationalism and Empire: The Habsburg Empire and the Soviet Union* (New York: St. Martin's, 1992).
30. One exception is the work of Fikret Adanir, "Religious Communities and Ethnic Groups Under Imperial Sway," in Dirk Hoerder, Christiane Harzigis, and Adrian Shubert, eds., *The Historical Practice of Diversity: Transcultural Interactions from the Early Modern Mediterranean to the Postcolonial World* (New York: Berghahn, 2003), pp. 54–86.
31. The boundaries differentiating between Muslims and the Peoples of the Book were meant to separate societies where these groups coexisted and mixed and socialized, necessitating

markers of difference. Among these were obligation to wear distinct clothing, refrain from public demonstrations of faith offensive to Islam, but also refrain from construction that overlooked Muslim neighborhoods, mosques, and buildings. See C. E. Bosworth, "The Concept of *Dhimma* in Early Islam," in Benjamin Braude and Bernard Lewis, eds., *Christians and Jews in the Ottoman Empire: The Functioning of a Plural Society* (New York: Holmes and Meier, 1982), pp. 37–55. Other classic statements include Hamilton Gibb and Harold Bowen, *Islamic Society and the West: A Study of the Impact of Western Civilization on Moslem Culture in the Near East*, vol. 1: *Islamic Society in the Eighteenth Century* (London: Oxford University Press, 1950), part 1; Yohanan Friedmann, *Tolerance and Coercion in Islam: Interfaith Relations in the Muslim Tradition* (Cambridge: Cambridge University Press, 2006). There has been a recent politicized argument on the *dhimmi* status that presents the standing and history of *dhimmis* in the Muslim world in a disquieting negative light. See Bat Ye'or, *The Dhimmi: Jews and Christians Under Islam* (Rutherford, NJ: Fairleigh Dickinson University Press, 1985); and a newer book by the same author, Islam and *Dhimmitude*: Where Civilizations Collide (Madison, NJ: Farleigh Dickinson University Press, 2002). These represent a variety of views of the relations between Muslims and *dhimmis*.

32. See especially Adanir, "Religious Communities and Ethnic Groups"; also, Cemal Kafadar, *Between Two Worlds: The Construction of the Ottoman State* (Berkeley: University of California Press, 1995).
33. Heath W. Lowry, in his *The Nature of the Early Ottoman State* (Albany: State University of New York Press, 2003), has a more pragmatic explanation for the openness toward non-Muslims. See also Karen Barkey, *Empire of Difference: The Ottomans in Comparative Perspective* (Cambridge: Cambridge University Press, 2008) for a more complete discussion of early Ottoman state making.
34. Barkey, *Empire of Difference.*
35. Mark Haberlein, "A Sixteenth-Century German Traveller's Perspective on Discrimination and Tolerance in the Ottoman Empire," in Gudmundur Hálfdanarson, ed., *Discrimination and Tolerance in Historical Perspective* (Pisa: Plus-Pisa University Press, 2008).
36. Stephen Fisher-Galati, "The Protestant Reformation and Islam," in Abraham Asher, Tibor Halasi-Kun, and Bela K. Kiraly, eds., *The Mutual Effects of the Islamic and Judeo-Christian Worlds: The East European Pattern* (New York: Columbia University Press, 1979), p. 58.
37. Quoted in Susan Ritchie, "The Pasha of Buda and the Edit of Torda: Transylvanian Unitarian/Islamic Ottoman Cultural Enmeshment and the Development of Religious Tolerance," *Journal of Unitarian Universalist History*, 30 (2005): 48–49. See also Leslie C. Tihany, "Islam and the Eastern Frontiers of Reformed Protestantism," *Reformed Review: A Journal of the Seminaries of the Reformed Church in America* 29 (1975): 52–71; and Gustav Bayerle, *The Hungarian Letters of Ali Pasha of Buda, 1604–1616* (Budapest: Akademiai Kiado, 1991).
38. See other examples of interreligious, interethnic relations within a larger framework of toleration: Marketa P. Rubesova, "Living in a Multicultural Neighborhood: Ottoman Society

Reflected in Rabbinic Responsa of the Sixteenth and Seventeenth Centuries," in Lud'a Klusakova and Laue Teulieres, eds., *Frontiers and Identities: Cities in Regions and Nations* (Pisa: Plus-Pisa University Press, 2008), pp. 137–52; Elena Brambilla, "Convivencia Under Muslim Rule: The Island of Cyprus After the Ottoman Conquest (1571–1640)," pp. 121–38, in *EU-Turkey Dialogue, A Cliohworld Reader*, http://www.cliohworld.net/. On the other hand, Charles H. Parker in his "Paying for Privilege: The Management of Public Order and Religious Pluralism in Two Early-Modern Societies," *Journal of World History* 17, no. 3 (September 2006): 267–96, associated the religious pluralism in the Ottoman Empire with not only insensitive management of diversity, but sees no constructive or beneficial aspect to Ottoman rule, assessing it as hierarchical, discriminatory, and persecutory even if they managed to coexist with non-Muslims.

39. Charles Ingrao, *The Habsburg Monarchy, 1618–1815* (Cambridge: Cambridge University Press, 1994). p. 5.
40. Robert A. Kann, *History of the Habsburg Empire, 1526–1918* (Berkeley: University of California Press, 1974), pp. 48–49.
41. Ibid. pp. 29–30.
42. Martin J. Wein, "'Chosen Peoples, Holy Tongues' Religion, Language, Nationalism and Politics in Bohemia and Moravia in the Seventeenth to Twentieth Centuries" *Past and Present* 202 (February 2009): 41.
43. Daniel Nexon, "Religion, European Identity and Political Contention in Historical Perspective," in Timothy A. Brynes and Peter J. Katzenstein, eds., *Religion in an Expanding Europe* (Cambridge: Cambridge University Press, 2003), pp. 256–83.
44. Robert A. Kann, *History of the Habsburg Empire, 1526–1918* (Berkeley: University of California Press, 1974), 137–39; Jaroslav Panek, "The Question of Tolerance in Bohemia and Moravia in the Age of Reformation," in Grell and Scribner, *Tolerance and Intolerance,* pp. 231–48; Wein, "'Chosen Peoples, Holy Tongues,'" p. 42.
45. Robert Bireley, S.J., "Confessional Absolutism in the Habsburg Lands in the Seventeenth Century," in Charles W. Ingrao, ed., *State and Society in Early Modern Austria* (West (Lafayette, IN: Perdue University Press, 1994), pp. 36–53.
46. R. Po-chia Hsia, "The Jews and the Emperors," ibid., pp. 71–80.
47. Wien, "'Chosen Peoples, Holy Tongues,'" pp. 48–50.
48. Lois C. Dubin, *The Port Jews of Habsburg Trieste: Absolutist Politics and Enlightenment Culture* (Stanford: Stanford University Press, 1999). Even though this book is about the later period of Habsburg-Jewish relations in Trieste, Dubin provides a nice historical analysis of the early compacts.
49. David F. Good, *The Economic Rise of the Habsburg Empire, 1750–1914* (Berkeley: University of California Press, 1984), p. 28. See also Ingrao, *The Habsburg Monarchy*, pp. 159–68, for an analysis of the fiscal problems of this empire.
50. Herman Freudenberger, "Government and Economy: Introduction," in Ingrao, *State and Society in Early Modern Austria*, pp. 141–53.
51. Ingrao, *The Habsburg Monarchy*, pp. 164–65.
52. Adanir, "Religious Communities and Ethnic Groups," p. 67.

MODERNITY, STATE, AND TOLERATION IN INDIAN HISTORY

Exploring Accommodations and Partitions

SUDIPTA KAVIRAJ

THERE IS A common prejudice in modern social sciences that views the question of toleration through a simple linear narrative and presents a plausible progressivist view of the relation between religion, modernity, and the practice of toleration. I would like to suggest that this belief is detrimental to a real understanding of historical evidence, drawing primarily on the complex experience of the Indian subcontinent.

WHAT IS WRONG WITH COMMON MODES OF SEEING THE PROBLEM

Modern social science absorbed from the Enlightenment a persistent tendency to present a narrative of linear development of human civilization in which each successive stage is viewed as an improvement on the previous one, and at the time of the rise of modern social theory this form of thinking was also permeated by an uncritical Orientalist prejudices against other cultures. Developments in modern Europe were usually considered the final achievements of humanity in every field; although it was at times acknowledged that previous cultures had startling achievements to their credit, these were nearly always considered deficient in relation to the full achievement of humanistic principles in European modernity.[1] As religious toleration was considered a significant value of social life, it was given a genealogy that accorded with these two background beliefs.[2] Instances of religious accommodation from around the world were often collected and compared condescendingly with the achievements of the modern Western rationalist state, which realized principles of political toleration in religious life. Applying the same historiographic principles to an understanding of Indian history, colonial historians, who were the first to produce modern Indian historiography, often spoke approvingly of earlier imperial states and rulers like Asoka, the Mauryan emperor who pledged nonviolence after a devastating war in Kalinga, and the Mughal emperor Akbar as rulers who "anticipated" modern principles of toleration between different faiths. But the underlying premises of that historiography always regarded these situations as *episodic*—transient periods of accommodation in a history marked by unremitting religious hatred. Careful analysis shows both sides of this picture—of the past and the implicit one of the present, which persuades us to picture the past in that precise way—to be misleading. Equally misleading is the tendency, deeply embedded in "universal histories" of nineteenth-century Europe, that saw histories of all cultures at all times trying to resolve the central problems of modern life and coming up with imperfect solutions.[3] This view is misleading on at least two separate counts: in suggesting, first, that the solutions devised by such rulers were similar in principle to modern secularism, only less perfect, and, second, that the nature of conflict between religious groups in premodern times was fundamentally the same as in modern history. Evidence from Indian history encourages us to think of comparative history in a more decentered fashion—i.e., not with the presumption that all previous history is failed attempts to achieve modern solutions. It serves to show that religious diversity was a question faced by entirely different cultures at very different historical moments, and they strove to find solutions to these questions that were entirely disparate, but comparable. In this chapter I shall present four episodes from a long and complex history—to illustrate the patterns of political construction by means of which societies sought to bring some resolution to this fundamentally contentious question.

WHAT IS INTERESTING ABOUT INDIAN HISTORY

In European history the question of religious conflict increasingly became a serious intellectual and political issue after the Reformation. All major religions develop great internal diversities of doctrine and observance through historical evolution; this was true of European Christianity. But for a long time those diversities did not lead to a serious political conflict that threatened to destroy the entire civilization of Europe. Christianity in Europe faced two kinds of challenges from diversity. Enclaves of other religious groups, especially Jewish groups, existed within a primarily Christian continent, but the Jews of Europe never had either the numbers or the political organization to act as serious contenders to Christian hegemony.[4] Second, periodic eruption of heterodoxies remained relatively minor, so that the Church successfully policed and contained them through its internal mechanisms of social control. These asymmetric challenges to Catholic orthodoxy were contained partly by religious mechanisms of control like the Inquisition and partly by direct use of political power. After the conquest of Spain for Catholicism, and the expulsion of Jews and Muslims, Europe did not face serious challenges arising out of religious diversity until the Reformation. Although for centuries, Europe faced the *external* threat of Islamic military power, in recurrent wars with the expanding Ottoman Empire, Islam never occupied a stable internal region within European Christian space. The Turks failed to infiltrate middle Europe in sufficiently large numbers until the late twentieth century.

The contrast with the Indian case is interesting—first, because of the sheer length of time over which religious diversity constituted a source of social and political "conflict" in the subcontinent and, second, because the two forms in which religious diversity can emerge in a society were both present in India.[5] The first instance of religious diversity—between Vedic religion and Buddhism—arose through a process of schism, much like the case of European Christianity during the reformation. The second major instance of religious diversity came through the arrival of Islam, leading after the thirteenth century to a major presence of Islam in the society and polities of the Indian subcontinent.[6] Indian history thus shows both routes to religious diversity—through internal evolution of a religious field and through the entry and entrenchment of a religion from outside leading to large-scale conversion.

CONFLICT BETWEEN VEDIC RELIGION AND BUDDHISM

Religious diversity became a source of social contention and destructive political conflict when Buddhism and Jainism arose to challenge the dominance of Vedic religion (which is often unmindfully called ancient Hinduism). The character of this diversity was both like and unlike the schism of European Christianity. It was like the Christian schism in the sense that evolution of these religious doctrines came from within the internal development of existing religion: it was a process in which a society once professing a single religious faith gradually came to face the challenge of contending and seriously critical views. In another respect the Buddhist schism was quite different from the division of Christianity. Buddhism, in particular, but also many of the reform religious sects assailed the *varna* hierarchy—the *sociological* structure of castes attached to Vedic religion. Buddhism offered a challenge not merely to religious doctrines and observances (which could also be deeply contentious: for instance, the central place of sacrifice in the Vedic system of *karma* and the Buddhist injunction against the taking of life in the name of religion), but it also proposed a serious modification of the hierarchic practices of the social order. Modern nationalist authors interpreted the Buddhist threat to Vedic religion as a global rejection of caste practice, probably an anachronistic, excessively radical portrayal. Recent scholarship suggests more cautiously that the Buddha's challenge was to the dominance of the Brahmin caste stratum, rather than for an abolition of the entire caste order, probably connected to the fact that he came from the *varna* of political rulers, and his religious teachings spread widely among *sresthis*, merchant groups thriving in this material culture. But historic differentiation of religious culture after the rise of Buddhism produced another significant effect. Although the field of religious life split primarily between the two major systems, Vedic Mimamsa and Buddhism,[7] it also led to a finer process of fragmentation. The rise of other doctrines and their contending sects—like the Jainas who shared a great deal with Buddhists—and the implicit differentiation among the "orthodox" about how the Buddhist heterodoxy should be met created a field of immense doctrinal and observational plurality. Instead of splitting into two massive systems that could engage a struggle until death, religious life went through a period of great philosophical questioning, doctrinal differentiation, and institutional fragmentation—moderating to some extent the ferocity of a purely binary confrontation. Four different aspects in this development should be disentangled for closer analysis:

a) the map of *doctrinal* differences,
b) the manner in which religious diversity affects the *structure of society* and its established group interests,
c) the response of the holders of *political power* to the emergence of religious diversity and the potential of conflict,
d) intellectual strategies fashioned by philosophers to deal with fundamental differences.

Doctrinally, Buddhist faith rejected fundamental ideas of Vedic religion. It assailed two related fundamental Vedic doctrines—that purity of ethical life is less important than performance of propitiatory ritual practices, which would purify or redeem an individuals' life irrespective of his moral attentiveness and probity.[8] Against this highly ritualistic conception of religious life, early Buddhism presented a spare, deeply ethical counterconception that nearly dispensed with the idea of God, not to speak of the innumerable deities of conventional Vedic worship. Some of their background beliefs—like transmigration of the soul and the cycle of rebirths—Buddhists shared with Vedic believers. With further evolution of Buddhist religion, finer philosophical differences emerged and led to fierce intellectual debates; but by the nature of these debates these were confined to specialist intellectuals like philosophers and logicians. Ordinary people were unlikely to be keenly interested in the disputes about the nature of negation or the temporal unity of selves.

Rejection of ritualism was inextricably connected to a challenge to the power of the religious elite—Brahminical groups who were allowed by the rules of the caste order to officiate at the sacrificial ceremonies and controlled cultural power over ancient Indian society. In its historical evolution, Buddhism later developed elaborate institutions of priesthood,like the monastic orders of Bhikkhus and Sramanas whose members renounced the life of householders and preserved the institutional and doctrinal order of the Buddhist faith. The Brahminical order lacked such a disciplined and highly institutionalized ecclesiastical structure: its priestly class of officiating Brahmins represented a more diffuse and unorganized elite. Simply by questioning ritual supremacy and the "purity" of the Brahmins,[9] and allowing lower-status groups like merchants, ritualized outsiders like lower artisanal castes, and women a place in religious life and an equal place in worship, Buddhism undermined fundamental social principles on which the Vedic order rested. It is plausible to believe that this relative egalitarianism/antihierarchical ideology drew converts to Buddhist religion, and clearly, for several centuries, ancient Indian society was split by the competitive presence of the two major religious orders until the decisive decline of the Buddhist alternative at the end of the first millennium. This terminal decline raises a number of explanatory puzzles.[10]

An analysis of the global situation of religious diversity in ancient India shows some interesting features of religious contestation. First of all, it is clear that, in a society marked by the dominance of a single religious faith and its attendant institutions, religious elites like the Brahmins enjoyed undivided social dominance, and usually they exercise some social-ethical superiority over the wielders of political power.[11] A schism in the dominant religion, interestingly, opens an opportunity for political elites, wielding royal power and using their obligation to provide protection for all their subjects to use this principle to turn the tables on religious elites. When a society has a plurality of religious elites, and they dispute each others' claim to exclusive moral dominance, royal authority can emerge as a mediator and the true preserver of social order, and this reverses the relation between religious and political power. It becomes the social task of the political rulers to secure a state of affairs that keeps religious disputes within reasonable limits. Notably, this can happen only if political elites do not directly take sides in disputes between religions. Ancient Indian history shows both kinds of examples. At the time of intense conflict between Vedic and Buddhist religious systems, some political rulers participated enthusiastically in the conflict between the two religions, since it was plausible to interpret the contention as one between good and evil. Buddhists regarded the Vedic features of ritualism, Brahminical hierarchy, and animal sacrifice as ethically repugnant and morally reprehensible. Vedic supporters viewed Buddhists as people who undermined the structure of social and normative order and questioned scriptures which had superhuman authority and sanction behind them.[12] Early religious conflict in India demonstrated why these disputes can easily become uncommonly bitter and violent. Refusal to believe in religious doctrine is viewed by believers not as a defiance of important legal systems of human creation but of injunctions possessing extrahuman, divine sanction. Defiance of human authority might be seen as detestable but within the limits of tolerance, calling for forbearance of something repugnant, but of divine authority it is regarded as ethically unbearable. When a religious dispute is seen thus as a Manichaean division between good and evil, it is tempting on the part of religious elites to enlist the power of secular rulers. Ancient Indian history, and particularly religious lore, offers numerous instances of this response to the conflict between Vedic and Buddhist religion.[13]

But it appears that a more common response of political rulers toward the challenge of religious diversity was a different strategy. Inscriptional and literary evidence indicate that more commonly ancient rulers applied an implicit distinction between private belief and the public sphere of religious life of the state, and although kings often declared their private religious faith, they desisted from converting that into a state religion, which immediately implied inferior or contested status for people of opposing or different religious persuasions. Evidence points to a common practice where kings would provide patronage to different religious groups and sects, would allow the existence of their religious institutions—like Buddhist monasteries and opulent Saiva temples—patronize schools for the philosophical pursuit of religious doctrines, and simply tolerate the diversity of faith observances of their subjects, unless these threatened what they regarded as the basic order of decency and domesticity. An ancient Sanskrit drama, the *Agamadambara*, by the celebrated Kashmiri Saiva philosopher Jayanta Bhatta, is fascinating not merely because of its presentation of intricate philosophic disputes but also its basic picture of the political sociology of an ancient kingdom.[14] In the play the king follows principles of government that were widely adopted by political elites in the entire subcontinent.

In terms of sociological theory, two features appear to be significant in this historical period. It shows first that there are two basic possibilities: either the political regime participates in the disputes of religious ideas, converting the question into one of good and evil, which draws the political state into religious wars and moves inevitably toward a religious homogenization of the principality. It seems that more commonly Indian rulers followed the alternative option—of viewing different religious paths as different approaches to resolving an uncommonly difficult question, of right and wrong in the human condition—and adopted an attitude of neutrality. By implication, this forced them to institute a division between two roles of the ruler—his *individual* path of good religious life and his *public* obligation to allow all his subjects to follow a religious path of their choice without hindrance from the state or other faiths. This required an implicit distinction between something like personal religion and state religion and the two functions of the king—as a good person and a good ruler. This strategy worked on the basis of a loose connection between the ruler and the collectivity of his subjects. Characteristics of belief were not seen as transferable from the society to the government: the government or regime was not a regime of its people in the modern sense, which requires a much tighter connection between the properties of the "people" and the properties of the state and its governing class. The clearest expression of this theory of rule in the context of deep religious diversity is emblematically contained in the Asokan edicts, which state explicitly that all *pā⊠sandas* (religious faiths) are welcome in the empire. One edict recommends, as a way of assisting religious accommodation, that even in the midst of religious disputation "adherents should exercise moderation in praising their own faith."[15]

With the rise of modern history, the strange decline of Buddhism became a puzzle and a matter of intense dispute. Some modern historians simply concluded that absence of evidence of persecution against religious groups simply indicates the erasure of evidence by powerful interests. (Just as, in a different field, the lack of evidence of large peasant uprisings simply means for some modern historians the suppression of their history. On the other hand, more textually oriented historians argue that this way of thinking simply turns European history into a normative frame through which Indian history is not merely interpreted, but even its factual base is conceived. Peasant uprisings must have happened all over the world at all times, only in some cases their evidence is either lost or successfully suppressed.) The intriguing question of the disappearance of Buddhism raises similar historiographic puzzles. A strand of modern historiography, on the basis of evidence that Buddhist *viharas* or monasteries were demolished by hostile monarchs,[16] paints a picture of religious conflict in early medieval India remarkably similar to European history of the sixteenth century. Actually, this similarity of construction is the point of historiographic contention: it is precisely the similarity to European history that makes this case plausible to some and entirely unconvincing to others. Other interpreters of this history, like P. V. Kane, provide an equally unpersuasive theory that Buddhism declined simply because of the degradation of its principles into licentious tantric doctrines and sexual practices, which ordinary householders mainly rejected out of moral repugnance. This remains a puzzle for historians of religious life: it is hardly likely that Buddhism could have been eradicated from India either by simply moral revulsion of ordinary householders against abhorrent sexual deviance or by systematic political persecution.

The "disappearance" of Buddhism raises another interesting question. It is incontrovertibly true that, after the tenth century, Buddhist religion declined in even those parts of India where it had enjoyed a dominant ideological presence. From both Kashmir and Bengal, in two extremities of North India, Buddhist religion totally disappeared. Organized Buddhist religious life—through the community of the *sangha* and the powerful institutional presence of the Viharas which acted as powerful centers of congregational and intellectual life—slowly declined; and evidence suggests that Buddhist scholars and religious elites responded to a combination of pressures and incentives to migrate with their knowledge systems to Tibet. Yet, the triumph of Vedic religion over the Buddhist challenge was a contradictory and complex affair. Kashmiri Saiva religion played the preeminent role in the intellectual contest against Buddhist doctrines and philosophic schools and, in a sense, secured the "triumph" against the heterodoxy. Yet Saiva doctrines absorbed significant complexes of ideas from Buddhist thought in several fields. Some of their philosophical speculation, it has been argued, drew major ideas from Buddhist philosophers. Saiva religion abandoned the strict Vedic adherence to the birth-based precedence of caste and evinced a far softer attitude toward the question of hierarchy. Even Sankara, who is a major figure in the struggle against Buddhist doctrines and often shows an ambiguous attitude toward caste practice, was regarded by later interpreters as a *pracchanna bauddha*—a hidden Buddhist.[17] Later texts show a more ambiguous approach toward caste hierarchy, less certain about the justifiability of birth-based distinctions.[18] The *Sukraniti* states, "Na jatya brahmnascatra ksatriya vaisya eva na, Na sudro na ca vai mleccho bhedita guna-karmabhih."[19] Not merely the ethical spirit behind the statement, but even its peculiar locutions are notably similar to the strictures against the Brahmins in the *Dhammapada*.[20]

Finally, in actual observance of popular religion, numerous Buddhist practices, occasionally associated with tantrism and more permissive sexual rules, remained influential. It appears that some of these strands of inexplicit forms of Buddhist religion revived and reentered the Hindu mainstream through Vaisnava, Saiva, and Sakta religious traditions, all of which selectively absorbed Tantric elements. The historical fate of Buddhism thus showed a strange and complex pattern—of explicit conflict between two traditions in philosophic and institutional terms and yet a contrary history of popular accommodation and absorption, a tendency to tolerate heterodox practice subsumed under a vague, often perfunctory, acceptance of an orthodox order. This also points to a long-term tendency toward constant interpenetration and mixture of religious ideas and observances, so that characterization of beliefs made sense only at a high level of doctrinal or philosophical abstraction. At lower levels of popular practice, it often became hard to distinguish between strictly Hindu, Buddhist, or Muslim religious practice or, inside Hinduism, between Saiva, Vaisnava, and Sakta sects. This spirit of something going beyond ecumenism is captured in a verse from the *Subhasita-ratna-bhand-agarah*:

yam saivah samupasate siva iti brahmeti vedantino
bauddhah buddha iti pramanapatavah karteti naiyayikah
arhan-nityatha jainasasanaratah karmeti mimamsakah
sohyam ho vidadhatu banchitaphalam trailokyanatho harih[21]

Read carefully, this verse makes some interesting moves regarding the grounds of religious accommodation. It not merely tolerates other religious paths, extending its hospitality to cover most of the significant religious traditions in India.[22] In a surprising move, both imprecise and radical, it does not merely recognize the value of all religious paths, but turns all forms of the divine into various names of one single God, who is worshipped by all. The absences in this passage are insignificant philosophically, because it obviously contains a principle that can be extended to other faiths.[23]

CONFLICT AND ACCOMMODATION IN MEDIEVAL INDIA

Buddhist and Jain religions emerged as heterodoxies from inside the field of Vedic religious orthodox beliefs, as schisms or consequences of a process of religious differentiation. Islam came from outside—by two quite dissimilar routes. Small communities of Islamic believers existed in enclaves on the western coast, primarily connected to the long-standing trade links with the Arabian peninsula.[24] But the major entry of Islam occurred through the expansion of Islamic political empires into Afghanistan and further into the North Indian delta from the thirteenth century. However, the substantial presence of Islam in medieval India was primarily due to large-scale conversion. After the establishment of a segment of the Ghaznavid Empire in the region around Delhi, the kingdom evolved into an independent political entity, inaugurating a long period of uninterrupted political dominion over North and Central India by Islamic dynasties, which ended only with the rise of the British power in the mid-eighteenth century. During a period of nearly seven centuries, large parts of India saw two major changes related to the presence of Islam—the conversion of large communities to Islamic faith and establishment of political rule by Muslim elites in not merely the major parts of the North Indian space but also in settled regional kingdoms in major centers of North, South, and Eastern India. Bengal and Kashmir—two regions once dominated by Buddhist presence, became regions of dominant Muslim faith. Interestingly, in the main part of the subcontinent, despite long and uninterrupted periods of Islamic political governance, Hindu sects constituted the statistical majority—a fact that would play a major role in the political dynamic of modern India.

The entry of Islam into medieval Indian society brought in a new, harder form of religious diversity. Prior religious life in India was marked by a great diversity of religious beliefs—between "Hindu" strands on the one side and Buddhists and Jains on the other—but, additionally, there was considerable differentiation amongst "Hindu" sects of numerous kinds, Saivas, Vaisnavas, and Jains in South India and among Vaisnavas, Saivas, and Saktas in the North. However, it could be argued that these religious groups shared some common fundamental beliefs and could be viewed as different segments of a vast common group that outside observers like the Islamic scholar Al-Biruni would classify as a single, but internally heterogeneous faith community.[25] External groups regularly made incursions into India before the entry of Islamic empires; some of them came as military conquerors, but stayed on as inhabitants, eventually losing their ethnic and religious distinctiveness. Presumably, the religious self-definitions of these groups and their sociological organization were weaker, to allow the encircling Hindu society to absorb them into the highly mobile and flexible arrangements of caste society.[26] Most of these groups of immigrants disappeared without trace in the dynamic structure of Hindu society, often embedded as distinct caste groups linked to specific occupations. Islamic groups possessed much sharper doctrinal self-definition, more effective military power, and a distinctive sociological structure, which prevented a similar incorporation into the Hindu caste hierarchy.[27] Remarkably, Islamic empires in North or Central India rarely attempted a serious process of conversion of the common population to Islam, and Al-Biruni's (973–1048) account already showed that observers assumed the long-term coexistence of these two religions in the same society as a settled fact of social life.[28] Medieval Indian society demonstrated religious diversity—like medieval Europe or the Islamic Middle East, but on a different scale and form. In

Europe small Jewish communities existed inside a predominantly Christian society and political order. Persian and Ottoman Empires of the Middle East contained long-standing Christian and Jewish communities,[29] but these were relatively small groups that did not disturb the primary Islamic character of these societies. The presence of Islam in medieval Indian society was on quite a different scale, and, crucially, the Islamic empires presided over a society of predominantly Hindu subjects. This produced two requirements for the political order and social structure. The political order had to find a way of balancing the faiths of the rulers and the large majority of their subjects. The society had to develop arrangements for the coexistence of two religious faiths that were significantly different in some ways.

Coexistence of two religious orders created an unusual state of affairs in medieval India. A primary point of doctrinal dispute between the Hindu sects and Islam was the question of idolatry. Islamic faith considered making images of God sacrilegious because no finite image could produce an adequate representation of His infinite qualities. By contrast, the Hindu religious imagination was compulsively productive of icons and images. Under early Islamic rule some Hindu and Buddhist temples were destroyed, though the impulse behind that may have been a combination of secular considerations of gathering wealth rather than establishment of true belief.[30] Hindu religious practice continued to thrive in the Islamic empires, and Muslim rulers appeared content to impose a tax on nonbelievers (*jaziya*) that made them eligible to equal political protection by the state. The interpretation of the *jaziya* has proved a contentious theme in recent historiography. Modern historians often make an anachronistic argument about the tax, viewing its imposition as a mark of *discrimination* against a religious community, a sign of inferior status.[31] Hindu nationalist historians rehearsed the instances of temple destruction and imposition of the religious tax: Islamic historians, accepting the same view of the tax, try to show its leniency, the numerous instances of exception.[32] But the tax had another side that is entirely disregarded in modern discussions. By the payment of the tax, groups that professed other religious faiths became entitled to equal protection from the Islamic state: the payment of the tax constituted a sign of fealty toward Islamic political authority by the other religious groups, and its acceptance constituted an obligation of nondiscrimination in security on the part of the Islamic state. Thus imposition of the *jaziya* by a devout religious ruler meant, on one side, that these groups were of a different religious faith, but also, on the part of the ruler, an acceptance of a *religious* duty to provide security to subjects of other religions.

Despite deep and fundamental doctrinal differences, in some ways the social order of the Hindus and Muslims appear remarkably similar. Both religious doctrines stressed limitations on the powers of the political "sovereign": the *constitution of society*—the order of everyday life—was subject to an imperturbable, unchangeable order set down by the rules of religion and interpretable by religious experts—the Brahmins and the ulema—and beyond the powers of secular authority to destroy or to modify significantly. The constitution of society, therefore, was kept outside the purview of political power, providing both stability to social life and an important limitation on the power of the rulers and their propensity to tyrannical rule.[33] Both religious orders therefore implicitly ruled out social engineering on a vast scale that is taken to be the privilege of modern sovereign states. This underlying sociological similarity of the two religious communities was reinforced by a further inexplicit factor—the productive structure of society was regulated by an occupational grid of the caste order. Converts to Islam remained *economically* integral parts of the caste-based occupational order,[34] and since conversion happened primarily in groups rather than by individual decision, change of religious faith did not subvert the occupational structure of caste society. Even after conversion to Islam, a group of fishermen, or weavers, would still remain in their hereditary occupations, and thus segments of caste society. This seems to be a partial answer to the puzzle—why Muslims and Christians in Indian society appear to be unproblematic members of the caste order, despite the egalitarian doctrines of their religious faith.

Two types of responses by political authorities to the evident fact of religious diversity can be discerned from the numerous historical chronicles of medieval India. In the absence of precise historical statistics, it is hard to surmise how the communities were spatially distributed or their precise numbers. In early stages of the Delhi sultanate, political elites were distracted by constant political upheaval and quick turnover of dynasties. Constant reconfigurations of alliances among military and political elites kept them entirely absorbed in affairs of the state. Iltutmish, the second ruler of the Slave dynasty, when pressed by priestly groups to show more ardor for imposition of Islamic laws, made practical points of expostulation. As long as Muslim rulers were a small minority in the society, it was unpractical; if larger numbers converted to Islam, in future, it might become possible to follow more exact Islamic legal rules, in effect, shifting the responsibility on to the religious leaders.[35] This practical rule of general noninterference in the social affairs of their Hindu subjects appears to have been the dominant political practice.[36] It can be suggested, inferentially, from the reproach more orthodox writers directed at political rulers that they appeared, in their view, not to make serious efforts for the conversion of their subjects. Barani, the major chronicler of the Delhi sultanate, commends Sultan Allauddin Khilji for adopting measures which reduced the status of the Hindus both politically and economically.[37] It can be inferred from this that he disapproved of statecraft that avoided taking sides in the religious question and did not view the state as a vehicle of the expansion of Islam. Such scholarly reproaches, and evidence of occasional urging from orthodox religious leaders that the state should view itself as an arm of the Islamic faith, only proves that these policies were exceptions, not the rule. By and large, political power allowed the practice of different religious faiths in social life, and the period of the sultanate was marked by a form of practical coexistence of the two large religious communities.

Another trend of interaction emerged in medieval India that was driven by a religious, not political impulse. Contrary to the casual "clash of civilization" thesis, which suggests that religious cultures, when they are brought into contact historically, inevitably produce political and ethical conflict, much evidence points in the opposite direction. It is true that religious systems of thought tend to associate their own peculiar principles with the sanction from God and therefore tend to induce conflict with contending demands of different moral principles claiming divine origin. In India a major source of ideological conflict between Hindu and Muslim faiths was the question of images and iconoclasm. The Hindu religious world teems with images, because Hinduism persists in thinking complex thoughts through an imagic translation that makes them more intelligible, memorable, and aesthetically available. Original doctrines of Islam were hostile to the idea of trying to capture the infinite quality of God in necessarily finite images; and it generated a powerful philosophical justification of strict monotheism, deeply critical of the idea of image worship. Despite these deep differences, Sufi traditions of worship developed an interest in Hindu traditions, particularly in the fields of literary composition, music, and art. Saints of various Sufi persuasions and their artistic representatives, like the poet Amir Khusrau, devised forms of worship and artistic production around them (like Qawwali singing) that sought points of convergence and exchange with Hindu devotional traditions. Transforming the original idea of a transcendent God, who could not be grasped by the intellectual faculty of the human mind or be encompassed by its aesthetic imagination, into a being who could be reached only by a perfected love, Sufi mystics inaugurated a new kind of devotional culture that made it easy for Hindu religious devotees to understand and interact with their language of worship. By the fourteenth and fifteenth centuries, religious reflection in India produced forms of devotion that transcended the intellectual and imaginative barriers between the two religions. Kabir's poems often invoke a God who is impossible to describe in terms of either religion, who lives inside or close to the human heart—a radical rejection of orthodoxies that undermined all symbols of religious division. "Na main devala na main masjid na kabe Kailas mein, Moko kahan dhundo re bande main to tere pas mein."[38] Through further evolution of these intellectual moves in Sufi religious thought, by the eighteenth century saints like Bulleh Shah could develop a closely reasoned doctrine of mutual respect and interchange between the two main religious communities. It displayed two powerful arguments, moving beyond the injunction of tolerance as bearing practices that were repugnant in the interest of social peace into suggesting that different religious paths were leading to the same God.[39] Often, religious thinkers make startling remarks about social identity.[40]

Traditions of accommodative religious reflection in India have been generally acclaimed for their tolerance; but their philosophic moves deserve more detailed analysis. From an examination of Sufi thought in Kabir and Bullhe Shah, we can observe some of the most radical steps in religious reasoning. First, they reinterpret religious diversity in a radically different way from the orthodox of the two faiths: instead of agreeing with the divisive orthodox belief that one's own religion's road to God is the true one, and that the others were erroneous paths at best, if not direct roads to a damning life of ethical perdition, they consider the different roads to God as different paths invented by the human imagination to grasp an entity who is inherently beyond its powers of cognitive capture.[41] God's infinity is thus turned into an argument for accommodation of divergent religious paths, as contextually determined and adequate ways of approaching his nature. Given this admission of the lack of fit between finite human intelligence and God as an infinite object, religious diversity is turned from a worrisome problem into a field of parallel experiments from which devotees of each religion had to learn. The difference of other religions, thus, is turned around, from the threat of untruth into a partnership in the same deep religious quest that, by the nature of the object it seeks, can never be concluded. No single path can ever be exhaustively right, and therefore all remain instructive and valuable. Both Kabir and Bullhe Shah make a further move by introducing two other ideas. If God is infinite, omnipresent, and therefore present in and to every seeking, he is inside every human being in some sense, in Kabir's wonderfully complex phrase, "main to tere pas mein," in which the two meanings of "being close to you" and "being inside you" cannot be disentangled.[42] The phrase can also mean a combination of "being near you" and "being within your grasp." If God is present everywhere, so that everything is an intimation of his existence, and an invitation to see him, and if he is inside every morally thoughtful person, external signs of his presence become "meaningless." He does not exist in or is equivalent to either the temples of Hindus or the mosques of the Muslims; in the extreme move of Bullhe Shah, these external symbols can be destroyed or dispensed with. In poetic composition the philosophic order of derivation is reversed: because God lives inside very heart, breaking a temple or a mosque is not a destitution of the divine from this world. Finally, if God and a worshipful life are conceived this way, the road is opened toward a more radical line of thinking: we can move into "a world of the blind" where no one asks for one's caste or sect, no one minds how others live. At the end of this line of reasoning, it is possible to arrive at the luminously ambiguous end where the devotee can utter a strange skeptical question: "Bullha, kaun jane main kaun?" a self-addressed question, "Who knows who I am?" Inattentively, we can view this as a poetic equivalent of a Kantian attributeless self, the basis of modern liberal conceptions of tolerance. In fact, however, this is a very different idea that wishes to extend toleration not by becoming blind to others' attributes but transcending them. It is interesting to note, however, that the practical consequences of philosophically divergent arguments can be entirely convergent.

It could be objected that this tradition of religious accommodation represented a small field of intersection between the two religious communities that lived their everyday lives primarily according to more orthodox interpretations of what their faith demanded. Real social life in India was marked by peaceful coexistence with a sense of strong difference, rather than a visionary attempt at the mixture of multiple religions. And, in any case, it could be argued, this is evidence drawn primarily from the realm of religious and philosophical thought. Actual arrangements in common public life showed remarkable parallel developments. If rulers of the sultanate period allowed the practice of Hindu religion by default—without serious ideological justification–major figures of the Mughal Empire (sixteenth through eighteenth centuries) fashioned both principled arguments and institutional practices that supported religious toleration explicitly. Historians of political thought have pointed out that Mughal rulers came from a peculiar regional history inside the Islamic world. Khorasan, the region from which the dynasty emerged, witnessed the rise of a flourishing Islamic culture that later fell under imperial control by the non-Islamic Mongols, and its intellectuals developed intricate arguments for toleration of the subjects' faith by conquering rulers by drawing on the resources of Aristotelian political theory. *Siyasatnameh*, a major text from Khorasan, argued that since provision of security to subjects was an obligation of all rulers, if security of subjects was expanded to include security of their mental life of beliefs, this derived a responsibility of non-Islamic rulers to protect the religious life of their Muslim subjects. Mughal rulers followed these principles in administering their kingdoms. Application of this political theory of rule was not surprising except in one highly significant respect. People subjected to political rule of another religion might, unsurprisingly, advance arguments of this kind; but rulers who are secure in their political power are not under similar pressure to accept them. The extension of these ideas by Babar, the first Mughal ruler, to his dominions in North India showed something more than the inertia of a received tradition, but rather a vivid understanding of the complexity of political power in a society of religious plurality. Such ideas about imperial rule in a mixed society were further elaborated in utterly remarkable ways by Akbar. The most notable aspect of Akbar's political practice was the direct connection between his religious explorations and modification of political institutions. Seriously interested in religious questions, Akbar appears to have initiated religious discussions among the differing strands of Muslim religious schools, but was driven by their contentiousness and mutual disrespect to seek a wider exploration of religious ideas, drawing in Zoroastrians, Catholics, Jains, and eventually the great variety of Hindu sects into a vast, unending exploration of religious truth and ideals of good life. His explorations were so unorthodox and his conduct so unconventional that orthodox Muslim chroniclers were convinced that he was no longer a true believer in Islam,[43] and some Christian missionaries visiting his court kept on reassuring the Church of the imminence of his conversion.[44] Clearly, these representations failed to capture the true nature of his explorations, which were probably hard to characterize within the existing religious languages. Later he invited a select intellectual elite to an order called Din-I-Ilahi, which modern interpreters have similarly struggled to describe—because it defied the normal definitions of religion. Hostile colonial historians portrayed it as an autocratic vision of imposing a new religious doctrine by the power of the state—a reading hardly confirmed by the lightness of touch with which it was pursued.[45] It appears in retrospect that it was not a religious system, rather a theory of comportment—both intellectual and practical—in a complex field of religious diversity, which surpassed the current languages of thought and practice.

In line with his realization that no religious orthodoxy deserved to be credited with a full understanding of religious life and the nature of God, Akbar devised institutional forms in his empire that reflected the benign implications of this pluralism. It was not skepticism about religious truth itself, unlike the road taken in Europe after the scientific revolution, but a skepticism about the absolutist claims of all faiths. During the second part of Akbar's reign, when he slowly extricated himself from the tutelage of orthodox counselors, he adopted policies unprecedented for his age –removal of the *jaziya*, implicitly according Hindus equal religious status inside the political realm, welcoming scholars and intellectuals from other religions into the religious debates and discussions held in his Ibadat Khana (the house of worship) and extending patronage to Sanskrit scholars and intellectuals.[46] These policies were continued by his successors, until the time of Aurangzeb, who interpreted his obligations to Islam in a more conservative fashion. Politically, Akbar's empire was based on a growing system of alliances with subsidiary Hindu rulers, and his administration, particularly its revenue system, was run by immensely powerful Hindu officials like Todarmal. At the high point of Mughal rule, large segments of social life—like the realm of commerce—remained primarily under the control of Hindu merchants, and in several fields of government, like revenue and general administration, the state pursued a policy of employing in high positions officials from both religious communities. In art and literature especially, the Mughals followed a policy of wide-ranging patronage, under which not merely court artists or intellectuals but also independent Sanskrit scholars and intellectuals participating in the thriving intellectual life in Varanasi enjoyed stipends, prizes, and general royal acclaim. As the Mughal Empire fell into decline in the eighteenth century, through a few short, disastrous reigns after Aurangzeb, the dominance of a single empire over a large, politically united territory crumbled. It was replaced by a messier tapestry of smaller kingdoms and Nawabis. During this period of descent into more complex system of smaller regional states, the older culture of religious accommodation and political exchanges remained, continuing the Mughal cultural heritage and political doctrines as a social common sense.

These two diachronically separate narratives of religious strife and attempts at resolution—in ancient and medieval India—show remarkable similarity. Precisely because it is hard to suggest a direct continuity between the statecraft at the end of the first millennium and in the sixteenth to eighteenth centuries, their similarity appears striking. In both periods the political class in North Indian society faced a problem with the same sociological structure: how should political authority deal with a given, unalterable situation of religious diversity? Brutal forms of political power could have been used to turn the society into a religiously homogeneous field, but this faced two difficulties. Political authority before the invention of modern states were comparatively ineffective in realizing large, abstract goals of state policy, and even ferocious use of force might have failed to get the desired results. Secondly, use of force in religious matters can always give rise, as Locke vividly argued, to the problem of dissimulation of belief.[47] To the people who pursue serious religious conversion, use of force is never a guarantee of a true ethical change.[48] Two approaches to religious diversity are apparent in the range of political events in these two stages of Indian history. Political rulers often simply adjust to the fact of religious diversity and practically define a field of public political action from which religious life is exempted. Effectively, this separates public life into two separate fields—of religious and mundane matters—and left religious life to a kind of self-regulation, without political interference. Rulers in the situation fictionally described in the *Agamadambara* follow a policy of benign neglect, of practical noninterference in the face of religious diversity. Indirectly, this also imposes an obligation on the religious groups to keep their differences within reasonable limits, as Dhairyarasi's speech recommends.[49] Delhi sultans appear to have followed this strategy. But there is also a second, more complex policy, under which the ruler makes a distinction between his *personal* life as a religious individual and his *public* role as ruler of the principality. In his personal capacity he has the same obligation to lead an ethical life as all other individuals and can choose a particular religious persuasion. In his capacity as the ruler of the state, he would provide patronage to all communities of worshippers amongst his subjects. There could thus be two quite different arguments for leaving the subjects' religious life alone. The first argument was against overreach: the political power of the state was not an effective instrument to forcibly produce religious homogeneity in the subject population. The second argument was for ethical respect for all religious creeds from a perception of the philosophical difficulty of knowing the infinite nature of God and his creation and the problem of undecidability of one single pattern of truly moral conduct. Though the two arguments were based on entirely different philosophic considerations, their practical implications for state policy were similar. Premodern Indian history does not offer a romantic picture of uninterrupted religious harmony, as nationalist narratives often claimed; but there are intelligible techniques of

tunity for large-scale conversion to Christianity. But colonial administrators showed a surprising lack of enthusiasm for these conversion projects and expressed fear that interference with religious practice might lead to rebellion, an unnecessary cultural provocation that might undermine the new empire.[51] In line with this perception, British authorities often interpreted the rebellion of 1857, exactly a century after the decisive battle of Plassey, as a response to religious interference.[52]

The colonial state continued to follow a policy of noninterference in religious affairs, a role that the British, as outsiders, could claim to play better than the Mughals. The most significant changes in the colonial period came from an altogether different source. The British colonial state, once it was properly established, could not carry on the pretense of mere succession to the "marginal" Mughal state, because the introduction of modern state processes fundamentally altered the nature of the relation between the state and the population under its control. Intellectuals from all segments of the diverse Indian society wondered deeply about what made colonialism itself possible: how could such a small number of officials from an imperial center so distant control a society of such vast proportions. For most of these intellectuals the answer lay in the nature of the modern state, particularly what Foucault has analyzed as its disciplinary techniques. Observant nationalists were proto-Foucauldian. The European state was not simply a state in a different geographical region with a different administrative principle: it was an entirely different kind of machine, one that supervised the systematic generation of entirely new types of collective intentionalities and resultant forms of collective action. It was the utterly superior effectiveness of the modern state-machine that explained the unprecedented capacity of European states to expand their political dominion over other continents. The historic process through which this state emerged and its final shape was an object of endless fascination for Indian political intellectuals from the nineteenth century. This transformation consisted of two different processes: first, one through which conventional empires crumbled and were replaced all over Europe by nation-states. Empire-states in European premodernity, and their vestiges even in modern times, like the Austro-Hungarian Empire, had unstable territorial borders and great internal diversity.

In most cases these states did not seek to establish a tight relation of mutual self-ownership between the people and the state. This relation was viewed as exigent, external, and loose, not animated by any deeply emotive cultural principle. Nation-states that replaced older empires were different in every respect. Territorial boundaries of nation-states became relatively stable, if not fixed, after the initial period of general transition from empires to nations as Europe's primary political form. This, in turn, was seen as normatively justified, because each state was supposed to be the state *of* a specific people, a homogeneous group united in a Herderian fashion by their unique language and its culture. Access of unprecedented power to the European states was seen as a combination of *nationalist* cultural homogeneity and *disciplinary* political technique. The idea of the European nation-state, based on a culturally homogeneous people, intensively mobilized by disciplinary apparatuses of control, exerted a tremendous fascination on the political imagination of early modern India—both attracting and alarming political leaders and intellectuals.

ENUMERATION PROCESSES

A transformation that the colonial state initiated without clear perception of its long-term consequences was the process of enumeration, resulting in the production of a new objectified picture of the state's two major constituents, its territory and population. Mapping the space of the subcontinent with modern cognitive techniques produced, for the first time, a reliable territorial picture of this space. This made possible the obsession of modern states and nations with a new kind of territoriality. Perhaps even more significant for modern political life were the techniques of gathering statistics for populations, an indispensable constituent process of modern governmentality. Joining these two types of objectified knowledge, it became possible for the first time in history to produce a picture of a world in which mapped territories were inhabited by counted populations: everybody interested in political life knew how many Hindus, Muslims, Christians, and Sikhs resided in which towns, villages, and districts, along with the numbers of different castes, of language speakers. For the life of religious communities, this counting process produced new pictures of these collectivities as comprehensive entities—numbers of all Hindus, Muslims, and Christians. These large, abstract, statistical conceptions created a new ontology of populated space, superseding premodern conceptions of religious sects, which were more the objects of face-to-face personal experience. Earlier, in real religious life, in places of worship, in fields of everyday social interaction, people met individuals of differing sects performing ordinary acts of religious life. The new abstract enumerated communities were quite different in character—monstrously large in numbers, surpassing all possible scale of everyday social action, looming over a new kind of political field in which these were to be seen as putative agents of political action. This led to a highly significant reallocation of functions within what we call religion—besides its metaphysical-ethical functions is added a new political function. In time, the metaphysical-ethical side of religion is gradually restricted to private observance, and the new political identities of religious groups dominate interchanges in the public sphere. The religious community is reconceived—from being primarily a *community of worshippers, it is viewed, and views itself increasingly as a community of collective actors.*[53] The enumeration process inaugurates what is a new ontology of religious communities, not just a new epistemic for the social world. It changes not the ways of seeing communities, but ways of being communities. Existence of religious communities acquires an entirely new dimension and a new meaning. This new understanding of communities fatally crossed the emerging understanding of the nation-state, creating an understandable apprehension among groups who feared that they might become minorities in modern political orders. But another crucial new idea regarding the state contributed to this sense of foreboding.

STATE AS AN INSTRUMENT OF REFLEXIVE ACTION OF SOCIETIES

In premodern India, as we saw, both Hindu sects and Muslim believers held an underlying common belief that the constitution of society was divinely sanctioned and beyond the powers of the mundane state to reconstitute. Secularity in one sense signals the dismantling of this fundamental idea of unchangeability of the social order of things. Infusion of modernist ideas first destroys uncritical acceptance of the rules of traditional social order like caste restrictions and exclusions, but eventually these partial rejections generate a larger, more fundamental sense of the *plasticity* of the social world. Not only are particular social rules transformable, but the entire order of society can be changed to conform to ideals conceived by critical political thought. But this possibility of global social change, which captures the imagination of the nineteenth century, requires an instrument for the accomplishment of these transformations. Gradually, the state comes to be seen as the instrumentality for such reflexive changes of society—massive transformations in which the society views itself as an object of transforming action and alters its own structures. This is the truly significant meaning of the state's "sovereignty"—a sovereignty against its own society. The function of the sovereign state is only partly to defend itself from aggression of other states and secure its borders; its primary function becomes the organization of reflexive action upon the structure of society itself—through a constant expansion of its taxation base and its bureaucratic apparatus.

In Indian political thought, from the late nineteenth century, these new perceptions about the state combine to produce an entirely new field of questions. Enumeration of social groups, particularly of these abstract religious communities, and a clear picture of their habitational patterns induce political actors to think in terms of majorities and minorities—both locally and nationally. Early moves toward limited representative institutions encourage these trends. It becomes clear to perceptive observers of political life that concepts of nationalism and representative politics are transforming the idea of the state from a distant ruling mechanism into a more powerful and intrusive machine, and the new state was based on a new kind of tight relation with its people, through influential ideas of popular sovereignty.

Paradoxically, although Indian intellectuals received Western modernist ideas as "emancipatory," it is clear that, in their reflections on the transforming nature of political life, some ideas about the state coming from modern Europe are seen as bearing deeply problematic implications. Some of the most perceptive and influential thinkers of modern India begin to raise serious questions about the appropriateness of the state structure of modern Europe in Indian conditions of deep religious and social heterogeneity. Interestingly, among modern thinkers, Gandhi, Iqbal, and Tagore—three of the most influential authors of the early twentieth century—express significant anxieties about the modern state, despite their grave differences on various fundamental questions. In the early twentieth century two kinds of critical arguments are advanced by intellectuals that were to become highly consequential. Gandhi and Tagore viewed the European nation-states with alarm, not so much for their internally exclusivist character as for their tendency to behave in an aggressive imperialist fashion against their colonies and against each other. And both saw the external aggressiveness of European nationalism as being connected to the internal aggressiveness of atomistic individuals fostered by the capitalist economy. As Ashis Nandy has pointed out, both considered modern nationalism to be an ideology centered on the primacy of the state and sought expressions of patriotism that avoided the state-centric visions common to ordinary modernists.[54]

Iqbal evinced an anxiety for the future that also focused on the European nation-state as the paradigmatic form of modern political organization. He saw the pressures of a homogenizing culture in European nation-states and expressed concern about the fate of minorities in India. If the nation-state was democratic because it was in a sense the state of the people, the vehicle of popular sovereignty, this was likely to work as long as the states were culturally homogeneous, if citizens possessed one single national identity. If the citizenry was constituted by different religious communities, the tight connection between the state and the nation, its exclusive people, would work against minorities, and the conflict of majority and minorities would break it apart. Modern nation-states were intrinsically inhospitable to minorities. The new optics of majorities and minorities produced a contradictory effect -heightening both the attraction and fear of the nation-state. As early nationalism began to coalesce and evoke a sense of a rising people, minorities felt an intensifying anxiety about their place in this future state.[55] If the state became a new kind of state *of* the people, what would happen to those who might not easily fit the self-definition of this people? Ironically, some of these critical reflections did not explore a radical rejection of the form of the nation-state as a feasible historical possibility, instead seeking a nation-state of their own. Those who were alarmed by the logic of the nation-state saw their only remedy in the creation of another nation-state—which, ironically, would not remove the problem but shift its sufferings onto some group other than one's own. Since individual identities were always multiple,[56] any nation-state based on this form of purity of the people was a chimera; all majorities could contain minorities with a slight shift in the criteria of identities. The cult of the European-style nation-state—which sought to unite a territory with a people with a common history, common language, common culture, and common religion—led to an impasse, a future of either unremitting conflict within states or an endless process of fragmentation. The partition of British India demonstrated both the immense power of this form of thinking and its fatal flaws. The idea of partition, proposed by the British and accepted by the leadership of the two new states, was a desperate attempt to find a Westphalian solution to the question of religious diversity in the subcontinent. Its subsequent history showed the immensity of this reckless miscalculation. Despite a partition, claiming an immense toll of human misery, what it sought to achieve eluded the two successor states. Indian history was not successfully forced into the patterns of the European. After partition, India retained a very significant Muslim minority, so the question of how to deal with them remained a critical question of institutional construction. Pakistan, initially under the illusion of religious homogeneity, soon realized that unity in one dimension of identity could be ripped apart by other diversities, and the treatment of internal diversity continued to be the crucial test of the viability of a state.

The process of constitution making in India illustrated the difficulties of applying to an intrinsically diverse society the form of the European-style nation-state. The institutions that were devised after independence departed from some central premises of that state form and constructed a legal edifice built on quite different premises, some of which, purely sociologically, resembled premodern techniques of statecraft.[57] The constitution rejected the idea of a confessional basis of the state and interpreted secularism not as a rejection of religious life but as equal respect to all religious faiths,[58] anchoring the state not on the marginalization of religious beliefs but on accommodation. It abandoned the idea of a single national language, despite fierce advocacy from the supporters of Hindi, and declared fifteen languages to be "national languages" of India—a politically intelligent, if administratively inconvenient device.[59] Although the constitution was primarily based on a liberal conception of rights conferred on individuals, it sought to reassure minorities by offering them collective rights to preserve their faith and cultural forms.[60] In other words, it sought an institutional translation of the principles of premodern statecraft into the sociological conditions of modern existence. The modern Indian state is, paradoxically, based on the direct repudiation of some of the fundamental attributes of the modern state in Europe. Demands of political modernity in Indian history could be met only by innovation and improvisation of institutions, not by plagiarizing European constitutional ideas.

This narrative of toleration in Indian history runs against the grain of much modern historical writing. From the mid-nineteenth century, writers of modern history about India's past habituated their readers to a narrative of a very different kind. The long centuries of premodernity were interpreted by colonial historians as a period in which Hindus, conceived in the modernist way as a "people," nation, or race, were conquered and subjugated by Muslims. And their subsequent history was seen as a chronicle of unceasing religious tension, modeled after the history of Europe in the period of religious wars. Ironically, this was a deeply anachronistic application of modernist categories of collectivities to times when such identities would have been unintelligible to historical actors. Cases of conflicts between social groups were read as a long history of religious animosity that ended only with the establishment of the modern, unfanatical colonial empire that brought the sobriety of rational mediation between fanatical warring faiths. Modernity, on this conventional historical understanding, ended a period of hostility between irrationally irreconcilable religious communities. It appears in retrospect that this history was itself a major obstacle to a sober understanding of the record of the Indian past. And we require a constant critical analysis of the history of writing history.

NOTES

1. Though this might appear a hazardously wide-ranging claim, a comparison between the views of, say, Kant, Hegel, and the Scottish Enlightenment thinkers like Smith and Ferguson would confirm this. Despite their significant differences on many questions, they share these two common beliefs: that there is a linear development in the history of the West and that the last stage reached in Western modernity constitutes a higher achievement in social ideals than in other cultures. Thus the European present was superior in this regard not merely to the European but all other pasts.
2. I want to call them background beliefs because these were often unstated, but, precisely because they were unstated, it was hard to subject them to critical attention.
3. One great example of such intellectual history, and also, incidentally an illustration of its influence, was Karl Popper's vastly influential study, *The Open Society and Its Enemies*, based on the dubious hypothesis that the struggle between an open and a closed society, a coded version of the cold war, was a universal question and started in ancient Greece.
4. For analyses of the place of Jews in Europe, particularly in the period of early modern state development, see Ira Katznelson, "Regarding Toleration and Liberalism: Considerations from the Anglo-Jewish Experience," in Ira Katznelson and Gareth Stedman Jones, eds., *Religion and the Political Imagination* (Cambridge: Cambridge University Press, 2010).
5. Conflict is put inside quotes because of a large indeterminacy of reference. For this kind of analysis it is essential to devise a finer conceptual terminology that differentiates between distinct states of affairs that are all indifferently designated as "conflict"—indifference between different religious communities, differences that are not significant, differences in which each community views the other's practices as repugnant but allows them, differences in which they try to apply pressure, differences that lead to violent conflict. Clearly, these are very different conditions of difference, and their distinctions need to be registered in our terminology.
6. It needs to be emphasized, though, that the spread of Islam in India was primarily through conversion of others to Islam rather than an influx of Islamic groups from outside: so that Indian Islam is primarily, in this sense, an internal phenomenon.
7. *Mimamsa* was the self-appellation used by authors of Vedic hermeneutics.
8. The entire section of the Dhammapada consisting of the Buddha's sayings on the Brahmins is full of this strand of thinking. *Dhammapada* (Calcutta: Jignasa, 1973), "Bahmanabaggo," section 26, pp. 131–45; *The Dhammapada*, trans, Juan Mascaro (Harmondsworth: Penguin, 1973), section 26.
9. The Buddha's question to the Brahmans: "kim te jata hi dummeha, kim te ajinasatiya/ abbhantarm te gahinam bahiram parimajjasi" (what does your matted hair mean, man of an evil intelligence, your inside is polluted, you labour cleaning the outside), *Dhammapada*, the Bahmanabaggo, p. 135; *The Dhammapada*, p. 90.
10. See P. V. Kane, *History of the Dharmasastras*, part 2, ch. 25, (Poona: Bhandarkar Oriental Research Institute, 1977), 5:1003–30, seeks to fashion an explanation of this decline.

11. Ritualistically, in the *varna* hierarchy, the Brahmin is superior to the kshatriya, holders of political power.
12. The Vedas are famously regarded as "apauruseya," which is often taken to mean "of divine creation" in modern Hindu discourse, though some eminent premodern philosophic interpreters regarded them as texts whose creators could not be captured within the range of human memory, rather than as texts of divine composition. This line of reasoning is followed, according to Kane, by Sankara, see Kane, *History of the Dharmasastras,* part 2, 5:1202 , and also by Jayanta Bhatta in the play *Agamadambara Much Ado About Religion*, trans. Csaba Dezso (New York: New York University Press, 2005), act 4.
13. It is interesting to note that modern nationalist writers who were particularly sensitive to the disruptive potential of religious conflict returned to interpret these legends—to extract a lesson for modern secularism. See, for instance, Tagore's poetic recreation of the story of a maid in the royal household of Magadha who preferred to sacrifice her life in the cause of Buddhist worship, defying an order the king, who reneged on Buddhism and returned to Vedic rituals. In Tagore's subtle retelling of the story, the Vedic religion thus became associated not merely with animal but with human sacrifice. Rabindranath Tagore, "Pujarini," in *Sanchayita* (Kolkata: Visva Bharati, 1972), p. 339.
14. Bhatta, *Agamadambara.*
15. "Inscriptions of Asoka," in *Corpus Inscriptionum Indicarum,* ed. E. Hultzsch (Delhi: Indological Book House, 1969), vol. 1.
16. For which there is some elusive and indecisive evidence in the textual archive; see, for instance, the references to the Sunga ruler and Pusyamitra's relentless hostility toward the Buddhists. Kane, *History of the Dharmasastras*, vol. 5, part 2, p. 1008.
17. Sankara's famous composition about the self, the *Atmasatkam* or *Nirvanasatkam*, says: "na me mrtyusanka na me jatibheda/ pita naiva me naiva mata na janmah." Ostensibly, this abandons the moral claim of the caste order; but the song is not about the phenomenal self, but the true self of the soul. The refusal of the claims of caste thus remains ambiguous.
18. These are hard to date, but can be surmised , from internal textual evidence, to have been composed after this age, like the significant dharmasastra text, *Sukraniti.*
19. *Sukraniti,* sloka 29–30. Here, in this sublunar state, who is a brahmana, kstariya, vasiya, sudra, or mleccha is not determined by birth, but by their qualities and achievements/attainments (*guna-karmabhih*).
20. "Bahmanavaggo," *Dhammapada.*
21. "Let Him, whom the Saivas worship as Siva, and as Brahma by the Vedantins; as the Buddha by the Buddhas, and as the karta by Naiyayikas, skilled in logical proof, as the Arhat by those who follow the Jaina regulations, and as Karma by the Mimamsakas—Hari, the Lord of all that is valuable in the three worlds—fulfill your wishes." Kane, *History of the Dharmasastras*, Subhasitaratnabhandagara (Bombay: Nirnayasagar Press, 1935), 15, verse 27.
22. It does not include Islam or Christianity, but its date is hard to determine. Its logic remains accommodative, but ambiguous. If it deliberately excludes Islam, that gestures toward the idea that these sects are all objects of toleration, but others, like Islam, are not. On the

other hand, if toleration can be granted to such divergent faiths, it could also be extended to others.

23. This tradition of devotion is carried on in modern times most obviously by figures like Ramakrishna Paramhansa and Gandhi. For instance, his famously favorite bhajan, "Raghupati Raghava Raja Ram," contains an evocation of the same principle, "isvara allah tere nam, savko sanmati de bhagavan"—*isvara* and *allah* are your names, grant everyone good intention/faith.
24. Ibn Batuta, visiting India during the reign of Muhammad Tughluq, visited some of these coastal communities, and describes their peculiar practices. Ibn Batuta, , ch. 18, in *The Travels of Ibn-Battuta in the Near East, Asia and Africa 1325–1354,* ed. and trans. Rev. Samuel Lee (New York: Dover, 2004), p. 169ff.
25. See *Al-Biruni's India,* ed. Edward C. Sachau (New Delhi: Rupa, 2012), for a detailed critical discussion, especially ch. 13, pp. 17–44; David Lorenzen, "Who Invented Hinduism?" *Comparative Studies in Society and History* 41, no. 4 (October 1999): 630–659.
26. For an excellent account of the mobility and absorptive impulse of Hindu society, see Nirmal Kumar Bose, *The Structure of Hindu Society*, trans. Andre Beteille (Delhi: Orient Longman, 1970).
27. Though Islamic groups remained religiously distinct, they could not escape the economic and productive incorporation into the caste order. For the paradoxical existence of caste among Islamic groups, see Imtiaz Ahmad, ed., *Caste and Social Stratification Among Muslims in India* (Delhi: Manohar, 1978).
28. *Al-Biruni's India,* ch. 2, 32–39.
29. For an excellent analysis of the Ottoman Empire, see Karen Barkey, *Empire of Difference: Ottomans in Comparative Perspective* (Cambridge: Cambridge University Press, 2008).
30. Romila Thapar, *Somanatha: The Many Voices of History* (London: Verso, 2005).
31. This argument forgets that this idea of discrimination requires as its background condition a belief in political equality of the modern kind.
32. Syed Ameer Ali, *The Spirit of Islam* (Whitefish, MT: Kessinger, 2003). On the question of temple destruction, see Richard M. Eaton, *Essays on Islam and Indian History* (Delhi: Oxford University Press, 2002).
33. Interestingly, the *Manusmrti's* section on Rajadharma stresses the importance of rulers following moral rules. For similar injunctions on Islamic rulers, see Nizam al-Mulk, *Siyasatnameh* (Bombay: Shīrāzī, 1911 [1330]).
34. To use a useful though anachronistic concept.
35.

> It is recorded in Saahifa-i-Nat-i-Muhammadi that one day the ulama of the Court of Iltutmich (1211–36) went to the sultan and said that since the Brahmins were the worst enemies of the Prophet of Islam, devotion to the Prophet enjoined upon the King of Islam to force the Brahmins either to change their faith or to suffer execution. Iltutmich was rattled to receive this demand from the court ulama. He replied he would give an answer the following day. The next days the king's minister told the ulama that since the Muslims in the kingdom were like "salt in food," their demand could not possibly be met in such a

situation. However, he said, when the situation changed and the population of the Muslims increased it might be to act according to the demand of the ulama.

S. Nurul Hasan, pp. 66–67.

36. S. Nurul Hasan, *Religion, State and Society in Medieval India*, ed. Satish Chandra (Delhi: Oxford University Press, 2005), ch. 6.
37. Zia ud Din Barani, *Tarikh I Firuzshahi* (Calcutta: Bibliotheca Indica, 1862 [1357]).
38. I am not in the temple, nor in the mosque, not in the Kaba, nor in Kailas. Where do you seek me (in vain), my servant, I am beside/inside you/yourself.
39. "Gal samajh gaye to raulan ki? Ram rahim se maulan ki?" (If you know the truth, there is hardly any occasion for conflict; who needs God/s beyond Ram and Rahim?) or "Mandir dha de, masjid dha de, dha de jo kuch dasde, par kisi ka dil na dha de, rab wahi bic wasde" (Break the temple, break the mosque, but never break anyone's heart, because that is where God resides). In the first quote, the word *Ram rahim* is ambiguous and can be glossed in various ways, and the conjunction "and" can be read in two ways. The first reading would see them as separate images of God, but both equally divine, but a second can read the "and" as suggesting that these are two names of the same God. The second reading is given greater credence by the fact that the original Punjabi verse does not use a conjunction.
40. Again, to take illustrations from Bullhe Shah, consider the following two lines: "Cal Bullhe cal utthe caliye, jitthe sare anne / na koi kise jat pachane, na koi sanu manne" (Bullha, let us go to a land of the blind, where no one knows another's caste, and no one minds what I do); and, finally, the astonishingly generous refrain of one of his famous songs: "Bullhe, kaun jane main kaun?" (Bullha, who knows who I am?).
41. Echoes of this line of thinking can be found among modern believers as well. Sudipta Kaviraj, "On Thick and Thin Religion," in Katznelson and Stedman Jones, *Religion and the Political Imagination*, pp. 343–44.
42. Tagore translates this phrase as "lo! I am beside thee." Rabindranath Tagore, *Poems of Kabir* (Calcutta: Rupa).
43. Badayuni, a major historian of Akbar's times, often expresses such disillusionment. Compare Badayuni, and Abul Fazl. Al-Badaoni, *Muntakhab-ut-Tawarikh,* trans. W. H. Lowe (Calcutta: Baptist Mission, 1884); Abu' l Fazl Allami, *Ain-i-Akbari*, trans. H. Blochmann (Calcutta: Asiatic Society of Bengal, 1927).
44. Makhan Lal Ray Choudhury, *Din-I-Ilahi* (Calcutta: University of Calcutta,1941), p. 19.
45. Vincent Smith, see the critical discussion in Ray Choudhury, ibid.
46. But Akbar's achievements should be assessed in its historical context, which would reveal his decisions to have been far harder than secular history suggests. He was widely regarded with intense disapproval and at times considered an apostate who had really abandoned Islam. Jahangir, his son and successor, comments cautiously but also judiciously that his father was an extraordinary individual who could do things that were impossible for ordinary persons. Jahangir stresses that he himself was a believing Muslim and much less adventurous in religious quest than his father. *Tuzuk-i-Jahangiri* (Delhi: Munshiram Monoharlal, 1968). Badayuni, the chronicler of his reign, wrote disapprovingly of his ecumenism.

Religious figures like Shaikh Ahmad Sirhindi considered him an apostate and held an entirely different view of the purpose of *jaziya.* He was, S. Nurul Hasan writes,"very keen that infidels should be kept in a state of degradation and humiliation." Hasan, *Religion, State and Society in Medieval India*, p. 96. "He elaborates this point in a letter to Murtaza Khan: 'The main reason for taking jizya is to degrade and humiliate them, so much so that because of its fear they may not be able to dress well and live in grandeur. . . . It does not behove the kings to stop jizya. God has instituted it to dishonor them. It is intended to bring them into contempt and to establish the honour and might of Islam.'" Ibid., p. 96, quoting from *Maqtoubat-i-Imam-i-Rabbani;* see ibid., pp. 95–99.

47. John Locke, *Essay Concerning Toleration* (New York: Cambridge University Press, 2010).
48. Abul Fazl quotes Akbar to this effect. Abu'l Fazl Allami, *Ain-I-Akbari*, book 5: "Comprising the Happy Sayings of His Majesty and Conclusion," 424–524.
49. *Agamadambara,* act 4.
50. The most famous example of this version of history is James Mill, *History of British India* (London: J. Madden, 1848), especially chapter 10.
51. For a theoretical statement of this argument, cf. J.S. Mill, *On Liberty*, in *Utilitarianism, Liberty and Representative Government* (London: Dent, 1972).
52. For British policy and Islamic responses, see Humeira Iqtedar, "Colonial Secularism and Islamism in North India: A Relationship of Creativity," in Katznelson and Gareth Stedman Jones, *Religion and the Political Imagination,* pp. 235–53.
53. Nandy indicated this change in his work on secularism through a distinction between religion as faith and religion as ideology. Ashis Nandy, "The Politics of Secularism and the Recovery of Religious Toleration," in Rajeev Bhargava, ed., *Secularism and Its Critics* (Delhi: Oxford University Press, 1998), pp. 321–44.
54. Ibid.
55. Cf. Mohammad Iqbal, *Address to the Muslim League* (Allahabad, 1930), *Speeches, Writings and Statements of Iqbal,* ed. Latif Ahmed Sherwani (Lahore: Iqbal Academy, 1977), 3–26.
56. For a brief statement of this argument, Kaviraj, "On Thick and Thin Religion," pp. 352–54.
57. With some simplification, it can be said that the ideas of federalism and secularism that work in the Indian political system bear a closer resemblance and owe a great deal more to premodern traditions of statecraft than to modern European ones.
58. For an explication of its bases, see Rajeev Bhargava, "The Distinctiveness of Indian Secularism," in T. N. Srinivasan, ed., *The Future of Secularism* (New York: Oxford University Press, 2009).
59. This is captured from a slightly different perspective in Juan J. Linz, Alfred Stepan, and Yogendra Yadav, *Crafting State-Nations: India and Other Multinational Democracies* (Baltimore: Johns Hopkins University Press, 2011).
60. Constitution of India, article 32.

MUSLIMS AND TOLERATION

Unexamined Contributions to the Multiple Secularisms of Modern Democracies

ALFRED STEPAN

ALMOST A DECADE ago I helped launch a debate asking how we should we interpret the following set of facts. For more than thirty-five years *not a single* Muslim has lived in an Arab majority state that has been considered a democracy by any of the three most utilized social science annual reports on the status of political rights and civil liberties in the world. In sharp contrast, even when we exclude the 160 million non-Arab Muslims living in democratic India, the same three reports indicate that there are more than over *300 million* Muslims living in non-Arab Muslim majority countries that are now democracies—Indonesia, Turkey, Senegal, and Albania.[1] These facts lead to a simple but powerful conclusion. If a set of countries shares a major variable (in this case Islam), but can be divided into two different subsets with sharply different political outcomes (in this case democracy), the shared variable cannot explain the variation. This means that Islam, taken by itself, cannot explain why Arabs are democratically "underperforming" or why, from a soci-economic viewpoint, Indonesia, and Senegal are democratically "overperforming."[2]

Since the start of this "Arab, More Than, Muslim Democratic Exceptionalism" debate much has been written to explain the persistence of authoritarian regimes in Arab countries and about Islam and violence. Nevertheless, how *democracies* in Muslim majority countries emerge and function remains understudied and undertheorized, and that is my task in this chapter. I am not a specialist on Islam, but I have written extensively on democracy, especially democratization, the growth of human rights in some once authoritarian regimes, and the emergence of interfaith religious tolerance or intolerance. It is from this perspective of democratization that I hope to make some contribution to our still neglected study of democracies in Muslim majority countries. The study of such democracies must begin with a discussion of democracy itself.

WHAT DOES DEMOCRACY REQUIRE AND NOT REQUIRE?

Democracy is a form of governance of a state. Thus no modern polity can become democratically consolidated unless it is first a state. Therefore, the nonexistence of a state or such an intense lack of identification with the state that large groups of individuals want to join a different state or create a new independent state raises fundamental and often unsolvable problems.[3] Democracy is a system of conflict regulation within the territory of a state that allows open competition over the values and goals that citizens want to advance. In the strict democratic sense, this means that as long as groups do not use violence, do not violate the rights of other citizens, and stay within the rules of the democratic game, *all* groups should have the right to advance their interests, both in society and in politics. This is the minimal institutional criterion of what democratic politics does and does not entail.

What does this core institutional requirement imply about religion, politics, and what I call the "twin tolerations"? Specifically, what are the necessary boundaries of freedom of elected governments from religious groups, and what are the necessary boundaries of freedom of religious individuals and groups from government? From the perspective of the twin tolerations, democratic institutions must be free, within the bounds of the constitution and human rights, to generate policies. Religious institutions should not have special rights, constitutionally embedded or not, that allow them to unilaterally impose public policies on democratically elected governments. At the same time, individuals and religious communities, consistent with my institutional definition of democracy, must have complete freedom to worship privately. More than this, as individuals and groups, they must also be able to advance their values publicly in society and to sponsor political organizations and movements, as long as their actions do not impinge negatively on the liberties of other citizens or violate democracy and the law.[4] This institutional approach to democracy necessarily implies that no group in society—including religious groups—can a priori be prohibited from forming a political party. For example, Christian Democratic Parties of Germany, Italy, Belgium, Holland, and Austria not only participated as key European political actors in the politics of their own countries, but they were crucial builders after World War II of the major new political organization of Europe, the European Union.[5] Constraints on political parties, religious or not, may only be imposed *after* a party, by its actions, violates democratic principles and the democratic constitution. The judgment as to whether or not a party has violated democratic principles should not be decided by parties in the government, but by courts interpreting a democratically crafted constitution.

Within this broad framework of the necessary tolerated freedoms of the democratic state from religion, and tolerated freedoms of religious individuals and organizations from the democratic state, an extraordinarily range of quite different patterns of state-religion relations can, and do, coexist with the twin tolerations necessary for a democracy.

Let us explore this argument further by our second question. What are the *actual* patterns of relations between religion and the state in long-standing democracies? Some classic arguments about the conditions necessary for democracy to coexist with religion resonate powerfully in current political discussions but are dangerously misleading. Until they are corrected, they will continue to have unfortunate consequences. They present a distorted story of how democracy actually emerged and operates in the West and they contribute to increasingly widespread political beliefs that that many non-Western religions, especially Islam, are incompatible with or, worse, systematically hostile to democracy

The first misinterpretation is the mistaken *factual* assumption that democracy always requires a strict separation of church and state. Of course, such a separation did emerge from the first two democratizing revolutions in the West, the American and the French Revolutions. But, if we examine the actual practices of the current twenty-seven European Union member states, we discover that *none* of them now (even France) has a strict separation of church and state and that *most* of them have arrived at collaborative arrangements with religion. Consider the following: 100 percent of EU member states give funding for religious schools or for religious education in state schools, 89 percent have religious education as a standard optional offering in state schools, 37 percent of them help collect taxes or money for (some) religions, 33 percent give some funding to religious charitable institutions, and 19 percent have established religions.[6] These figures alone make it absolutely clear that complete separation of religion and the state is neither a necessary condition for democracy to function nor the norm in contemporary European democracies.

The second misinterpretation of the West is an insufficient recognition that Christianity has had an intolerant past. Indeed, the preeminent historian of Christianity, Diarmaid MacCulloch, categorically asserts that "western Christianity before 1500 must rank as one of the most intolerant religions in world history."[7] The West was also "multivocal" concerning democracy. By multivocal I simply mean that during and after the Reformation in the sixteenth century virtually all variants of Western Christianity still had antidemocratic voices and doctrines, as well as some democratic voices and doctrines. For example, in the Roman Catholic Church, Pope Pius IX's 1864 "Syllabus of Errors" condemned the separation of church and state, socialism, and "progress, liberalism and recent civilization." But in the Second Vatican Council (1962–1965), which brought the pope and all the bishops of the church together in reformist discussions, all these condemnations were reversed, and democracy, and even what the council called a "preferential option for the poor" and the "priority and unviolability of human rights," were endorsed.[8] John Calvin (1509–64) allowed neither inclusive citizenship nor any form of representative democracy in Geneva when he founded Calvinism because, as Michael Walzer writes, Calvin "found no human community capable of organizing itself and appointing delegates. . . . Particular officers were created only by God."[9] Yet later Calvinist reformist thinkers—such as Hugo Grotius (1583–1645) helped turn Holland into a leading example of religious tolerance in Europe. Lutheranism, for over three hundred years, particularly in northern Germany, theologically and politically accepted a form of authoritarian direction of government so that a good Lutheran's concentration on salvation would not be weakened by participation in politics. Indeed, after World War II in Germany there was an extensive critique of the negative political consequences of such a religiously inspired refusal to participate in democratic politics, a critique that came to be described as the path "from Luther to Hitler."

My central point is that all these major West European Christian denominations had authoritarian dimensions. But other aspects of Christian doctrines and practices more congruent with democratic values were also present. We need to have a careful analysis of how such doctrines and practices became the dominant, but never the only, voices in the multivocal Christian tradition.

The third misinterpretation relates to and/or normative philosophical values. John Rawls, arguably the most influential political philosopher in the English language in the twentieth century, once famously argued that citizens "ought" to take matters of religion "off" the political agenda. For Rawls, such restriction of religion to the private sphere was necessary for the building of the philosophical consensus he argued was required for liberal democracy.[10] But following such advice would make it virtually impossible to socially construct the twin tolerations in those political systems where the citizens are deeply religious but profoundly divided over democracy. An essential part of the historical political process by which Christian multivocal denominations and democracy become reconciled and compatible with the twin tolerations of democracy was precisely through public argument and negotiated agreements about the correct role religion would play in society. Indeed, historically, in every part of the world, democratic thinkers of whatever denomination or religion (including Islam), have had to constantly challenge, in the public arena, the ideas and actions of their antidemocratic co-religionists. To be effective, they had to advance religious, as well as political, arguments for the twin tolerations and democracy.

The fourth misinterpretation, building upon the first three, is to argue that modernization and democracy require the waning of religious faith and the growth of secularism.[11] This was both the empirical prediction and normative prescription of most of the founders of sociology.[12] Democracy and the twin tolerations certainly demand respect by religions of the authority of democratically elected officials and the core institutions they craft. But the twin tolerations do not require less religious belief or practice for either the development of democracy or modernization. Countries like the United States mix modernity, democracy, and some of the highest levels of religious practice in the world. As I shall document later, India for the last thirty years, and Indonesia for the last twenty years have increasingly democratized and modernized while the level of religious belief and practice has intensified. Countries can also be secular but undemocratic, such as Syria, Libya, not to speak of Turkey under Atatürk. Thus strict secularism is neither a necessary nor a sufficient condition for democracy. Significantly, none of the first three winners of what is called the Nobel prize of political science, the Skypte Prize (Robert Dahl, Juan J. Linz, or Arendt Lijphart) have ever included the word *secularism* in their definitions of the requirements of democracy.[13]

I will use the word *secular* in this chapter, but only with a major qualification. As I shall document, there are in Western democracies, and in non-Western democracies such as India, Indonesia, and Senegal, at least four distinctive types of secularism that satisfy the requirements of the twin tolerations and democracy. It thus makes more sense for us to speak of "multiple secularisms" for many of the same reasons that S. N. Eisenstadt and Sudipta Kaviraj use the concept of "multiple modernities."[14]

This is a politically important distinction because some non-Western countries are repeatedly urged to conform to *the* Western style of secularism before they can be considered real democracies. But in the United States and Western Europe there are three sharply different kinds of secularism: 1) relatively strict separation of church and state, as in the United States and France (but even these two countries have crucial differences because the separation in the USA was "religiously friendly," whereas in France it was "religiously hostile");

2) democracies with established churches that by the late nineteenth century respected the twin tolerations (all the Scandinavian democracies and the UK); and 3) democracies, such as Germany, Holland, Belgium, and Switzerland, that do not have established churches but follow a constitutionally embedded, religiously friendly model of secularism that is so distinctive and important that it deserves to be given a name. I call it positive accommodation.: "positive" to differentiate it from the French-style hostility to religion and "accommodation" to differentiate it from any form of strict separation of church and state. "Positive," because, as Germany's leading analyst of state religion relations in Germany, Gerhard Robbers, has written, "Neutrality . . . means *positive neutrality*. This concept obligates the state to actively support religion and to provide for the space religion needs to flourish in the polity. This makes possible and requires for example that the state include religious needs in planning law. This concept of positive neutrality is predominant in the official discourses and not only in law. It is actively supported and implemented by the courts and state officials."[15] The word *accommodation* is also crucial because this model accommodates the major traditional religions in numerous areas.[16]

With these important caveats about democracy clear in our minds, let us now explore how democracy has emerged and functions in two Muslim majority countries, Indonesia and Senegal. Both countries, and also India, have a state-religion-society pattern that is consistent with democracy, but quite different from the Western European or U.S. patterns we have just described.

AN EMERGING PATTERN OF DEMOCRACY IN MANY COUNTIES WITH LARGE MUSLIM POPULATIONS

With the exception of Turkey, whose politics for much of the last sixty years was closely related to variations of an often "religiously hostile" French type of *laïcité* separation of religion and the state, most of the Muslim democracies I have studied, especially Indonesia and Senegal—like India—have crafted a new "religiously friendly" model of religion-state-society relations.[17] Hindu majority India is not, of course, a Muslim majority democracy, but India does have a "minority" of approximately 160 million Muslims, giving it, after Indonesia and Pakistan, the third most populous Muslim population in the world, and the Indian model of politics toward religion and democracy was constructed partly to respond to this reality.

State-religion relations in Indonesia, Senegal, and India are "twin tolerations"–supportive and have five characteristics that to some extent *all* of these three countries share.

First, they are more officially *co-celebratory* of a wider variety of religions than any of the three Western varieties of secularisms we have discussed.

Second, they are close to the "positive accommodation" model found in such countries as Germany, except whereas in Europe accommodation is *intra-Christian*, in Indonesia, Senegal, and India accommodation is *interfaith*.

Third, unlike those European democracies where religious homogeneity facilitated democratic coexistence with established churches, in Indonesia, Senegal, and India many key political leaders recognized religious heterogeneity of belief and intensity of religious practice as sociological facts that required the political choice of pluralism and thus all of them, therefore, struggled against the establishment of an Islamic state or any use of shari'a as the obligatory and only source of law.

Fourth, given the opposition of some Islamic leaders to measures necessary for the advancement of rights and the twin tolerations, key reforms are often only made after some religious leaders argued *from within Islam* or because of the moral necessity of these reforms and worked in *alliances with secular state officials* to help implement them.

Fifth, given the multivocal, sociological fact of antidemocratic and intolerant elements within Islam, key Islamic activists against such intolerance and for democracy could not afford to follow any early Rawlsian prescription to keep religion "off the public agenda." Rather, they acted on the conviction that they could best contribute to making pluralism and democracy the consensual option in their Muslim majority states by putting *Islamic democratic arguing* on their agenda.

In the remainder of this essay I will attempt to illustrate briefly each of these five points:

1. CO-CELEBRATORY

Since religion is a part of their life that some citizens value deeply, all West European democracies, no matter how secular, and whatever one of the three "multiple secularisms" is preeminent in their country, still have some religious holidays where employers, both state and private, *must* give a paid public holiday to all their citizens. "Separatist" France has six such holidays, "established" Norway and Denmark and once established Sweden now have a total of thirty-one such compulsory paid holidays, and "positive accommodation" Germany, Netherlands, and Switzerland have twenty-three. However, *not one* of these sixty religious holidays is for a non-Christian minority religion. All are for the Christian majority religion.

What is the practice in Muslim majority Indonesia and Senegal, and in India with its 160 million Muslims? In all these deeply religious countries, religion is publicly acknowledged by the democratic state as being an important part of the private and public life of all citizens, and there is a great effort for state and society to "co-celebrate" or, in Charles Taylor's sense, to "recognize" the diverse and intense religious identities. Given the great religious diversity in Indonesia and in India, this means that there are actually *more* holidays for minority religions than for the majority religion. In Indonesia there are six mandatory holidays for the religion of the Islamic majority (87 percent) of the population, but a total of seven for the minority religions, Hinduism, Christianity, Buddhism, and Confucianism. India is federal, so there is some variation within states, but the majority Hindu religion only has five compulsory, paid religious holidays, and, all together, Muslims, Sikhs, Christians, Jains, and Buddhists get twice as many, ten. In Senegal, during the nineteenth century, Catholics were a major presence in the four major coastal cities of Senegal, and elaborate "rituals of respect" were developed to create and maintain good relations between Muslims and Catholics, between both religious leaders and laical state officials, and between the four Sufi orders.[18] In the twenty-first century, well less than 10 percent of the population is Catholic, but over 40 percent of the compulsory religious holidays celebrate Catholic feasts. Secular state officials are "co-celebrants" at major Muslim and Catholic holidays, and the Sufi and Catholic religious leaders attend major state functions.

TABLE 9.1 COMPARISON OF PAID RELIGIOUS HOLIDAYS IN FOUR STATE-RELIGION-SOCIETY MODELS

	SEPARATIST			ESTABLISHED CHURCH			POSITIVE ACCOMMODATION			CO-CELEBRATORY		
Country and majority religion	France Christian	Turkey Muslim	USA Christian	Denmark Christian	Norway Christian	Sweden Christian	Germany Christian	Netherlands Christian	Switzerland Christian	India Hindu	Indonesia Muslim	Senegal Muslim
Paid religious holidays for majority religion	N = 6	N = 2	N = 1	N = 11	N = 10	N = 10	N=8*	N =8	N = 7*	N = 5	N = 6	N = 7
Paid religious holidays for minority religion	N = 0	N = 0	N = 0	N = 0	N = 0	N = 0	N = 0	N = 0	N = 0	N = 10	N=7	N=6

* Individual Swiss cantons and German Länder have additional paid religious holidays, decided on by local governments. In Switzerland eight additional holidays are celebrated by between one and fourteen Swiss cantons (Corpus Christi – 14, All Saints' Day – 14, Saint Berchtold's Day – 13, Assumption – 13, Immaculate Conception – 10, St. Joseph's Day – 6, Epiphany – 4, St. Peter and Paul – 1). In Germany six additional holidays are celebrated in between one and eight German Länder (Corpus Christi – 8, Reformation Day – 5, All Saints' Day – 5, Epiphany – 3, Assumption Day – 2, Repentance Day – 1).

SOURCE: http://www.qppstudio.net/publicholidays.htm.

Significantly, excluding *laïcité* Turkey, the other most highly ranked Muslim majority country on these three democracy indexes is Albania, and it has this same pattern of public religious holidays. Albania has large Roman Catholic and Orthodox Catholic religious minorities, which together are accorded five national holidays, whereas the Muslim majority has only three holidays. During the period when Mali was also a democracy it exhibited the same cocelebratory pattern as in Indonesia, India, and Albania. See table 9.1.

2. INTER-FAITH POSITIVE ACCOMMODATION

In Western Europe the "positive accommodation" pattern was historically constructed and negotiated over hundreds of years, initially as a way to accommodate conflicts *within* the Christian religions, and later between Christianity and liberalism, both of which often distrusted, and attempted to curtail, the other. These accommodations often took the form of socially constructed institutional arrangements that, once created, often took on "path dependent" qualities and were even conflated over time with fixed normative values. This model accommodated the major traditional Christian religions in numerous areas. For example, in Germany the state accommodates the two largest Christian churches, Catholics and Protestants, by helping them collect a church tax. According to Robbers, "the rate of the church tax is between eight and nine percent of the individual's wage and income liability. . . . Approximately 80 percent of the entire budget of the two major religious communities, the Catholic and the Protestant Churches . . . is covered by the church tax."[19] With these monies the social power of the two major churches is not only accommodated, but reinforced. "Hospitals run by religious communities, which in some parts of Germany make up the majority of the available hospital beds, are thus part of the public-run financing systems for hospitals."[20]

By the late 1990s many of the positive accommodation countries like Germany, Holland, Belgium, and Switzerland experienced growing difficulties accommodating new immigrants from religions, such as Muslims, who had not been a party to the highly negotiated, often even consociational, agreements. A particular, for some no doubt "convenient," sticking point with

Muslims was that a key vehicle for accommodating religions was to give them subsidies and space in the public sphere in their capacity as "hierarchically organized public corporations." This formula implicitly excluded most Muslim organizations because, owing to Islam's inherent, but not necessarily undemocratic, structures, most of the Muslims in Europe are not in hierarchical organizations.

Indonesia and India were vastly more religiously heterogeneous than Germany, Holland, Belgium, or Switzerland, so if they were to accommodate religions they had to invent more inclusive formulas than Europe, and in fact they created formulas of accommodation that were inherently more interfaith friendly. Religious holidays for virtually all religions was one such form of interfaith accommodation. There were many others. In India, against a backdrop of the partition, all religious communities could run schools, organizations, and charities are eligible for state financial support. The norms and practices of India's positive accommodation model are so pervasively accepted that the Hindu nationalist Bharatiya Janata Party did not dare, when it was head of the ruling parliamentary coalition, not to honor the tradition of giving extensive state subsidies to help Muslim citizens make the hajj to Mecca.

In Indonesia the Ministry of Religion granted official recognition and some subsidies to five different religions. I have talked with the heads of all these different religions and each one stressed that they valued official recognition in one key respect; it means that if Muslim extremists want to burn down their churches, or to thwart their schools, they have the right to immediately call for state police protection.

In Senegal the state extends substantial accreditation to Catholic schools and helps subsidize pilgrimages to Rome for some Catholics.

3. SOCIOLOGICAL FACTS AND POLITICAL CHOICES: THE NONESTABLISHMENT OF ISLAM

No Muslim majority country with reasonably high democratic ranking (Indonesia, Senegal, Turkey, or Albania) has established Islam as the state religion.[21] From the viewpoint of democracy, this was critically important; if shari'a were ever accepted as *the* only source of law in a policy, this would be a direct violation of the twin tolerations because elected democratic legislators could not create the constitution of the country or be the fundamental source of lawmaking in the polity.

Each country has a contextually distinctive complex of reasons why it has not become an Islamic state and made shari'a the only source of law. Let us take a look at the reasons why this has been resisted in Indonesia. In Indonesia, with its 240 million citizens, 206 million of whom (86 percent) are Muslim, why did Indonesia never create an Islamic state?

The most influential actors and arguments were Indonesian, and the state-religion model that has emerged is "multivalued" (to use a term from Isaiah Berlin). This includes a positive value attached to a successful and peaceful territorial nationalism in Indonesia itself, which is seen as vastly more important than pan-Muslim nationalism. There is also a positive value—or at least the positive recognition—of Indonesia's inherent diversity and a positive interpretation of what Islam entails, and does not entail, concerning religion and public life.

In Indonesia, an archipelago of thousands of islands, the island of Bali has a Hindu majority population, and many of the smaller outer islands have Catholic or Protestant majorities; Buddhist and Confucian Chinese businessmen are prominent in the major cities; several varieties of Islam exist in the country; and there are also strong animist traditions. In this context, some Islamist groups demanded a shari'a state, in which Islamic law would be the law of the land and apply to everyone. During the constitution-making moments of 1945, 1955, and again after the recent democratic transition began in 1998, a shari'a state was demanded, but rejected. Shari'a as an obligatory state policy for all citizens in Indonesia was rejected because it was perceived by religious minorities, as well as many Muslims, secular or not, as a policy that would create threats to Indonesia's territorial integrity, social peace, and way of life. It is legal for a party in Indonesia to campaign in its platform for a shari'a state, but it is a vote loser. Votes for such pro-shari'a parties in the general elections of 1999 were 15 percent, in 2004, 12 percent, and in 2009, only 7 percent.[22] Some parties like the Prosperous Justice Party (Indonesian: Partai Keadilan Sejahtera), which have a normative preference for shari'a law, have not put it on their party platform on the last two elections because they appreciate that it will not help them politically.

The diversity within Islam in Indonesia also prevents any one variant of Islam becoming a state-endorsed version. As part of the resistance to authoritarianism, some Muslims in Indonesia pushed for a shari'a state, arguing that it would put constraints on the military dictatorship. But the democratic struggle itself, and awareness in mainstream Islam that an extreme version of shari'a would tear the country apart, led to the defeat of any proposals for shari'a being the only source of law.

Indonesia certainly has some shari'a laws and is a case of "legal pluralism," which alarms many observers. However, it is important to note that some long-standing democracies, like England and Canada, also have an element of legal pluralism. John Bowen has documented how and why a form of legal pluralism is used in London where some shari'a family councils can give an Islamic (but not an official English) divorce that would allow, for example, an abandoned wife with children to get a religiously sanctioned divorce, on the one hand, and thus be eligible to possibly remarry and remain a good Muslim, while, on the other hand, seeking legal redress and state enforced payments for herself and her children via a secular British court.[23] In Toronto this informal legal pluralism existed for many years for the Jewish community and in the United States many Catholics, in essence, use a form of legal pluralism in that they seek annulments from the Catholic Church (which will, if granted, allow remarriage in the eyes of the church), but they also seek a legal divorce from the state.[24]

Indonesia has the two largest member-based Islamic organizations in the world, both of which have taken strong positions against Indonesia as an Islamic state and the establishment of shari'a as the only source of law. Both also were strongly supportive of the democratic transition in 1998. One association, Nahdlatul Ulama (NU), has an estimated 35 to 40 million members, drawn from a largely tolerant, rural religious tradition, built upon Javanese layers of animism, Sufism, and a somewhat syncretic Islam. In a survey undertaken in 2002, 42 percent of Indonesian respondents identified themselves as belonging to the NU community and another 17 percent said they felt close to NU although they were not affiliated. Thus what NU argues about policies about the state and religion would seem to be very important because of their large number of followers.

While I was in Indonesia, I spoke twice, for about two hours each, with Abdurrahman Wahid, universally called Gus Dur, the three times–elected president of NU, and later president of Indonesia. He was a broad and brilliant conversationalist. Stretched out on a sofa in his relatively modest house in Jakarta, he looked at me and used a metaphor that I have often heard in Indonesia: if I could imagine a large floor map of Europe and the Middle East, and if I threw a carpet over it the size of Indonesia, I would have covered everything from Dublin to Bagdad.[25] For Gus Dur, the great size and linguistic, religious, and ethnic diversity of Indonesia was a *sociological fact* that called for a *political choice* of pluralism.[26]

The other large Islamic civic association in Indonesia is Muhammadiyah, a more urban organization having what they call a rational direct engagement with the Qur'an, with approximately 30 million members, thousands of schools, and hundreds of hospitals. Amien Rais, a former president of Muhammadiyah, speaker of the Consultative Assembly, and presidential candidate, is, like Wahid, a public intellectual. He gave the following interview to me, which was relayed to Indonesia on television, about why he opposed Indonesia becoming a shari'a state.

"First of all," he said "the Qur'an does not say anything about the formation of an Islamic state or about the necessity and obligations on the part of Muslims to establish a shari'a or Islamic state. Secondly, the Qur'an is not a book of law but a source of law. If the Qur'an is considered a book of law, Muslims will become the most wretched people in the world. . . . We should not establish Islamic justice, as it will create controversy and conflict. Indonesia should be built on the principles of Pancasila to be a modern state and to allow every citizen of Indonesia to pursue his or her aspiration."[27]

4. ARGUMENTS FROM WITHIN ISLAM FOR REFORMS AND COOPERATION WITH THE SECULAR STATE ON REFORM IMPLEMENTATION

In the cases of Senegal and Indonesia, the constant mutual public displays of respect between religions and the state has facilitated policy cooperation even in some sensitive areas of human rights abuses. It has also facilitated an atmosphere where religious leaders have felt free to make arguments *from within Islam* against practices and policies that violate human rights.

When I argued in "The World's Religious Systems and Democracy" that all religions are multivocal, I drew the conclusion that this necessarily implied, *contra* John Rawls, that it would be mistake to "take religion off the agenda."[28] I did so because proponents of some human rights violating policies often use religious arguments to support their positions. A counterresponse that at least partially employs powerful religious reasons for respecting these threatened rights is thus particularly useful.

Ideally, the response against violations of human rights is not only from abroad, in the name of "universal human rights." The most effective counter-response is by a local authoritative figure who, from within the core values of the religion and culture of the country, makes a powerful religiously based argument against the specific practice that violates human rights. Let us look at some examples of Senegalese state/religion policy cooperation in the area of human rights.

The Campaign Against Female Genital Mutilation (FGM) in Senegal

A variety of national and international feminist and human rights movements wanted to ban the practice of FGM, but had been countered by powerful religious-based attacks. In the end, secular movements in the government and some national and international NGOs were greatly helped by religious leaders. The secretary general, N'Diaye, of the National Association of Imams of Senegal (ANIOS), publicly argued that there is nothing in the Qur'an commanding the practice and that there was no evidence that the Prophet had his own daughters circumcised.[29] A law banning female circumcision was passed in 1999. To avoid the law being a dead letter, ANIOS enlisted the help of government health authorities to train imams in how to speak authoritatively about the health problems circumcision presents and to help with anti-FGM talks by imams on radio and television. Since patterns of female circumcision are closely related to perceptions of marriage eligibility, the government, ANIOS, and national and international women's rights organization worked together with entire adjacent villages to develop policies of "coordinated abandonment" of female circumcision so as to preclude jeopardizing marriage prospects within participating villages.[30]

Despite this law banning FGM, it helps make the law an increasing social reality if the most authoritative religious bodies in the country continue to campaign against the practice so that it is increasingly delegitimated in the religious norms and social practices of the country. To help advance this crucial goal, Professor Abdoul Aziz Kebe, coordinator for the Tivaouane-based largest Sufi order in Senegal, the Tijans, wrote a powerful forty-five page attack on FGM. The report systematically argues that FGM is a violation of women's rights, bodies, and health, with absolutely no justification in the Qur'an or in approved hadiths. Kebe argues that not only is there no Islamic justification for FGM, but that, given current medical knowledge and current Islamic scholarship, there is a moral obligation for communities and individuals to bring a halt to FGM. The report was distributed by Tijan networks, secular ministries, and the World Health Organization.[31]

Female circumcision is still a problem in Senegal, with an estimated 28 percent of women from the ages of fifteen to forty-nine having undergone FGM according to UNICEF. However, the same source lists Egypt at 96 percent. Senegal's three contiguous Muslim majority countries have much higher rates: Mali, 92 percent, Guinea, 95 percent, and Mauritania, 71 percent. It should be acknowledged that ethnic traditions as well as social policy are important. The Wolofs traditionally have not practiced FGM. However, it is worth noting that among ethnic groups that have a high rate of FGM, the rates inside Senegal are lower. For example, the Pular in neighboring Mali have more than a 90 percent rate and the Pular in Senegal have a 62 percent rate.[32]

Anti-AIDs Policies in Senegal

Another area of policy cooperation between religious and secular authorities concerns AIDS. A United Nations Development Program report on anti-AIDS policies in Muslim majority countries notes that

> in Senegal, when political leaders realized that a change in sexual behavior was necessary to contain HIV/AIDS they undertook multiple strategies, an important one of which was to enlist the support of religious leaders. Religious leaders were given training to equip them with knowledge for advocacy work. HIV/AIDS then became a regular issue of Friday prayer sermons in mosques throughout the country and religious leaders talked about HIV/AIDS on television and radio. Brochures and information were distributed through religious teaching programs. Since the early 1980s, Senegal has managed to keep their HIV prevalence rates low, less than 1%.[33]

Some observers may think that the Muslim pattern of male circumcision alone accounts for this low AIDS rate. However, they should bear in mind that AIDS rates in some other Muslim majority African states, where male circumcision is also the norm, such as Chad, Guinea, Eritrea, Mali, and Djibouti, are two to five times higher. This is, of course, not to speak of the extremely high AIDS rates in some non-Muslim states such as South Africa, 21 percent, and Botswana, 37 percent.[34]

Indonesia: Secular/Religious Policy Cooperation: Education and Family Planning

In Indonesia in particular, but also in Senegal, the combination of positive accommodation toward religions, with some financial aid to religious schools, has opened the way to forms of active policy-making cooperation between the "co-celebratory" secular state and religions. For example, in Indonesia, if a religious school wants official recognition, there has recently been a growing process of consensual co-design of books on the history of religion by state authorities from the Ministry of Education and religious leaders from major Muslim organizations. Robert W. Hefner and Muhammad Zaman have recently edited an invaluable book that reviews madrasas in eight different countries. One of the most inclusive and tolerant systems described in the volume, and the one that now works most cooperatively with a democratic state, is in Indonesia. Their article on Indonesia shows how NU and Muhammadiyah have made substantial contributions to this educationally high quality and politically pluralist outcome.[35] The positive engagement of both the state and religious organizations in providing education has resulted in the fact that basic literacy for boys and girls is now virtually universal by the time they reach the age of fifteen. Young women, fifteen to twenty-five, and young men of the same age have achieved virtual parity with 98–99 percent literacy.[36]

In contrast, in Pakistan, in the same age range, only 79 percent of boys are literate while only 58 percent of girls are: a virtual forty point difference to Indonesia's literacy rate for girls. Unlike Indonesia, Pakistan has an often a hostile relationship between religion and the state, and cooperation between the state educational authorities and religious authorities is so tenuous that there only fourteen hundred registered madrassas but fifteen thousand unregistered madrassas in the Northwest Frontier Province alone.[37] In fact, the provincial secretary for education in this Pakistani province stated that no one from his office has ever visited any of the unregistered madrasas.[38] In this near "stateless" territory, fundamentalist money, armed insurgents, and teachers, many from outside Pakistan, fuel intolerant, antidemocratic hate factories in a way that is unconceivable in Indonesia or Senegal.

For the last thirty years in Indonesia there has also been a growing cooperation between religious officials and secular state officials to provide more family planning opportunities for women. Indeed, Indonesia is held out by many in the World Bank and the United Nations as having the most exemplary family planning program of any country in the developing world, whether they are Christian, Buddhist, Hindu, or Muslim.[39]

5. PUTTING DEMOCRACY, TOLERANCE, AND ISLAM "ON" NOT "OFF" THE PUBLIC AGENDA

I have already made theoretical and historical arguments against the early Rawlsian injunction that religion should be taken "off" the public agenda. In the case of Islam and democracy in the contemporary world, I believe the case for some major activists putting Islam and democracy "on" the public agenda is strong in general, and particularly in four arenas: 1) core scholarship within Islam about religion and the state, 2) public intellectuals, 3) civil society, and, 4) political society. Consider the following.

Core Scholarship

Assume a political situation within a polity where arguments are fairly commonly disseminated in the public sphere by religious and scholarly actors who make the case that modern democracy is incompatible with one or more of the following requirements of a good Islamic society: the need for a worldwide Islamic caliphate (and thus the illegitimacy of any democracy located in only one state); the requirement that God (not citizens or electorates) governs and thus God-given sharia, not man-made laws must be obligatory for all; or the assertion that the content of a Muslim state is spelled out in binding (and democratically restrictive) detail in the Qur'an. If a situation like this exists, and it does in many polities, the chances of tolerance and democracy becoming a consensual sentiment in that polity is much greater if excellent Islamic scholarship is carried out and incorporated into public debates that confront these arguments and help citizens create an "imaginary" of committed Muslims living, indeed, in Taylor's sense, flourishing, in a democracy.[40]

Public Intellectuals

The chances for democracy becoming a consensual value in the politics of the polity will be even greater if some of the intellectuals who are engaged in core scholarly or at least conceptual development of a beneficial relationship between Islam and democracy are also public intellectuals. The task of such public intellectuals is to challeng antidemocratic arguments supposedly based on Islam as soon as they are articulated and to offer credible and attractive democratic alternatives in the public sphere via the creative and constant use of popular and elite press, radio, and television.

Civil Society

The chances for winning Gramscian "hegemony" for democratic values and practices, and protecting a possible democratic transition and consolidation with "moats," will be vastly increased if some of these public intellectuals are also leaders of major civil society organizations active and influential in the public arena. This is so for two reasons. Leaders of such organizations have many followers. This raises the costs for the authoritarian regime of imprisoning, torturing, censoring, exiling, or assassinating major visible civil society leaders. Such leaders, if they are doing their job, might also create massive member networks engaged in activities that can become increasingly supportive of a more inclusive democratic politics and even available for resistance to the authoritarian regime.

Political Society

Finally, if some of these civil society leaders become active in political society, this might increase the impact of their ideas in public life, help legitimate all necessary formal institutions of democracy for their followers, and ideally give them incentives and opportunities for entering into pro-democratic alliances and coalitions with secular activists who share democratizing goals with them.

In my judgment none of the activities by religious actors in these public arenas violates the twin tolerations or democratic practices, indeed, they advance them. Let us look at some actual examples of such activists drawn from the Indonesian case.

INDONESIA AND FOUR MAJOR ISLAMIC AND DEMOCRATIC ACTORS IN THE PUBLIC SPHERE

In the Indonesian case there are at least four major actors with a strong base and foundation within Islam who participated in all four public arenas and who played critical roles in transforming Indonesia into a twin tolerations supportive polity and now almost a consolidated democracy: Gus Dur, Amien Rais, Madjid and Maarif.

Abdurrahman Wahid, popularly known as Gus Dur, came from a family of the Islamic elites from East Java. Wahid's grandfather, Hasyim Asy'ari, was one of the founders of Nahdlatul Ulama while Wahid's father, Wahid Hasyim, was Indonesia's first minister of religious affairs. Educated in

Indonesian Islamic boarding schools (*pesantren)*, at Al Azhar University in Egypt, and at the University of Baghdad in Iraq, Wahid's family and educational credentials gave him significant authority to speak on theological questions. He used that authority to promote religious pluralism on theological questions, to institutionalize that discourse within civil society, and to mobilize the public behind democratic opposition to the authoritarian military regime of Suharto.

In the 1970s Wahid began promoting religious pluralism among Muslims on the grounds that such diversity was a blessing (*ikhtilāf al-umma, ra'ma*) rather than an obstacle to developing a strong community. This vision put him in opposition to the more formal approach to shari'a being put forward by advocates for an Islamic state.[41] Elected to the chairmanship of the 40-million-member NU in 1984, Wahid used his platform to modernize Islamic education, build civil society, and train a new generation of public intellectuals. In doing so, he influenced young scholars who are today at the forefront of promoting religious pluralism and democracy, including Masdar Mas'udi, Ulil Abshar-Abdalla, and Luthfi Assyaukanie.[42] He gave these young intellectuals an institutional platform on which to speak by helping found NGOs: Lakpesdam (Institute for the Study and Development of Human Resources), LKiS (Institute for the Study of Social Knowledge), and P3M (Association for the Development of Pesantren and Society).[43]

Wahid also mobilized civil society in order to promote political reform. The Forum Demokrasi (Forum for democracy), which he created in 1991, made a point of having a broad base of interfaith and secular members and was important in mobilizing a democratic opposition to Suharto. Wahid himself was one of the most visible voices of democratic reform in 1997. Rather than contributing to political conflict or discord, the political power of Wahid came directly from his authority as an Islamic scholar and his leadership of an Islamic civil society organization.

A note on the NU: the NU has a network of at least 6,840 Islamic boarding schools, many health clinics, a labor union, two of the world's largest women's organizations, effective environmental organizations that are part of Indonesia's green movement, a daily newspaper, a publishing empire, youth and college wings, and influential political parties. Given this base, the arrest or torture of Wahid would almost certainly have caused a grave crisis for the military regime and was virtually sociologically impossible.

Another advocate for Islamic pluralism and democracy is Ahmad Syafi'i Maarif. Maarif defended his dissertation at the University of Chicago under the tutelage of the famous Islamic reformist Fazlur Rahman. Based on the inability of the Pakistani and Indonesian parliaments to incorporate Islamic law into governance, Maarif called for the reformation of shari'a. "As has been stated repeatedly before, the entire edifice of the present sharī'a is already too outmoded to be implemented in the present age. Therefore, if the Muslim umma is really serious and sincere in its demand, a comprehensive and responsible ijtihād to reformulate the sharī'a becomes absolutely imperative."[44] The bulwark of the dissertation is focused on Islamic reform and not on political reform. Yet in the conclusion Maarif links the two. "This creative development is only possible, when intellectual fear and laziness as evidenced in many Muslim counties not excluding Indonesia, come to an end. Intimately related with this is the fact that the fresh spirit of ijtihād ought to be strongly encouraged; and this can only survive and bear fruit in a democratic environment. Indonesia at the present juncture is not a good instance for this, unfortunately."[45] As one of the country's most prominent reformists, Maarif's arguments had significant implications for reformist thought and action.

Maarif was appointed head of Muhammadiyah in 1998, and later elected, and held that position until 2005, thus heading Muhammadiyah throughout the most critical seven years of the democratic transition in Indonesia. In addition to supporting democratic reforms, he institutionalized his arguments for Islamic reform through his NGO, the Maarif Institute. Like Wahid's work with P3M, the Maarif Institute has helped give young Muhammadiyah intellectuals a voice though the Young Muhammadiyah Intellectual Network (Jaringan Intelektual Muda Muhammadiyah), which supports emerging activists like Hilman Latief, Moeslim Abdurrahman, and Tuti Alawiyah Surandi. These intellectuals are likely to become the leaders of civil society and agents of democratic consolidation in Indonesia's fledgling democracy.

Maarif has also tried to combat the voices of uncivil movements. He signed on to a 2009 petition by a group of activists who filed a petition asking the constitutional court to revoke a 1965 Blasphemy Law, deemed as discriminatory against certain religious groups. The 1965 law has been used to restrict the rights of the minority groups and other religions outside of the six recognized ones.

While Wahid and Maarif's leadership in civil society and political society has been crucial to the success of Indonesia's democratic transition, there is no intellectual voice that has been as influential as that of Nurcholish Madjid. One of the leaders of the intellectual "renewal" (*pembaharuan pimikiran*) movement in Indonesian Islam beginning in 1970, these thinkers "embraced the demographic realities of the country through appeals to democracy and pluralism informed by both Universalist ideas and the historical traditions of the region."[46] The reform movement was sparked by frustration with the stagnation of the Islamic reform movement since the 1950s and relative to the changes among other groups in Islamic civil society.[47] Through letters, newspaper columns, and speeches in 1970–1972, Madjid called for the "desacralizing" of human institutions that were seen as divinely sanctioned, particularly political parties and the state. He became famous for his slogans, "Islam yes, Partai Islam no" (Yes to Islam, no to Islamic parties) and "Tidak ada Negara Islam" (There is no Islamic state). In his writings Madjid argued against those working for an Islamic state, particularly the followers of Muhammad Natsir in Dewan Dakwah Islam Indonesia (DDII). Madjid also developed the concept of *masyarakat madani* (civil society), which became influential in the 1980s within the burgeoning NGO community.

Like Wahid and Maarif, Madjid has been supported by civil society organizations and in return created institutions to promote his views. When he began to espouse his idea of desacralizing politics, he was the president of the influential Islamic Students' Association (Himpunan Mahasiswa Islam). He went on to create the Paramadina Foundation, whose "primary concern has been to preach and develop the notion of an inclusive and tolerant Islam. To serve this purpose, Paramadina offers a series of intensive courses on classical as well as contemporary Islam across difference religious schools (*madzhab),* within both the *sunni* and *syi'i* traditions."[48] He has also engaged in public political debates; in the mid-1990s Madjid called for genuine multiparty democracy and later used his platform as a moral voice to personally urged Suharto to step down in May 1998, even while the president tried to rally Muslim support.[49] In a country where Islam is already on the table, Madjid used his religious and political authority to push Suharto out of office.

Amien Rais has also been crucially engaged in the political integration of Islam and democracy. Rais earned a PhD in political science from the University of Chicago with his thesis "The Moslem Brotherhood in Egypt: Its Rise, Demise and Resurgence." While Rais shares Maarif's roots in the Muhammadiyah, he is also close to the Islamist DDII and was critical of the *pembaharuan* movement's willingness to accommodate the Suharto regime.[50] Instead, his focus has been on promoting social justice and economic equality though Islamic mechanisms such as the *zakat.*

Rais's activities in civil society include membership in Muhammadiyah's Majelis Tabligh (propagation committee), after which time he was elected vice chairman of the central board in 1990 and chair in 1995. Politically, Rais was active in the Muslim Scholars Association (Ikatan Cendikiawan Muslim Indonesia, ICMI), which was used to mobilize political support in the Islamic community for Suharto. Yet, despite being a creation of the regime, Rais's voice was not eclipsed by Suharto; Rais was forced to resign from ICMI in 1997 after his outspoken criticism of the regime. Rais then went on to play a crucial role as one of the leaders and mobilizers of the student movement against Suharto, activities that were instrumental in Suharto's decision to resign.

In 1998 Rais established the National Mandate Party (Partai Amanat Nasional) to mobilize Muhammadiyah and other plural Muslim voices in democratic politics. The fact that he participated in the creation of a party that competed in electoral politics, and that he also became the chairman of the Consultative Assembly that debated and refused to accept shari'a, was important for the normalization of Islamic involvement in democratic politics in Indonesia.

I could have mentioned many other prominent Indonesian activists who were involved in two, three, or even four of these arenas.[51] However, in sharp contrast, Mirjam Künkler, who has a forthcoming book on the failed democratization movement in Iran and the successful democratization movement in Indonesia, does not think that any person in Iran in the last twenty years has been able to sustain activity in more than one, or at most two, of these arenas.

There were in Iran, of course, some outstanding scholars who wrote on the need for more democracy in Islam in general and specifically in Iran, such as Abdolkarim Sorroush, but none has been able to be as active in civil or political society in ways comparable to the Indonesians I have discussed because of credible threats of imprisonment, torture, exile, and sometimes even death. Likewise, I have discussed the analysis of these actors in the five arenas with a number of scholars who have done or are now conducting research in Egypt. To date, no one has made a convincing case that there is a single person who is effective in all five arenas in Egypt. In fact, many of the people who became prominent have rapidly been silenced by censorship, imprisonment, or exile.

NOTES

1. The three most widely used surveys are Polity IV, created by Ted Gurr, Freedom House's "Freedom in the World Survey," and the Bertelsmann Transformation Index. Polity IV uses a twenty-one-point scale for democracy with -10 being the worst possible score (Saudi Arabia) and +10 the best (Scandinavian countries). Countries with a +7 score or higher are generally considered democratic. Freedom House annually classifies the status of political rights and civil liberties in most countries around the world on a scale between 1 (free) and 7 (unfree). The Bertelsmann Transformation Index, a new index from Germany, has been published in 2003, 2006, and 2008. For the purposes of this essay, it is important to stress that these three different surveys have somewhat different criteria of democracy, almost no overlapping experts, and employ different methodologies to reach their scores, but Indonesia, Senegal, and India are all ranked, by all three poles, as democracies. Based on my independent field research in all three countries, I too classify them as democracies.
2. For comparisons of this set of non-Arab countries with large Muslim populations with Arab countries see Alfred Stepan, with Graeme Robertson, "An 'Arab' More than 'Muslim' Electoral Gap," *Journal of Democracy* 14. no. 3 (July 2003): 30–44, and the debate about this article with our response in the same journal in 15, no 4 (October 2004): 140–46.
3. See Juan J. Linz and Alfred Stepan, *Problems of Democratic Transition and Consolidation: Southern Europe, South America, and Post-Communist Europe* (Baltimore: Johns Hopkins University Press, 1996), pp. 8–12.
4. I develop, conceptually, empirically, and historically, the roles of the "twin tolerations" in "The World's Religious Systems and Democracy: Crafting the 'Twin Tolerations,'" in my *Arguing Comparative Politics* (New York: Oxford University Press, 2001), pp. 213–55.
5. See the classic book by Stathis N. Kalyvas, *The Rise of Christian Democracy in Europe* (Ithaca: Cornell University Press, 1996).
6. All data are collected from the "Religion and State Dataset" gathered by Jonathan Fox, Department of Political Studies, Bar Ilan University. The data are reported in Jonathan

Fox, "World Separation of Religion and State Into the Twenty-First Century," *Comparative Political Studies* 39, no. 5 (2006): 537–69. For a more detailed analysis of this data, see Jonathan Fox, *A World Survey of Religion and State* (Cambridge: Cambridge University Press, 2008).

7. Diarmaid MacCulloch, *The Reformation: A History* (New York: Viking, 2003), p. 653.
8. Daniel Philpott, "The Catholic Wave," in Larry Diamond, Marc F. Plattner, and Philip J. Costopoulos, eds., *World Religions and Democracy* (Baltimore: Johns Hopkins University Press, 2005), pp. 102–16, and R. Scott Appleby, "Vatican Council, Second," in Robert Wuthnow, ed., *Encyclopedia of Politics and Religion,* 2d ed. (Washington, DC: CQ, 2007), 2:919–21.
9. Michael Walzer, *The Revolution of the Saints: The Origins of Radical Politics* (Cambridge: Harvard University Press, 1965), quotes from pp. 55 and 60.
10. John Rawls, *Political Liberalism* (New York: Columbia University Press, 1996), see pp. xviii, 133–72.
11. For a powerful analysis of how these arguments became dominant in parts of the West, see Charles Taylor, *A Secular Age* (Cambridge: Harvard University Press, 2007).
12. See José Casanova's chapter "Secularism, Enlightenment, and Modern Religion," in his *Public Religions in the Modern World* (Chicago: University of Chicago Press, 1994), pp. 11–39.
13. There is no discussion of secularism in Robert Dahl, *Polyarchy: Participation and Opposition* (New Haven: Yale University, 1971); or in Arend Lijphart, *Patterns of Democracy: Government Forms and Performance in Thirty-Six Countries* (New Haven: Yale University Press, 1999). Juan J. Linz and Alfred Stepan, in *Problems of Democratic Transitions and Consolidation: Southern Europe, South America, and Post-Communist Europe* (Baltimore: Johns Hopkins University Press, 1996), devote ch. 3 to a typology of democratic, authoritarian, sultanistic, post-totalitarian, and totalitarian regimes, but we do not use "secularism" as part of our classification.
14. See S. N. Eisenstadt, "Multiple Modernities," *Daedalus* (Winter 2000): 1–30; and Sudipta Kaviraj, "An Outline of a Revisionist Theory of Modernity," *European Journal of Sociology* 46, no. 3 (2005): 497–526.
15. Gerhard Robbers, "Religion in the European Union Countries: Constitutional Foundations, Legislations, Religious Institutions and Religious Education; Country Report on Germany," in Ali Köse and Talip Küçükcan, eds., *State and Religion in Europe* (Istanbul: Center for Islamic Studies, 2007), p. 112 (emphasis added). In this same collection, Rik Torks, the author of the chapter on Belgium, which has many positive accommodationist features, makes very similar arguments: "The state positively promotes the free development of religious and institutional activities without interfering with their independence. In that sense, one might call this positive neutrality." Ibid., p. 58.
16. I discuss these three West European models of state-religion relations at much greater length in my "The Multiple Secularisms of Modern Democratic and Non-Democratic Regimes," in Mark Juergensmeyer, Craig Calhoun, and Jonathan Van Antwerpen, eds., *Rethinking Secularism* (New York: Oxford University Press, 2011).

17. So does the other highly ranked democracy with a Muslim majority, Albania. Space precludes a discussion of Albania in this essay.
18. See Alfred Stepan, "Rituals of Respect: Sufis and Secularists in Senegal in Comparative Perspective," *Comparative Politics* 44, no. 4 (July 2012): 379–401.
19. Ibid, p. 120. In some, not all, Länder, the Jewish authorities have a similar arrangement. In positive accommodationist Switzerland, "most of the 26 cantons financially support a form of Catholicism or Protestant Christianity and collect taxes on behalf of whatever church or churches they support. . . . Religious education is standard in Swiss schools, generally in the majority denomination of the canton, but classes in other religions are usually offered and students may opt out of the classes." Fox, *A World Survey of Religion and the State,* p. 131.
20. Ibid, p. 121.
21. And India, of course, does not have Hinduism as a state religion.
22. Jennifer Epley, "Voices of the Faithful: Religion and Politics in Contemporary Indonesia," PhD diss., University of Michigan, 2010.
23. John R. Bowen, *Blaming Islam* (Cambridge: MIT Press, 2012).
24. Ontario has had a long tradition of faith-based legal tribunals and the province formally established Jewish and Catholic tribunals in 1991. These religious courts were eliminated in 2005 after an enormous backlash against the Ontario attorney general's proposal to establish a Muslim tribunal. For an overview about these tribunals in Canada and Britain, see "Whose Law Counts the Most?" *Economist* (October 2010), accessible at www.economist.com/node/17249634. The report by the Ontario attorney general can be found at www.attorneygeneral.jus.gov.on.ca/english/about/pubs/boyd/executivesummary.pdf.
25. This actually seems true. Based on rough estimates, the distance between Dublin and Baghdad is 2,819 miles. The length of Indonesia is at least that.
26. For diversity as a "sociological fact" and pluralism as a "political choice," in Indonesia in general and in the speeches and actions of Wahid, see the chapter by Abdullahi Ahmed An-Na'im, "Indonesia: Realities of Diversity and Prospects of Pluralism," in his *Islam and the Secular State: Negotiating the Future of Shari'a* (Cambridge: Harvard University Press, 2008), pp. 223–66. For an analysis of Wahid's political discourse, also see the chapter, "Abdurrahman Wahid: Scholar-President," in John l. Esposito and John O. Voll, *Makers of Contemporary Islam* (Oxford: Oxford University Press, 2001), pp. 199–216.
27. See Alfred Stepan and Mirjam Kunkler, "An Interview with Amien Rais," *Journal of International Affairs* 61, no. 1 (Fall/Winter 2007): 205–18, a special issue on religion and statecraft.

    Pancasila consists of five interrelated principles that are fundamental to the Indonesian state: belief in 1. the one and only God; 2. a just and civilized humanity; 3. the unity of Indonesia; 4. democracy guided by the inner wisdom in the unanimity arising out of deliberations amongst representatives; 5. social justice for all the people of Indonesia.
28. See Stepan, "The World's Religious Systems," pp. 227–29.
29. See the long feature article in one of Senegal's leading newspapers, Habibou Bangré, "Croisade muselmane contre l'excision: Les imams rétablissent la vérité sur cette tradition," *Walfadiri,* June 8, 2004.

30. Ibid. A similar social policy of public pledges renouncing foot-binding in nearby Chinese villages with high patterns of intermarriages proved useful.
31. See Abdoul Aziz Kebe, "Argumentaire Religieux Musulman Pour L'Abandon des MGF's" (Dakar: Organisation Mondiale de la Sante, December 2003).
32. All FMG rates from UNICEF statistics (Multiple Indicator Cluster Servers, MICS 1995/2005) available at www.unicef.org/statistics/index_24302.html (accessed May 22, 2013).
33. "The Role of Religious Leaders in the Fight Against HIV/AIDS," United Nations, UNDP, November 30, 2006, p. 19.
34. See table 4 in UNICEF, www.unicef.org/sowc05/english/Table4_E.xls (accessed on May 22, 2013).
35. See the chapter by Azyumardi Azra, Dina Afrianty, and Robert W. Hefner, "Pesantren and Madrassa: Muslim Schools and National Ideals in Indonesia," in Robert W. Hefner and Muhammad Zaman, eds., *Schooling Islam: The Culture and Politics of Modern Muslim Education* (Princeton: Princeton University Press, 2007), pp. 172–98. For recent analogous processes in the educational system in Senegal, see my previously cited "Rituals of Respect."
36. World Development Indicators, World Bank. Numbers for Indonesia are from 2004. Numbers for Pakistan are from 2006. See http://data.worldbank.org/indicator; accessed November 4, 2010.
37. Christopher Candland, "Pakistan's Recent Experience in Reforming Islamic Education," in Robert M. Hathaway, ed., *Education Reform in Pakistan: Building for the Future* (Washington, DC: Wilson Center, 2005), pp. 151–53.
38. For Pakistan, see the volume that reviews madrasas in eight different countries by Hefner and Zaman, *Schooling Islam*, pp. 85–86.
39. For an excellent article on this, see Jeremy Menchik, "Secularizing Shari'a: Islamic Law and Family Planning in Indonesia, 1938–2005," *Southeast Asia Research* (forthcoming, 2014).
40. See Charles Taylor's essay "On Social Imaginary," available at http://blog.lib.umn.edu/swiss/archive/Taylor.pdf; accessed December 14, 2012. See also his *Modern Social Imaginaries* (Durham, NC: Duke University Press, 2004).
41. Michael Feener, *Muslim Legal Thought in Modern Indonesia* (Cambridge: Cambridge University Press, 2007), pp. 154, 157.
42. Assyaukanie has written an important book on multivocality in Indonesia and makes a strong case for a religiously friendly democratic secularism there. See Luthfi Assyaukanie, *Islam and the Secular State in Indonesia* (Singapore: ISEAS, 2009).
43. Greg Barton, *Gus Dur: The Authorized Biography of Abdurrahman Wahid* (Singapore: Equinox, 2007), pp. 161–63.
44. Ahmad Syafi'i Maarif, "Islam as the Basis of State: A Study of the Islamic Political Ideas as Reflected in the Constituent Assembly Debates in Indonesia (Chicago)," PhD diss., University of Chicago, 1983, pp. 279–80.
45. Ibid., p. 307.
46. Feener, *Muslim Legal Thought in Modern Indonesia*, p. 131.

47. Mohammad Kamal Hassan, *The Issues of Modernization and Its Impact on Indonesian Muslim Intellectuals: Nurcholish Majid's Attempt at a Theology of Development* (Plainfield, IN: Association of Muslim Social Scientists, 1978), pp. 12–13, 18.
48. Bahtier Effendy, *Islam and the State in Indonesia* (Singapore: ISEAS, 2003), 143, note 19.
49. Robert Hefner, *Civil Islam* (Princeton: Princeton University Press, 2000), pp. 114, 208.
50. Martin van Bruinessen, "Indonesia's Ulama and Politics: Caught Between Legitimising the Status Quo and Searching for Alternatives," *Prisma—The Indonesian Indicator* (Jakarta), no. 49 (1990): 62.
51. While I could have included numerous other leaders, a few specific ones deserve mention by name. Nassaruddin Umar, head of Islamic affairs in the Ministry of Religion, a prominent member of the NU executive board, and the creator of the Dialogue Among Religious Communities, is a self-proclaimed Islamic feminist whose writings on gender biases in qur'anic exegesis have proved vital to the Islamic women's movement in Indonesia. Maria Ulfah Anshor, the former chairwomen of one of the NU women's organization, Fatayat NU, is a member of parliament with the National Awakening Party (PKB) and has had significant impact on women's right through her organization and her writings on the diversity of opinion within the shari'a on women's rights and abortion. Azyumardi Azra is one of Indonesia's most prominent Islamic intellectuals, rector of the State Islamic University Syarif Hidayatullah-Jakarta, a prolific author, and was an adviser to vice president Yosef Kalla from 2004–2009.

CONTRIBUTORS

Karen Barkey is professor of sociology and history and director of the Institute for Religion, Culture and Public Life at Columbia University. She studies state centralization/decentralization, state control, and social movements against states in the context of empires. In her recent work she has also explored the issue of toleration and accommodation in premodern empires. Her research focuses primarily on the Ottoman Empire and, recently, on comparisons between the Ottoman, Habsburg, and Roman Empires. Her first book, *Bandits and Bureaucrats: The Ottoman Route to State Centralization,* studies the way in which the Ottoman state found new strategies of control and managed to incorporate potentially contentious forces into the Ottoman polity; it was awarded the Allan Sharlin Memorial Award for outstanding book of the year in social science history in 1995. Her recent book, *Empire of Difference: The Ottomans in Comparative Perspective,* is a comparative study of different forms and moments of imperial organization and diversity. *Empire of Difference* was awarded the 2009 Barrington Moore Award from the Comparative Historical Sociology section at American Sociology Association and the 2009 J. David Greenstone Book Prize from the Politics and History section at the Political Science Association.

Rajeev Bhargava, B.A. (Delhi), M. Phil, D. Phil (Oxford), is senior fellow and director, Centre for the Study of Developing Societies, Delhi. He was formerly professor at the Jawaharlal Nehru University and, between 2001 and 2005, professor of political theory and head of the Department of Political Science, University of Delhi. He has held visiting fellowships at Harvard, Columbia, Jerusalem, Bristol, and Paris. He is on the advisory board of several institutions and programs and was a consultant to the UNDP report on cultural liberty. His publications include *Individualism in Social Science*; *Secularism and Its Critics*; *What Is Political Theory and Why do We Need It?* and *The Promise of India's Secular Democracy*.

Akeel Bilgrami is the Johnsonian Professor of Philosophy, director of the South Asia Institute, and a faculty member of the Committee on Global Thought at Columbia University. Professor Bilgrami is the former chairman of the Philosophy Department from 1994–98 and the director of the Heyman Center for the Humanities from 2004–2011. He has two relatively independent sets of intellectual interests—in the philosophy of mind and language and in political philosophy and moral psychology, especially as they surface in politics, history, and culture. His books include *Belief and Meaning*; *Self Knowledge and Resentment;* and *Secularism, Identity, and Enchantment*.

Ira Katznelson, Columbia University's Ruggles Professor of Political Science and History, is president of the Social Science Research Council. His books include *Fear Itself: The New Deal and the Origins of Our Time*; *Liberal Beginnings: A Republic for the Moderns* (coauthored with Andreas Kalyvas); *When Affirmative Action Was White: An Untold History of Racial Inequality in Twentieth-Century America;* and *Desolation and Enlightenment: Political Knowledge After Total War, Totalitarianism, and the Holocaust*. He was president of the American Political Science Association for 2005–2006.

Sudipta Kaviraj is a professor of Indian politics and intellectual history at Columbia University. His research interests include Indian social and political thought, modern Indian literature and cultural production, the historical sociology of the Indian state, and the history of Western social theory. He received his Ph.D. from Jawaharlal Nehru University, New Delhi. His books include *The Unhappy Consciousness: Bankimchandra Chattopadhyay and the Formation of Nationalist Discourse in India*; *Civil Society: History and Possibilities,* coedited with Sunil Khilnani; and *The Imaginary Institution of India*. He is also the author of the classic article "An Outline of a Revisionist Theory of Modernity," which appeared in the *European Journal of Sociology*. Before joining Columbia University, he was chair of the Department of Political Studies at the School of Oriental and African Studies, University of London. He has also taught political science at Jawaharlal Nehru University and was an Agatha Harrison Fellow at St. Antony's College, Oxford.

Salman Rushie is the author of eleven novels including *Grimus*, *Midnight's Children*, (which was awarded the Booker Prize in 1981), *Shame*, *The Satanic Verses*, *Haroun and the Sea of Stories*, *The Moor's Last Sigh*, *Shalimar the Clown*, *The Enchantress of Florence*, and *Luca and the Fire of Life*. He is also the author of a book of stories and four works of nonfiction: *Imaginary Homelands*, *The Jaguar Smile*, *Step Across This Line*, and *Joseph Anton—A Memoir*. His books have been translated into over forty languages. A fellow of the British Royal Society of Literature, Salman Rushie has received, among other honors, the Whitbread Prize for best novel (twice), the Writer's Guild Award, and the James Joyce Award of University College Dublin. In addition, *Midnight's Children* was named the Best of the Booker—the best winner in the award's forty-year history—by a public vote. As an advocate of toleration, Rushdie has been honored with the Freedom of the City awards by Mexico City; Strausbourg, Vienna; and El Paso, Texas, and the Edgerton Prize of the American Civil Liberties Union. He served as president of the PEN American Center (2004–2006) and continues to work as chairman of the PEN World Voices International Literary Festival, which he helped to create.

Alfred Stepan is the Wallace Sayre Professor of Government, co-director of the Center for the Study of Democracy, Toleration and Religion, and former co-director of the Institute for Religion, Culture, and Public Life at Columbia University. He is a specialist on comparative democratization in the modern world and has taught at Oxford, Yale, and Central European University. His books include *Crafting State-Nations: India and Other Multinational Democracies,* with Juan Linz and Yogendra Yadav; *Problems of Democratic Transition and Consolidation* with Juan Linz; and *The Military in Politics: Changing Patterns in Brazil.* He also has edited two volumes published by Columbia University Press, *Democracy, Islam, and Secularism in Turkey* and *Democracy and Islam in Indonesia.* His thirteen books and edited volumes have been translated into more than a dozen languages including Chinese, Farsi, and Indonesian. In 2012 Professor Stepan received the Karl Deutsch Award from the International Political Science Association for his work in cross-disciplinary research. He is an elected member of the American Academy of Arts and Sciences and of the British Academy.

Charles Taylor is emeritus professor of philosophy at McGill University. Professor Taylor was the 2007 Templeton Prize recipient for progress toward research or discoveries about spiritual realities. He was the first Canadian to win the Templeton Prize. In 2008 he was awarded the Kyoto Prize in the arts and philosophy category. Among other books Dr. Taylor has written are *Hegel; Hegel and Modern Society; Philosophical Papers* (2 vols.); *Sources of the Self: The Making of Modern Identity; The Malaise of Modernity* (the Massey Lectures, reprinted in the United States as *The Ethics of Authenticity*); *Multiculturalism: Examining the Politics of Recognition; Philosophical Arguments; A Catholic Modernity?* and the award-winning *A Secular Age.*

Nadia Urbinati is the Kyriakos Tsakopolous Professor of Political Theory and Hellenic Studies at Columbia University. She specializes in modern and contemporary political thought and the democratic and antidemocratic traditions. In 2008 the president of the Italian Republic awarded Professor Urbinati as Commendatore della Repubblica (Commander of the Italian Republic) "for her contribution to the study of democracy and the diffusion of Italian liberal and democratic thought abroad." She is the author of *Representative Democracy: Principles and Genealogy*; *Mill on Democracy: From the Athenian Polis to Representative Government*; and is presently coediting Condorcet's *Political Writing* with Steven Lukes. She is also an editorial contributor to the Italian newspaper *La Repubblica* and publishes articles in the culture section of the Italian newspaper *Il Sole 24 Ore.*

Gauri Viswanathan is Class of 1933 Professor in the Humanities at Columbia University. She has published widely on education, religion, and culture; nineteenth-century British and colonial cultural studies; and the history of modern disciplines. She is the author of *Masks of Conquest: Literary Study and British Rule in India* and *Outside the Fold: Conversion, Modernity and Belief*, which won the Harry Levin Prize awarded by the American Comparative Literature Association, the James Russell Lowell Prize awarded by the Modern Language Association of America, and the Ananda K. Coomaraswamy Prize awarded by the Association for Asian Studies. She is coeditor of the book series *South Asia Across the Disciplines* published jointly by the Columbia, Chicago, and California university presses. She is also the editor of *Power, Politics, and Culture: Interviews with Edward W. Said.* She has received Guggenheim, NEH, and Mellon fellowships and has been a fellow at various inernational research institutes. Her current work is on modern occultism and the writing of alternative religious hisories.

INDEX